THE BUSINESS MANAGEMENT
AND SERVICE TASKS OF
THE SCHOOL PRINCIPALSHIP

THE BUSINESS MANAGEMENT
AND SERVICE TASKS OF
THE SCHOOL PRINCIPALSHIP

By

GEORGE W. HARRIS, JR., PH.D.

Professor of Educational Leadership
College of Education
The University of Tennessee, Knoxville

and

RUTH A.H. DAWES, M.ED.

Supervisor
Employment Services Division
City of Tempe
Tempe, Arizona

CHARLES C THOMAS • PUBLISHER
Springfield • Illinois • U.S.A.

Published and Distributed Throughout the World by

CHARLES C THOMAS • PUBLISHER
2600 South First Street
Springfield, Illinois 62794-9265

© *1988 by* CHARLES C THOMAS • PUBLISHER

ISBN 0-398-05420-7

Library of Congress Catalog Card Number: 87-25555

With THOMAS BOOKS *careful attention is given to all details of manufacturing
and design. It is the Publisher's desire to present books that are satisfactory as to their
physical qualities and artistic possibilities and appropriate for their particular use.*
THOMAS BOOKS *will be true to those laws of quality that assure a good name
and good will.*

Printed in the United States of America
SC-R-3

Library of Congress Cataloging-in-Publication Data

Harris, George W., Jr.
    The business management and service tasks of the school
principalship / by George W. Harris, Jr. and Ruth A.H. Dawes.
      p. cm.
    Bibliography: p.
    Includes index.
    ISBN 0-398-05420-7
    1. School management and organization—United States. 2. School
principals—United States.   I. Dawes, Ruth A. H.   II. Title.
LB2805.H33 1988
371.2—dc19   87-25555
                                                              CIP

PREFACE

School principals are primarily charged with the responsibility of providing instruction to the community's children. Supervision and evaluation of the various facets of the school's curriculum offerings takes a major portion of the building administrator's daily operational format. However, there is a segment of the building principal's tasks that receives little attention by administrative preparation institutions, or by school districts in providing for principal level inservice programs. This segment can be identified by building level business management and service tasks, or by the term—building level logistics.

Business management and service operations need to be governed by the principal (due to overall responsibility) or delegated to a member of the building level administrative team (an assistant principal). If delegation of the building logistical element takes place, the principal still needs to keep aware of the fact as to whether business management and service needs of the building are being met. There is need for a periodic appraisal system of the building's logistical effort in order to identify: (1) goal accomplishments; (2) adequate service and support procedures for the building's instructional program, (3) premium task performance by building level logistical personnel, and (4) adequate support from central office.

Proper planning procedures represent another key to having and maintaining an adequate business management and service effort within the building's operational format. The building's planning scheme as it regards logistical service and support endeavors needs to include subordinate leaders and their staffs. Building units (custodial, clerical, food service, etc.) along with their staffs should provide each unit leader with those requirements needed to accomplish unit goals. Each logistical unit leader would then have the necessary information to present to the principal those needs necessary for building support and overall building goal achievement.

This book has been constructed to provide the graduate student and the principal practitioner with a systematic presentation of business management and service tasks which are part of the building level administrative responsibilities.

Development of this book has been planned to provide both the graduate student and the practitioner with (1) the social, legal, and administrative framework, (2) building level managerial and logistical theory, (3) human resources and human relations, and (4) the managing of building level logistical tasks.

Part I (Foundations of the American Public School) brings forth America's educational philosophy from the colonial period to the late twentieth century. There is also a mixture of politics, economics, and the legal system and their influence upon American society and the individual school.

Another focus of Part I includes the principal's community relations program along with an overview of building level instructional leadership.

Part II (Managerial and Logistical Theory at Building Level) allows the reader an opportunity to observe overall building leadership, decision making, problem solving, and logistical foundations and management.

Part III (Managing a Most Critical Commodity: Human Resources) provides the reader with the establishing, maintaining, and providing innovative programs in the areas of human resources and human relations management.

Part IV (Management of Essential Logistical Activities). Here the reader will find information concerning building level involvement in the sectors of fiscal and electronic services, facility care and management, purchasing and stores management, food services, transportation services coordination, health services, and social services. Additional material is presented involving pupil personnel and office management procedures.

This book provides the graduate student in educational administration and the principal practitioner with a format for gaining knowledge in the area of building level business management and service task procedures. Another features of the book is that it also gives the reader an opportunity to witness the building level administrative blend between the instructional and logistical tasks.

ACKNOWLEDGMENTS

The authors acknowledge with thanks to the ALMIGHTY, our family members, our friends, and the late Leo Perry.

CONTENTS

PART TWO:
MANAGERIAL AND LOGISTICAL THEORY AT BUILDING LEVEL

PART FOUR:
MANAGEMENT OF ESSENTIAL LOGISTICAL ACTIVITIES

THE BUSINESS MANAGEMENT
AND SERVICE TASKS OF
THE SCHOOL PRINCIPALSHIP

PART ONE

FOUNDATIONS OF THE
AMERICAN PUBLIC SCHOOLS

CHAPTER I

AMERICAN SOCIETY AND THE
EDUCATION OF ITS PEOPLE

The roots of our national society took hold during the colonial period. With a diversity of religions, social classes, and ethnic groupings there was no evidence of a common acceptable American society. However, during the rebellion of the thirteen original colonies against the British Crown, a cohesiveness became evident. Cooperation between the thirteen colonies produced a solid effort in the American Revolutionary War which resulted in the overthrow of the British yoke of oppression.

Before the Revolutionary War there were various forms of public and private educational systems operating to help supply the mainly minimal needs of the various microcosmic colonial groups. The aftermath of the Revolutionary War brought the thirteen colonies into a more solid form of national unity. It created a cornerstone of America's original society—a society that constructed and satisfied the various needs of colonial and postcolonial life and its problems.

Public education being a need in the newly formed nation demanded an advocate to plant the seed of perpetuating democracy, liberty, and the newly found American way of life. These ideals of government had been paid for with the blood of patriots, Washington's Continental Army, and seamen of John Paul Jones' navy. The most prominent of the founding fathers to plant the seed of the American perpetuation of democratic principles was Thomas Jefferson. Jefferson's plan for a public school system for Virginia set the course for other states to later follow.

A. THE JEFFERSONIAN PHILOSOPHY OF EDUCATION

Aristotle in his works concerning politics takes aim at the community (which in turn is a segment of the nation's overall society) must have an aim toward a positive atmosphere. This thought is brought forth by Aristotle in the following statement:

5

"Every state is a community of some kind, and every community is established with a view to some good; for mankind always act in order to obtain that which they think good. But, if all communities aim at some good, the state or political community, which is the highest of all, and which embraces all the rest, aims at good in a greater degree than any other and at the highest good."[1]

In order to maintain the goodness or positiveness within community and the state there must be fostering process from one generation to that of another through a system of education. Likewise we can witness the perpetuation of negativism and wrongdoing being carried through government from generation to generation. Fascism and communism have presented vivid evidence of this fact. Since the Declaration of Independence, our nation kept the course of democracy through the proper education of its future citizens.

Thomas Jefferson in his famous quotation touches upon the attempt to remove ignorance (the key to negativism) in educating citizens to achieve the positive:

" . . . Preach, my dear Sir, a crusade against ignorance, establish and improve the law for educating the common people."[2]

Another supporting factor is brought out in a Jefferson letter to his friend, George Wythe in the discussion of an education bill that was being prepared for presentation to the Virginia Assembly:

"I think by far the most important bill in our whole code, is that for the diffusion of knowledge among the people. No other sure foundation can be devised, for the preservation of freedom and happiness."[3]

Jefferson's thoughts on using education as a means to preserve the positiveness or goodness of democracy has support to Aristotle's central political thought upon the aims of goodness within the state.

Jefferson with the aid of supporters in the Virginia Assembly made a series of attempts to establish a state system of education. These ideas were far ahead of their time, and were not popular with the wealthy Virginia planter class (that maintained the state's center of power). The Jeffersonian plan was to allow the state to assist in the elementary, secondary, and higher education aspects of public education. The zenith of his (Jefferson's) education plan was the establishment of the University of Virginia (which became a reality during Jefferson's lifetime).

Prominent issues in proposed bills which promoted public elementary and secondary education brought forth the following major points[4].

1. A free elementary education for all (male) Virginians. (The elemen-

tary program was to make its pupils knowledgeable in reading, writing ciphering, and the mastery of geography)[5].

2. County residents were to be taxed to provide revenue for operating the elementary schools.

3. The local area would also control the schools within its boundaries.

4. The establishment of county visitors from the residential lay public to oversee elementary education. This can be interpreted as an early form of the local board of education.

5. The division of the counties into wards (or present day townships). The residents of the wards with the advisory assistance of the visitors were to select land for the location of the schoolhouse, and a housing site for the teacher.

6. The residents of the ward would provide money or labor for building construction.

7. The residents of the ward would also be taxed for payment of the school site.

8. The elementary school would cover a period of three years. Those having a desire to enter the secondary ranks would be charged tuition. However, certain poor boys who were scholarly could be selected to move on to a more advanced ranking at the expense of the public purse.

9. The final point in Jefferson's plans called for the state to establish a university to provide for advanced professional instruction.

Most of Jefferson's bills were not passed in their original forms[6]. Some were heavily amended by political foes to allow loss of their original intent, plus the monster of legislative neglect took its toll on the Jeffersonian plan. However, Jefferson's influence did lead to the establishment of the University of Virginia (which is presently an American citadel of intellectualism and scholarly achievement). Credit must also be given to Thomas Jefferson for giving America direction to the road for establishing state systems of public education. Educating the populace is a dominant task in all of America's fifty states. This action has resulted in the perpetuation of America's democratic ideals for over 200 years.

B. HORACE MANN'S EDUCATION OF AMERICA

Unlike Jefferson, Horace Mann was a Northerner and native of Massachusetts. Mann gave his professional contributions to the state of Massachusetts during the mid-nineteenth century. The state of Massachusetts is considered by some scholars to be the pathfinder and early innovator of American public education.

Mann's greatest contribution to education came during his tenure as Secretary of the Massachusetts Board of Education. Horace Mann viewed the common school as a place for the common person. The common school allowed the common person to train himself/herself to make a citizenly contribution to America. The educated citizen would, therefore, reinforce the ideals of our nation. If America was to develop, Mann saw the need for public education to train the model American citizen concerning culture, morals and civic responsibility. His (Mann's) thoughts also stressed the optimism of enrichment, judgment, and intelligence.

During the early nineteenth century public schools in the United States as a whole and in the state of Massachusetts were basically under some type of local control. State influence was not dominant in nature. Mann as the first Secretary of the Massachusetts Board of Education had to construct the task of how to bring the highly dispered locally governed schools under the single roof of a state school system.

Morgan states that[7]:

> "Mann was convinced that 'in a Republic ignorance is a crime.' So clearly did he visualize the school system which would develop educated citizens that for more than a century the states have moved more or less steadily in the direction he indicated. He knew that sanitary and comfortable buildings were necessary to the health of the children. Teachers who had been given special preparation for their work were essential in the improvement of the curriculum. Statewide supervision was the first step in the provision of equal opportunities for all children. Finally the people themselves must be won to the support of the whole enterprise."

During Mann's stay (1837–1848) as Secretary of the Massachusetts Board of Education, he issued twelve annual reports to the state board of education. These reports were read throughout the United States and overseas. The reports were as follows[8]:

1. The First Report (1837)—Brought forth the duties of school committees with great emphasis on teacher selection. This report also attacked indifference of the lay public concerning the state of the Massachusett's public schools.

2. The Second Report (1838)—Involved Mann's concentration in the curriculum area of reading by advocating the word-method over the single letter method. Mann also brought forth a negative evaluation of the current reading books of the period.

3. The Third Report (1839)—At this point Horace Mann presented to the people their responsibility for school improvement, the evils of child labor, the need for good reading habits, and why there was a need to establish school libraries.

4. The Fourth Report (1840)—Mann advocated that the primary district system of school governance should be abolished and that union schools should be created for the purpose of grading and classifying students.

5. The Fifth Report (1841)—This report presented the advantages of education and its effect upon society and its support of business and the field of science.

6. The Sixth Report (1842)—Here Mann pushed for the need for a course of study to assist and prepare students to meet the challenges of daily life. This report also stressed the need for the study of physiology and hygiene.

7. The Seventh Report (1843)—Here Mann presented an additional push for curriculum in the schools concerning the following areas:
   a. Again, the word-method of teaching reading,
   b. Oral instruction,
   c. Elementary science,
   d. Language exercises,
   e. Geography,
   f. Music, and
   g. Drawing.

8. The Eighth Report (1844)—Here Mann pressed for proper governance and control of teacher institutes, the importance of teaching societies, and the study of vocal music in the public schools.

9. The Ninth Report (1845)—Here Mann emphasized the equality of school program offerings to all children regardless of socioeconomic status or local school district size. Points were also made concerning positive classroom management by the teacher.

10. The Tenth Report (1846)—In order to have a strong and permanent common school system there must be the following approach:
   a. That successive generations on a collective basis constitute one great commonwealth (Massachusetts).
   b. That the state is pledged for the education of all youth in order to insure proper citizenship.
   c. A pledge of proper stewardship of successive state school administrators.

11. The Eleventh Report (1847)—Presented a discussion of the relation of education and crime.

12. The Twelfth Report (1848)—Here Mann presented (as his final report upon resignation from office) the changes in Massachusetts education over the past twelve year period. Mann also reinforced the need to educate the state's youth for life in a democracy.

Mann's work in the state of Massachusetts presented a framework for education that has a dominant influence in the present day state education programs. Thomas Jefferson indicated direction which Mann followed and expanded upon (for the state of Massachusetts). Mann's ideas gradually caught on in other parts of the nation to where his basic principles of state educational operations are universal and in operation today. Horace Mann was a pathfinder who lighted the way for Massachusetts and the nation. He (Mann) established a more specific system (than Thomas Jefferson) to protect and perpetuate the ideals of a national democracy.

C. JOHN DEWEY'S OBSERVATION OF AMERICAN SOCIETY AND EDUCATION

John Dewey was an American educator and philosopher of the late nineteenth and early twentieth centuries. The core of Dewey's philosophical views of education rested in his philosophy of science. In Dewey's thinking science was appropriate to a panoramic presentation of numerous pragmatic circumstances. According to Archamboult[9] comprehension of Dewey's philosophy of education is dependent upon Dewey's thoughts of science. Dewey point of science rested upon the biological in which the individual searches for center of stability. The key points in Dewey's thought upon the scientific mode were: (1) Control; (2) Experiment; and (3) The Objective Tool. Through the use of the previously mentioned items, Dewey was of the opinion that this method could be used in all segments of individual actions in society[10]. Dewey further refined the scientific approach in which the individual confronted with a problem would move toward five stages between problem recognition and solution. They are[11]:

1. Suggestions—leaping forward to a solution.
2. Clarification of the problem which is to be solved.
3. The use of hypotheses.
4. Reasoning about the possible results of acting on one or another hypothesis and choosing one.

5. Testing the hypothesis by overt or imaginative action.

Dewey was highly interested in implications that were part of the scientific philosophy—that of: (1) objectivity, (2) honesty, (3) freedom, and (4) openendedness. These four points of the scientific philosophy opened the door to and coordinated well with the ideals of democracy. To Dewey democracy was a political manifestation of the scientific method. It (democracy) possessed a mixture of purposiveness plus objectivity, freedom and discipline, individual speculation and public verification[12].

America being founded upon democratic ideals tied in with Dewey's philosophy of the scientific method. Such a philosophy (Dewey's) would assist in maintaining and providing continuance to America's foundation of democracy through the scientific applications to education.

In observing education as a function of society, Dewey makes the following statement[13]:

> "We have seen that a community or social group sustains itself through continuous self-renewal, and that this renewal takes place by means of the educational growth of the immature members of the group. By various agencies, unintentional and designed, a society transforms uninitiated and seemingly alien beings into robust trustees of its own resources and ideals. Education is thus a fostering, a nurturing, a cultivating process."

Here Dewey shows that maintenance of society comes through the proper education of its children. Educational growth and physical growth are combined in order to turn out a civic minded and responsible individual. This is the aim of the American educational system in its responsibility to society. However, even with the providing of an educational net to grasp and educate the nation's youth, some children (through a variety of reasons) do not become contributing and responsible members to society. Some laypersons will state that our net of education has weakened allowing individuals to break through. Some segments of the populace will state the machinery (educational programs and personnel) are not of the best quality and are in need of an overhaul through a plan of quality control and assurance. Recent reports of America's students following scholastically behind in achievement when compared to other western nations, certain Asiatic nations, and certain Communist Bloc powers. Little do many of the adversaries of education realize that the American home is not of the same calibre that it was a generation or two ago. High divorce rates, an inflationary economy, single parent families, high unemployment, a high crime rate, and moral decay have all weakened American society. Education is in need of society's support (both from a monetary and moral point of view). In order to keep up the foundations laid by Jefferson, Mann, and Dewey there must be a meeting of the minds between education and the lay public. If education is to insure society's well-being, a conscientious effort must be made by both parties.

Dewey makes an excellent point of view in looking toward the environment having a strong influence upon children. It must be remembered that that environmental influence can either be positive or negative. Dewey reinforces this concept in the following statement:

> "The development within the young of attitudes and dispositions and progressive life of society cannot take place by direct conveyance of beliefs, emotions, and knowledge. It takes place through the intermediary of the environment. The environment consists of the sum total of conditions which are concerned in the execution of the activity characteristic of a living being. The social environment consists of all the activities of fellow beings that are found up in the carrying on of the activities of any one of its members. It is truly educative in its effect in the degree in which an individual shares or participates in some joint activity. By doing his share in the associated activity, the individual appropriates the purpose which activates it, he/she becomes familiar with its methods and subject matters, acquires needed skill and is saturated with its emotional spirit."[14]

D. THE RICKOVERIAN PHILOSOPHY CONCERNING THE DEFENSE OF AMERICA'S SOCIETY THROUGH EDUCATION

Admiral Hyman Rickover, who is considered to be the father of America's nuclear navy, noticed deficiencies among naval personnel assigned to him for the construction of naval nuclear power plants. The use of nuclear power supplies to operate the navy's submarines and surface craft called for a new breed of engineer and engineering methods. Rickover also pointed to the poor quality of workmanship involved in the construction of naval vessels. To Rickover the proper education and training of individuals in the technical areas was vital to America's defense. The negative personnel aspects of nuclear ship and submarine construction gave Admiral Rickover a springboard from which to attack the American educational system. Pungent points brought forth in Rickover's attack on education were: (1) that American students were not being properly prepared to meet America's technological needs, (2) a need for federal (not state) standard for teachers and teacher preparation, (3) the use of federal funds to raise the pay of teachers, (4) federal support to improve education, (5) condemned a wanting system of public education that was created by professional educators, (6) supported a de-emphasizing of the state boards of education system with more direction toward federal control and support, and (7) that American schools should adopt the more rigorous educational programs of the European schools[15].

Rickover constructed his criticism of the American educational system through his managing of personnel needs for the U.S. navy's change from a conventional to nuclear fleet. Only premium personnel were selected for this task. In observing those individuals that did not meet the navy's nuclear needs, Rickover came to the conclusion that an inadequate education was the center of the problem. This frame of thought indicated not only program quality, but that quality which concerns the training of the educational professional. The nuclear age (with its advanced technology) would require that public education produce a product that had the ability to comprehend and be capable of synchronizations with constantly changing technical demands.

In making the connection between education and national defense Admiral Rickover makes the following point:

> "... Only massive upgrading of the scholastic standards of our schools will guarantee the future prosperity and freedom of the Republic."[16]

Here one finds that education not only provides the vehicle for American society to maintain the democratic system (through the present and projected generations), but it also provides the mechanism for national defense. Those military services that have been provided to defend the nation (according to Rickover) must be properly educated by the civilian authorities to meet new technological demands. During the late 1950s and early 1960s the navy began its move from conventional sea power to that new age of nuclear powered surface and submarine fleet. Today one will find a substantial number of nuclear powered submarine and surface vessels in service.

Another point projected by Rickover is observing the need of adequately educated technical personnel to man the nuclear aged navy was brought out in the following quotation:

> "... Daily we become more dependent on other countries for the sinews of our economic and military power. We are deficient in eighteen of the thirty most important industrial minerals and we lack five completely; our oil production will pass its peak about 1965, twenty years before this happens in the world at large. Then we shall have to import oil or undertake the costly process of utilizing shale-oil deposits. It is possible that we may then have to operate with energy which is more expensive than that used elsewhere. This

will adversely affect our standard of living and our political power. Impercep-
tibly some of the foundations supporting our present prosperity in the world
have been getting weaker. As always happens when things are turned upside
down, it takes a while for people to readjust their beliefs to changed conditions."[17]

The Arab Oil Embargo of 1973 emphasized American dependency on
foreign oil and gave direction to national energy conservation. By this
time period, the American navy was heavily nuclearized which reduced
heavy oil dependency in fleet operations. The increased emphasis on
the use of nuclear and coal powered generators has created a demand for
adequately trained technical personnel. Technicians have developed
methods of reducing pollution problems that have been associated with
the use of coal.

Rickover's prophecy concerning the fact of energy problems under-
mining: (1) America's standard of living, (2) political power, (3) prosperity,
and (4) world position have been greatly influenced since the Arab Oil
Embargo of 1973. These problems have given an indication that our
public schools need the programs, tools and personnel to produce a
better product that will be able to provide the technical know-how for
civilian and military use. Education is indeed vital to the nation's defense
of its democratic principles.

E. THE INFLUENCE OF POLITICS AND ECONOMICS UPON SOCIETY AND EDUCATION

The American political and economical settings look toward education as a means of a dual guarantee. That is a political guarantee that
democracy, capitalism, and the free enterprise system are maintained
throughout future generations. The other segment of the dual guarantee
concerns the national economy. That is, for education to provide a
knowledgeable work force in both the technical and nontechnical fields.
A work force of this nature is needed to provide support to politically-
oriented capitalism and free enterprise thrusts. One can readily observe
the close (but separate) relationship between politics and economics.
Our national political and economic philosophies have resulted in America
attaining its superpower status. Currently there are some segments of the
political and economic communities that are concerned about our loss of
status in the world market due to foreign business and industrial
competition. Market offerings of lower prices, better quality and workmanship, and innovative product features has taken its toll upon Ameri-

can produced items. Some quarters of the economic and political camps also point to inflation, foreign energy dependence, and the demands of labor as contributing to our economic woes.

The economic and political machine also points to the outstanding educational accomplishments of our foreign competitors in their education systems. This alarm has introduced quality programs in their public school systems and institutions of higher learning. Our current political and economic problems have signaled the need for national action to rectify our slippage of the last two decades. If American is to keep its superpower status, there must be a change of direction in order to surpass foreign competition.

Education and Politics

A nation's citizenry is the key to providing and maintaining a particular form of government. America is considered to be the bastion of world democracy. In order that this position be kept, an excellent program of education is needed for all segments of society. Democracy needs its citizens to be properly educated as participants of the political system, and also to provide those leaders, technicians, and other specialists needed to operate the government and the private business sector.

Politics, knowing that its existence depends upon the educational process, supports and maintains education. The result of this mixture can be termed a dual-survival dependence. One cannot properly operate and maintain itself without the other. Politics provides the legal foundation, the state and local level tools and machinery, personnel needs, financial support plus other logistical support required for proper administration and operation.

Free Enterprise—America's Key Road to the Economic System's Freeway

A pure free enterprise system allows for an economic freedom granted on an individual basis. This allows business and industry to make its own economic decisions. The United States does not practice a pure form of free enterprise, because there are modifications of the system by governmental controls. Governmental modifications have been designed mainly to protect market interplay and the consumer. However, the American business machine has been allowed mostly to make decisions that are best for the various sectors of their respective markets. Not all of these decisions have provided a respectable and profitable gain. Profit and loss are the main ingredients of the free enterprise system. The success is a barometer of the nation's economic well-being. If the business and industrial sectors are profitable, they provide jobs, economic well-being, and a hopefully adequate standard of living for the citizenry.

Education's Support of the Economic System

Previous statements have pointed out the fact that education is a must in a democratic society. Education is also important in a democratic government's economic system. The quality of our families, community, states, and the nation depend highly upon the educational input to the national economy. There is also a dependency upon the national economy's various benefits to the nation and the individual. If the economic system of the nation is successful it can provide work, increased standards of living and financial support (through taxes and grants) to operate the public and higher educational systems.

Education provides a more specific support of the national economic system through the preparation of the citizenry in the basics of reading, writing, and ciphering. However, a more indepth observation provides individuals with the basic and advanced training needed for occupations of work in both the technical and nontechnical areas.

Business, industry and government distributes employment opportunities to the finished products of education. The better quality education's finished product (the graduate), the better the position of employment and advancement possibilities. Quality education can assist business, industry, and government in reaching their respective objectives. Positive contributions of the educational community should assist in providing for a more positive and panoramic position of the national economy. Education has become a vital link to the success of the national economy. Business, industry, and government are required to be influential in America's educational system. Coordination of this nature can assist education in its preparation of a knowledgeable and adequately trained work force.

F. MAINTENANCE OF THE STATUS QUO
AND THE DEMAND FOR CHANGE

Since the birth of our nation in 1776, education in one form or another has assisted our country in the maintenance of its democratic roots. However, the previous statement does not delete the attempts to topple America's political and economic system. One can look back to: the lingering loyalties of some citizens toward the British crown after the Revolutionary War, the events that led to the Civil War, the communist attempt to indoctrinate America's laboring class through the International Workers of the World (IWW) during the 1920s and 1930s, the German-American Bund (the Nazi Party) during the 1930s, the highly influential student organizations of the 1960s, the neo-nazi organizations, and other pressure groups which currently operate within the national boundaries. These radical organizations are locked into political programs that operate on extremes from communism to facism. One can hardly recognize the thin line that separate the revolutionary from the reactionary. Every political system attempts to grasp the status quo in order to maintain a survival of its current system. Education is a prime factor in the maintaining of any political system whether its a democratic, communistic or facist state. America has survived the attacks and attempts for monumental change such as the communistic takeovers of Russia, China, and Adolph Hitler's Nazi takeover of Germany.

America has witnessed a number of cultural changes that have come about through business, industry, technology, and organizations for change (for example ethnic, gender, religious, socioeconomic, professional, labor, and other politically forceful groups which have demanded breakdown of the status quo). One can look at the alterations in American life that has resulted from introductions of the railroads, electricity, artificial light, the automobile and trucking industries, air transportation, radio, telegraph, telephone, television, satellites, refrigeration, the deep freezing process, dehydration, product uniformity, audio and visual cassette production and recording, microwave cooking, computers, robotics, educational program advancement and opportunities, social class mobility, etc. It must be realized that innovation and alteration will continue as long as mankind exists under normal global conditions.

Another point which must be considered is that of observing, studying in depth, and refining knowledge of other cultures. For example, the new management techniques of Japanese industry which reduces to a lesser degree labor-management strife. This new management theory allows for pride in the product produced, worker input, and it increases quality standards. Another point is one European method of terminating assembly line production and using a team concept to totally produce an automobile. The appropriation of ideas and methods may also involve nontechnical situations such as medicine, dentistry, education, social programs, etc.

Society interacts with two classifications of change. They are: (1) change that is constructed. Constructed change has been formulated after detailed study, input from various sectors, and a projection is made. For example, the 1959 National Defense of Education Act (NDEA) which provided for increased and a more proficient undertaking for mathematics and the sciences. This particular avenue was to assist America in surpassing the Soviet Union in space exploration. Another example was the Nazi takeover of education in Germany during the 1930s. Censorship and the "burning of the books" paved the way for facist dominance of the young mind and a construction of the foundation which supported the mythical superman theory. (2) The second type of change involves that circumstance, or a series of circumstances that were not constructed directly by individuals of society. One can witness the present problems of the earth, air and water pollution problems, water scarcity, termination of various animal species, the increasing of established diseases, the introduction of new diseases such as AIDS, food shortages, moral decay (which fosters problems such as teenage pregnancies, teenage runaways, drug and alcohol addiction, etc.), and other impromptu problems that American society has been forced to contend with.

Both constructed and unconstructed change have a terrific influence upon society. This in turn forces society to place to impress upon the nation's educational system. Education reacts by allowing for research plus the development and implementation of new educational programs to meet society's needs. There are other specific segments of society that also place points of pressure upon the national educational system. They can be labeled as the segmented determinators for modification. They are:

1. The Power structure
2. Academic Organizations
3. Mores
4. Organized Pressure Groups
5. Conflicts

6. The American Legal System

7. Government (Local and State and National)

In looking upon the status quo and change a portion of both can assist the American system to hold on to its democratic ideals. But there is a need for constructed change to keep abreast of the world situation and to maintain leadership. There is also a need to meet unconstructed change in order to provide for a balance of the system.

G. SUMMARY

Society has more or less set the pace for program operation of the American educational system. Since the colonial period, our nation has witnessed a primary change of governmental attitude. A movement from a colony loyal to the British crown to that of a democratic type of government. Through the years (with some minor adjustments by various constitutional amendments and supreme court decisions) our nation has held itself in the realms of the status quo concerning democratic ideals.

Thomas Jefferson has given America the foundation of providing for the individual state (Virginia) to establish a program of education (elementary—college) for its citizens. Jefferson was of the belief that an ignorant society and a free society could not coexist. He (Jefferson) pointed to education as the vehicle upon which democracy would ride through the generations.

Horace Mann took the foundation of Jefferson, expanded it. He (Mann) called upon specificity to exploit the Jefferson's penetration of the gap of ignorance. Mann as Secretary of the Massachusetts Board of Education opened the door to the common person to train himself/herself in order to make a contribution to Massachusetts and the nation. One of Horace Mann's goals was to train and invest the responsibility of citizenship to the populace. Items such as proper teacher selection procedures, reading instruction, lay responsibility for public education, unified school districts, educational support for the economy and science, a course of study for daily living, curriculum improvement, control of teacher training institutes, the establishment of pedagogical societies, the equality of educational opportunities to all segments of society, advocacy for a strong common school supported by the people and the state, and education as a vanguard against crime and immoral conduct.

Mann's Massachusetts model for a state system of education became the prototype for other states to follow. Today one can find these basic elements in the various state educational programs.

During the late nineteenth and early twentieth centuries another American champion for education was brought forth in the personage of John Dewey, an educational philosopher. Dewey acquainted the philosophy of education to that of science and its biological foundations. Through this medium Dewey's key thrust rested upon the use of scientific practices in problem recognition and problem solving. Dewey was also of the opinion that the scientific philosophy harmonized well with the principles of democracy.

During the late 1950s and the 1960s another great champion for education's cause arose from the ranks of the military. Admiral Hyman G. Rickover, who is considered to be the father of America's nuclear navy. Rickover found during his quest for scientific and engineering personnel (to work in the designing and construction of nuclear submarines) that the premium individual were a rarity. He (Rickover) stated that the problem of finding qualified personnel was caused by the poor quality of the American educational system. Rickover proposed that America's students needed a proper preparation in the technical fields in order to meet America's technical needs. Rickover called for America to pattern its educational system after that of the British and other European school systems. Other points presented by Admiral Rickover were federal standard for teachers and teacher institutions. He (Rickover) also supported the raise of teacher pay in order to attract top quality people to the profession. Rickover was of the opinion that massive federal support would improve not only education, but the product of education.

Rickover was of the conception that properly educated individuals (especially in the technical fields) would help insure the nation in its task of protecting democratic ideals.

The political, economic, and educational climates are very heavily entwined in the operations and the destiny of our nation. Politics will demand that our school system operate on the preserving of democratic ideals, preparation of proper citizens. The political machine also provides support, maintenance, and control (by law) over the educational machine. Economics through the American free enterprise system is somewhat controlled by politics (through governmental regulations). However, the economy demands that education produce individuals that are trained to become a working part of the business, industrial, governmental sectors. The economic segment assists (through taxes) education in its operation. Education finds itself supporting the political machine through the training of citizenship and the preservation of democracy. Another contribution brought forth by the educational process is that of providing trained person power to the economic machine (business, industry, and government).

REFERENCES

[1]McKeon, Richard, Editor. *The Basic Works of Aristotle.* New York: Random House, 1941, p. 1127.

[2]Arrowood, Charles F., Editor. *Thomas Jefferson and Education In a Republic.* New York: McGraw-Hill, 1930, p. 23.

[3]Ibid., p. 22.

[4]Ibid., pp. 23–24, 49–75, and 79–87.

[5]Ibid., p. 103.

[6]Ibid., pp. 22–25.

[7]Morgan, Joy E. *Horace Mann: His Ideas and Ideals.* Washington, D.C.: National Home Library Foundation, 1936, p. 19.

[8]Ibid., pp. 24–28.

[9]Archamboult, Reginald D., Editor. *John Dewey on Education: Selected Writings.* New York: The Modern Library (Random House), 1964, p. xv.

[10]Ibid., pp. xv–xvi.

[11]Ibid., p. xvi.

[12]Ibid., pp. xvii–xviii.

[13]Dewey, John. *Democracy and Education: An Introduction to the Philosophy of Education.* New York: The Macmillan Company, 1916, p. 12.

[14]Ibid., p. 26.

[15]Rickover, Hyman G. *Education and Freedom.* New York: E. P. Dutton and Co., Inc., 1959, pp. 99–110 and 188–207.

[16]Ibid., p. 15.

[17]Ibid., p. 28.

CHAPTER II

THE LAW AND SCHOOL BUILDING
LOGISTICAL MANAGEMENT

A. FORMULATION OF A BUILDING POLICY BOARD

Problem Solving and Decision Making

Two managerial tasks that are authoritatively fixed and controlled by policy are:

1. Problem Solving—An action that involves singular or joint management input which attempts to find a solution to strife within or without the organization. These attempts can be labeled with an odds factor of a 50-50 chance (to pure solution of the problem at hand).

2. Decision Making—This action may be used in the above problem solving situation, or it may be involved in directing the organization (or a segment of the total organization) on a particular azimuth. The prime azimuth is selected after the detailed study of all known and projected possible options have been contemplated.

Problem Solving

Before delving into policy making a closer observation of problem solving is in order.

Problems are those obstacles within the organization that either terminate goal accomplishment, or decelerate the planned rate of time needed to accomplish a goal. Planned programs usually carry a fixed time block to signify the commencing point, the point of termination, and an evaluation plan to determine whether the goal has been met. A reduction in the time factor may hinder goal accomplishment and coordinate activities within other segments of the organization.

The presentation of a problem may have its origin internal or external to the organization. Origin of the problem can also be classified according to construction. This classification would be: (1) anthropomorphic or person problems; (2) problems created by fabrication; and (3) problems created by the natural environment.

The road to problem solving involves the following steps:

1. Identification of the problem through:
   a. Reporting
   b. Observation
   c. Nonaccomplishment of goal(s)
   d. Delays
   e. Quality control
   f. Quality assurance
   g. Appraisals
2. Construction of alternative plans to solve the problem.
3. Selection of one of the alternative plans (the one that best fits the need of the present situation).
4. Attempted or actual solving of the problem.
5. Evaluation of the problem solving process.
6. Repetition of the previous five steps if the problem has not been solved.

The task of problem solving may be carried out by one individual or a group of individuals. Group problem solving will allow for a variety of input (which can be considered and evaluated for use in the process). Regardless of the number of people involved, the previously mentioned six steps will remain the same.

Decision Making

The previously mentioned statements supported the fact that decision making can be a part of the problem solving task (Item 3 of the before mentioned problem solving steps). Another approach for decision making is the providing of an avenue for organizational direction. It (decision making) becomes a means of controlling the organization along with its human and mechanical subjects.

The decision making process can be arranged into a general-specific classification system. A detailed format is indicated by the following six primary classifications along with their secondary breakdowns:

1. Time—The decision making process in its relationship to time consumption may vary depending upon the demand situation.

Specific segments of time classification concerning the decision making construction process, plus the consumption of time needed to adequately and conscientiously complete the task at hand are:

  a. The less than normal rate—Demand weak.
  b. The normal rate—Demand normal.
  c. Impromptu—Demand intense (this situation may call for the need to overtake negative time loss).

2. Priority Establishment—Problems or events within the organization can be so numerous that the manager and/or managerial staff will feel the need to rank order the decision making process.

Specific points in the priority establishment area are:

  a. Requirement—Immediate
  b. Requirement—Routine
  c. Requirement—Routine Minus (Time is not a critical issue in this priority status).

3. Single Manager Construction—This particular action involves one manager's construction of the process leading up to the point of decision. There may or may not be subordinate staff input. However, no other direct managerial input (peer or superior) is involved. The single manager involved has decided or has been directed to attack the issue of concern.

Specific factors supporting this particular classification are:

  a. Timeliness and Convenience
  b. Requirement for a Directed Single Action Undertaking
  c. Situation Directed Single Action Undertaking

4. Multimanager Construction—A classification of this nature involves a mix of managerial input before the final decision is made (by the indicated, dominant or superior manager of the group involved). Input may or may not be made by subordinate staff members.

Specific features of this particular classification will involve the following members of the managerial hierarchy:

  a. Superior-Immediate Subordinate Managerial Staff Decision
  b. Superior-Subordinate Staff Decision
  c. Peer-Peer Decision

5. Postalternative Period Decisions (after-the-fact)—Decisions of this type are constructed and implemented when there are direct or indirect changes of operation within the organization. Decisions within this classification may be necessary to allow the organization to regain efficiency, synchronization, and various goal accomplishments.

Specific types of decisions in this sector would center around the following:

  a. Internal Alternative Directed Decisions

    b. External Alternative Directed Decisions
    c. Mechanically Induced Alterations Requiring Decisions
    d. Human Induced Alterations Requiring Decisions

6. Innovative Conversion Periods—New ideas, processes, material, and organizational schemes may well require decisions to be made in order to allow the organization to maintain its ongoing balance.

Those specific types of decisions involved with the aftermath of new introductory methods or items to the organization may be:

    a. New Policy Induced Decisions
    b. New Program Induced Decisions
    c. Reorganization Induced Decisions
    d. Decisions Brought About by New Objectives
    e. Decisions Due to Personnel Changes
    f. Decisions Influenced by New Material
    g. Decisions Influenced by New Financial Management Procedures

Democratic Decision Making

By having our foundation in a democratic country, democracy tends to be practiced within various governmental organizations (such as schools, governmental departments, etc.). However, realism and past experiences will forewarn those in administrative positions that: (1) conflict, (2) hostility, (3) rebellion, (4) apathy, (5) indolence, (6) treachery, (7) organized disruption, and (8) the possibility of subtle yet highly organized take-over attempts by subordinates or others within the organizational structure.

The principal should place himself/herself on a scale of elasticity when coming forth in the democratic decision making process (see Figure 1). An elastic situation is derived from the pressures brought forth from two areas. They are:

1. Internal Pressures—Stress in this area will come from conflict or various types of problems within the building organization.

2. External Pressures—Those matters of tension brought about by organizations or groups outside of the building organization. For example:

    a. Central Office
    b. Local Board of Education
    c. Governmental offices
    d. Citizens and citizen groups
    e. The community in general

Forces of the pressures previously mentioned can determine the amount

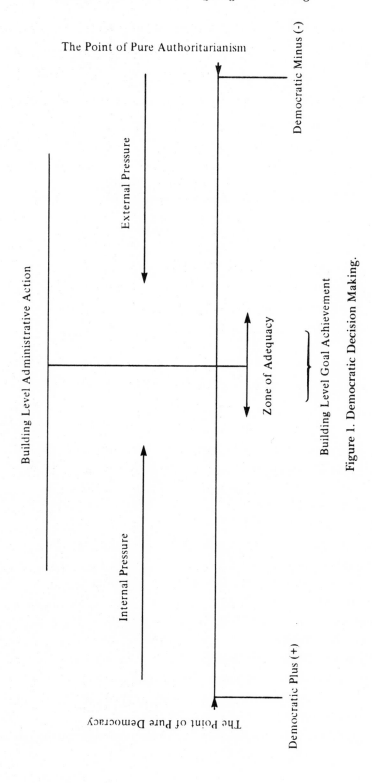

Figure 1. Democratic Decision Making.

of democratic leeway the principal will allow in the areas of decision making. One fact that the principal must keep in mind is that he/she is solely responsible for the decision that is made and carried out. The elasticity shown in Figure 1 illustrates the choice of the principal's zone of adequacy. The zone allows shifting from extreme polarization of pure democracy (democratic plus) or to the other extreme pole of pure authoritarianism (democratic minus). Operation at either of these extreme levels would be detrimental to the school and its goals. Therefore, an adequate operating point between the extreme point of polarization should be used. A response taken within the above mentioned region would assist the individual building in accomplishing its objectives.

Democratic decision making needs to be approached with caution. The principal must carefully measure his/her level of capitulation authority to subordinates. Responsibility always lingers after the decisive actions have taken place.

Legal Hierarchy and the Building Level Policy Book

School building policy is built upon the refinement of school district policy, state department of education rules and regulations, state board of education policy, and the state statutes. Those policies constructed at building level should be aimed at daily building operations and the facilities individual goals. The building administrator needs to realize that the authority which allows building policy to be constructed has a foundation at higher levels than the local board of education.

further basic elements in the law concerning public education can be found in the state constitution. Some states specifically outline the state's program of education. Other state constitutions may be broad and automatically delegate a further refinement of the public education program to the next lower level in the hierarchy—the state legislature. In fact further refinement may come at the lower echelons. Such as those previously mentioned. For example: the state boards, state education departments, local boards of education, the building level, and down to the classroom where policy is created by the classroom teacher.

The supreme level of the legal hierarchy is the Federal Constitution. From this legal document all legal operations within the public school domain, obtains the rights and powers to function according to the various appointed tasks. Education is not directly mentioned in the Federal

Constitution, however, there are two avenues of approach to the public school system which are mentioned in a circuitous manner. They are:

1. The Tenth Amendment which states the following[1]:

> "The powers not delegated to the United States by the Constitution, nor prohibited by it to the states, are received to the states respectively, or to the people."

With the task of public education not being mentioned in the United States Constitution and with no further mentioning of barring the process from taking place automatic delegation take-over. The next lower level of government—the states automatically take on the function of public education. This type of automatic delegation can also take place at even lower level superior papers (such as state constitutions, charters, etc.), government or governmental bodies that are subordinate to the federal government (state and local levels).

2. The second avenue of approach which leads from the Federal Constitution to public education is the general welfare clause found in the Preamble of the federal constitution[2].

> "We the People of the United States, in order to form a more perfect Union, establish justice, insure domestic tranquility, provide for the common defence, *promote the general welfare,* and secure the blessings of liberty to ourselves and our posterity, do ordain and establish this Constitution of the United States of America."

The general welfare clause has been legally interpreted to allow the federal government (through the legislative and executive branches) to support public education (among other general welfare tasks) in the United States.

The preceding information has illustrated that the seat of power is in the Federal Constitution, in delegation to state government, and in the state's delegation to the local boards and local school districts. Direction at this point will be the delegation of power and rights from the local school board and local superintendent to the building principal. This action gives the principal the right to build building level policy and enforce the same.

Formulating the Building Policy Book

Building level policies are usually somewhat specific statements which are in line with specific board of education policies. Building policy selects a course of action and certain zones of limitations for personnel functioning within the building area. The previously mentioned general term, personnel, can be further subdivided into the following groups:

1. Building level administrative team (principal, assistant principal, attendance officers, deans of girls, deans of boys, etc.).

2. Building level special support personnel such as guidance counselors, librarians, audiovisual personnel, athletic directors, coaches, school nurse, school social workers, school psychologist, audiovisual managers, etc.

3. Building level instructional staff (curriculum coordinators, instructional department chairpersons, teachers, and teacher aides).

4. The building level logistical staff (custodians, maintenance personnel, clerical staff, and food service staff, and school bus driver liaison and coordination).

5. Student personnel (those students that are permanently assigned to the building, and those students who may be assigned partially during the school day).

Building level policy is usually operational in nature and should assist the school building to function in a more smoother and synchronized fashion.

The school policy book needs to reflect the philosophies of:

1. Society in general
2. The community
3. The school district
4. The individual school

Policy can be solely fabricated by the principal with or without input of the school staff. Building policy can also be built by the building's administrative team with or without staff input. Whether or not to use staff input or even student input toward building level policy construction depends upon certain factors such as:

1. Leadership style of the principal.
2. The quality of the administrative team.
3. The quality of the teaching and nonteaching staffs.
4. The desire or nondesire of student input.
5. Individual school goals.
6. School district goals.
7. Community goals.
8. State goals.

The building policy book should be built from the following major procedural areas (in order to provide proper administrative supervision and control over the school's daily operations):

1. The instructional format by both grade level (for elementary schools) and subject matter (for middle and senior high schools).

2. Building level administrative team procedures (if the building administration is assisted by subordinate administrators).

3. Teacher personnel management.

4. Logistical personnel management.

5. Pupil personnel management.

6. Scheduling and space management.

7. Safety and security procedures.

8. Computer usage and security procedures.

9. Financial administration.

10. Logistical support systems management.

11. Procedures for interaction with the central office.

12. Procedures for interaction with the community and its members.

13. Procedures for interaction with governmental agencies.

14. Procedures for interaction with nongovernmental agencies.

Building level policy development and enforcement gives the principal and his/her administrative team a vital reference point and source of authentic knowledge. Policy needs to be clear, concise, and complete in order to prevent the confusion which can be caused by a variety of interpretations. Policy must also be in line with the local board of education, the state public education system and its constitution, the federal framework (if applicable) and the Federal Constitution.

B. PROPER MANAGEMENT OF THE BUILDING MAINTENANCE AND OPERATIONS PROGRAM

The building level administrator has direct responsibility for the maintenance and custodial operations of his/her school plant. Upper level responsibility usually includes central office administrative personnel such as the superintendent, the logistical or business manager, the director of buildings and grounds, and various curriculum directors (elementary, secondary, and special education, vocational education, etc.). The principal operates from his/her main source—the school plant. A principal has the direct task to supervise proper maintenance and custodial operations within the building.

Improper maintenance and custodial procedures in the building's internal and external activity zone can lead to possible legal action. Personnel and in some cases school districts may be held liable for property or personal damage or injury due to task liability. School plant care from both the maintenance and custodial sectors needs to be more than adequate. Maintenance and operational management planning should also be "before the fact" (concerning all known and possible injurious avenues of approach).

In order to reinforce the legal issue as it relates to maintenance and operations, the principal needs to start with a viable program of building safety. The safety program may be under the direct guidance of the principal, or it (the safety program) may be delegated to a lesser building administrator or staff member.

Planning for the building safety program should have the input of the entire building staff (administrational, instructional, and logistical). The overall intent of the safety program being planned should involve such items as:

1. Periodic general inspections.
2. Preventional procedures.
3. Maintenance program procedures.
4. Custodial program procedures.
5. Danger areas.
6. Potential danger areas.
7. Danger signs.
8. Storage procedures (especially chemicals and other flammable products).
9. Electrical systems and wiring.
10. Water and waste water systems.
11. Control and direction of traffic within the building.
12. Control and direction of traffic outside of the building.
13. Building site and grounds observation.
14. Hazard surveillance procedures.
15. Fire prevention program.
16. Close observation and supervision of heating, cooling and ventilating systems.
17. Close observation, supervision and security provision for computer, fire and burglar alarm systems.
18. Accident and injury prevention—classroom, interior, nonclassroom areas, and the building campus.

19. The enlistment of total staff cooperation and support of the safety program.

All possible building and site areas that harbor a potential for injuries or damages cannot be fully realized by any school's administration and staff, however, there is need for proper and intensive planning. The safety planning process (concerning building maintenance and operation) should include the establishment of a building policy available to both staff and students.

C. THE SAFETY AND SECURITY RESPONSIBILITY

Mention has been made concerning the building level safety program as it relates to care of the school plant through maintenance and custodial operations. The building's safety program has a direct linkup with security as a means of being "before the fact." State statutes usually require that security procedures be taken in school buildings. The principal is directly responsible to seeing that the specified security procedures are followed in his/her building. Central office administration and policies should give the building level administration direction. However, a principal may decide to improve upon central office security policy in order to better fit the needs of his/her building. This will also include consideration of the crime and vandalism climate of the surrounding community.

Safety and security procedures that should be monitored by the principal and his/her administrative team could possibly include:

1. Electronic and locking systems to deter unofficial entry into the school plant.

2. Safe and complex locking systems for the storage of funds on a temporary basis. All monies and checks should be deposited in a bank on a daily basis. A bank night depository system should be used to deposit funds received from evening extracurricular affairs (after bank closing hours).

3. Waterproof and fireproof complex storage areas for important papers, records (including student records), and computer software.

4. Electronic surveillance systems for building and grounds.

5. Adequate illumination for the building and exterior areas.

6. Emergency illumination for the building and exterior areas.

7. Electronic fire alarm system.

8. Computerized heating, cooling, and ventilation controls in order

to provide a more healthful atmosphere within the building. Proper functioning within these areas will provide for less structural damage which can be caused by fluctuations of temperature and humidity.

9. A more than adequate sanitizing and disinfecting effort within the school housekeeping program.

Safety and security should not be taken lightly by the building level administrative staff. A poor effort in these areas could have the possibility of leading into a tort action.

D. PROPER PLANNING COORDINATION OF EXTRACURRICULAR ACTIVITIES AND FIELD TRIPS

Extracurricular activities provide for the school and its student body a means to promote the cohesiveness for identification within and without a particular school. Extracurricular activities also provide an espirit de corps or group pride for the school body. Activities of this nature also provide the students with a secondary role (along with instruction being the primary role) that has foundation in the school's daily operation. Extracurricular activities may involve interscholastic athletics or special interest events, intramural athletics, or those special events within the building area. Some extracurricular functions may be coordinated with external organizations such as business, industry, government, services, and other organizations.

Extracurricular programs should be a mainstay within the overall school program. Proper administration of these activities will discount the old theory of, "all work and no play makes Jack (or Jackie) a dull boy (girl)."

The field trip has become an important element of the public school program. Johnston and Harris give support to this point of view by stating the following[3]:

> "...As a rule of thumb, each elementary school teacher might consider taking at least one field trip every three or four weeks. . . . Field trips are more important today than in former years because of children's homes (growing up places) are increasingly farther removed from other community activities. Urbanization, zoning and ease of travel separate residential and living areas from business, industry, government and other activities. Consequently, if we would have our children understand and appreciate the various elements of modern living, it seems essential for the school to overcome this segmentation of communities in the minds of students by frequent and varied field trips."

Extracurricular events and field trips have become a part of the daily school operation. However, care along with proper planning and program coordination should be carried out by building level administration and teacher personnel. Board of education policies may require coordination with central office personnel in the areas of curriculum, interscholastic sports, and/or transportation concerning field trips or extracurricular events. Careful planning and coordination can assist school personnel in being "before the fact" if a legal situation arises. Students that are participating in extracurricular events or field trips are owed a standard of care by the principal and his/her staff members (those individuals that are involved in a particular activity). The principal needs to have building level policies which guide, supervise, coordinate, and properly plan the event from the perspective of the building level. In providing for the welfare and care of participating students (in field trips and extracurricular activities) the school board and building policies will be enforced (at the school site and away). Tort liability situations can be well grounded if negligence by school personnel can be proven. By providing for an excellent "standard of care" (on the part of school personnel) through policies and policy enforcement, the better are the chances of school personnel overcoming a law suit attempt.

Another legal point that is in need of explanation is the legal concept of "in loco parentis." The definition of this legal term according to Jenson and Stollar is[4]:

> "In place of the parents; charged with some of the parents' rights, duties, and responsibilities."

In providing for the student participant's "standard of care," the principal and the teaching staff are also standing "in loco parentis" or in place of the parent. The courts for the most part have recognized this obligation of the school staff in tort liability litigation. Principals and teachers alike can be subject to legal action if the "standard of care" has been violated and negligence is proven. This position also holds true if school personnel have not made proper judgment in standing "in loco parentis." However, there are times when "in loco parentis" can be placed in favor of the principal or teacher in exercising the duties of their positions.

E. RECORD KEEPING AND PRIVILEGED COMMUNICATIONS

The process of record keeping actions of this nature may involve a number of items such as:
1. Teacher Personnel Records
2. Student Personnel Records
3. Logistical Personnel Records
4. Financial Records
5. Attendance Records
6. Transcripts or Grade Records
7. School Property Records
8. Other Miscellaneous Records

A number of school districts are converting from manually constructed bulky records to computerized record keeping. Problems have arisen concerning access to records by unauthorized parties, or by school personnel (without authorization of the student or his/her parents if a minor). Unlawful entry into electronic information systems has become a problem even when various combinations of codes and coding devices have been used. Manually-kept records are even freer to access, because of only locking devices used as security or openness to the record storage area may allow unauthorized entry.

The building principal needs to establish policies concerning records and other confidential items. This task should be completed in addition to board of education policies and central office directives. Building level policies in this area should be custom made to meet individual school needs.

Emphasis needs to be made concerning the personnel records of teachers and students. These customized policies should include:
1. Record construction,
2. Record access,
3. Record storage,
4. Record security, and
5. Authorized dissemination and manner of dissemination of recorded information.

The law provides for the protection of personal information and the extent to which and how it can be released. Many school systems will not release personal information unless it is approved by the student (or his/her parent or guardian if the individual is a minor). A practice of this nature protects the school district and its personnel from the responsibility of releasing information to unauthorized parties.

Kemerer and Deutsch make the following statement to those in support of the "inherent right to privacy"[5]:

"... These advocates claim that for privacy or the 'right to be let alone' to take hold in our society, there must be statutory protection of specific areas of privacy. The statutory approach would, it is claimed, in combination with case law help nationalize the right of privacy in a variety of contexts. The general concern of these advocates include:

1. More attention must be paid not only to the citizen's right of access about data concerning him, but also the avoidance of all unnecessary sharing of data stored in the filing systems and data banks of business, government and educational institutions.

2. More attention must be given to the dangers of gathering personal or group information, however service-oriented the original intention of the organization. A new sense that the organization has no right to inquire into certain areas of one's life needs to be defined and fostered."

A more pointed direction toward student privacy plus the allowing of students and parents to review school records was the passage of the 1974 Family Rights and Privacy Amendment or the Buckley Amendment, 20 U.S.C.A. 1232g. Kemerer and Deutsch bring forth the following comments concerning this amendment[6];

"The Buckley Amendment applies to most educational institutions in the country and is intended to protect the privacy rights of parents and students by providing rights related to the keeping of student records. Until the child is 18 years of age or attends college, parents exercise the right on behalf of their children. Abuse of student records had become commonplace prior to the passage of law. Much of the abuse was done unknowingly, yet the damage in terms of college rejections, lost employment opportunities, and tainted reputations was great. The Buckley Amendment seeks to eliminate such abuse by giving parents and students access to their records and the opportunity to challenge inaccurate, misleading or inappropriate information contained in them. The measure also limits the educational institution's disclosure of data to third parties without the consent of the parents or student ... "

The Buckley Amendment has had a profound effect upon custodial procedures concerning the recourse of students. Similar procedures and policies have been enacted by school districts to protect the privacy teacher and other staff personnel records. These individual have also gained the right to review their personnel records.

A principal must follow all federal and state statutes plus board policies concerning the keeping of personnel (staff and students) and other records. The principal and his/her administrative team must enforce all directives and policies in the area of record keeping if it is to be effective. Action in this area lessens the possibility of tort action by students and employees.

F. THE BUILDING LEVEL'S LEGAL RESPONSIBILITY OF FINANCIAL MANAGEMENT

Financial management at the building level is carried out by the principal directly, or it may be delegated to an assistant principal or a member of the clerical staff. However, the principal has sole responsibility for the financial management tasks and he/she should actively supervise this effort.

Building level financial management is supervised and coordinated by the central office. Financial areas in which there needs to be coordination with central office are:

1. The purchasing of supplies and equipment.
2. Fiscal period budgeting.
3. Accounting for building level fund activity.
4. Extracurricular fund raising.

Monies that are received daily by a typical elementary, middle, or senior high school can amount to hundreds or even thousands of dollars.

Common sense informs us that there must be some type of legal control to safeguard the public purse. Education is primarily a state function which in turn gives this function to the people or the public. Therefore, an accounting of the educational tasks must be given to the people. Supreme legal foundations in building level financial management will rest with the state. State statutes may be specific concerning building level financial procedures or they may be broad. If a broadness does exists delegation and a more specific direction is sometimes given by the state board of education or the state department of education. Financial management directives given at the state level will offer a uniformity of financial procedures at all of the state's local school districts and the school buildings within the local school district.

If there is involvement with federal funds, federal statutes will usually outline procedures for management and accounting practices. These procedures are customized to fit the goals and directions of the federal government.

Typical key points of building level financial management that may be state prescribed to the building level administrator could be[7]:

1. Adherence to rules, regulations, standards, and procedures of the state and other policies adopted by local boards of education.

2. To provide for the safekeeping and handling of all monies and other tangible property.

3. To submit reports and other materials on time as directed.

4. To deliver all financial records, books, ledgers, reports, etc. as directed by the superintendent and local board of education.

5. To be accountable for material located in the school including its security, inventory control, care, and utilization.

6. To follow the prescribed procedures regarding purchasing.

7. To notify the superintendent and/or responsible central office personnel when theft, misplacement, or destruction has taken place.

8. To obtain written permission from the local superintendent before disposing of a transferring from the superintendent's jurisdiction any items for which the superintendent is custodian.

9. To maintain and keep records current by removing materials that have been superseded in accordance with instructions.

Other directives by the state to the local school district and the individual school building may be in the areas of:

1. Accounting procedures.

2. Auditing procedures.

3. Local school board financial policy direction.

4. Student activity fund procedures.

5. School building internal financial control.

6. Safekeeping procedures for building funds.

7. Insurances.

8. Property management and liquidation procedures.

9. Fund investments.

10. Deficits and deficit avoidance.

Local boards of education must work within the framework of the state. Financial management policy constructed by the local board must have its groundwork according to state law (and directives from the state board of education and the state department of education). However, local boards may refine or become more specific than state laws and directives. Local school district policy may in addition to the state's position require additional components (concerning financial management) that will be of concern to the building administrator.

Principals also have the option of refining state and school district level directives to meet the individual needs of the building. Again, mention needs to be made that upper governmental level (state and school district) direction must be respected and allowed to serve as foundational supports.

G. HEALTH LAWS AND CAFETERIA SERVICE

Principals usually do not have direct control over the food service operations within the building. The major thrust for the food service operation will most likely come from the school district's central office. Central office organization usually contains an operations slot for a supervisor of cafeteria or food services. The position of food service supervisor will most likely require a dietician's license along with the experience of administering mass institutional feeding. The food services supervisor many times has a direct line of authority and communication with the individual school cafeteria manager. If the school district has a centralized or regionalized food service preparation center, the central office food service supervisor will be in direct contact with the managerial staff of the food preparation center.

There is need for the principal to have an understanding of the laws involved in food service operations. A prime reason for this particular knowledge is the fact that his/her student body and staff will partake of meals prepared by the food service staff. The mere fact of meals being served in the principal's building places a portion of responsibility within his/her responsibility zone.

Food programs by the U.S. Department of Agriculture are offered by federal statutes to the states are[8]:

1. National School Lunch Program
2. School Breakfast Program
3. Other Miscellaneous Programs (such as milk programs, child nutrition programs, etc.)

The states will usually reinforce the federal programs by statute to include[9]:

1. Eligibility.
2. Coordination between state departments of education and local boards.
3. Reimbursement procedures.
4. Reporting requirements.

5. Record maintenance.

6. Minimum requirements for individually participating schools.

School food service operations must also comply with food health laws. The main foundation of food health law is at the federal level which concerns adherence to the Federal Food Drug and Cosmetic Act. This federal statute prohibits dispersal of contaminated foods, drugs, and cosmetics in the United States. The food section of the act establishes standards concerning ingredients, illegal foods, legal additions to foods, and the labeling of foods[10].

Enforcement of the Federal Food, Drug and Cosmetic Act is carried out a federal agency of the United States Department of Health and Human Services. This agency is called the Food and Drug Administration (FDA) and is involved in (1) investigations, (2) coordination with federal courts concerning legal actions against violators, (3) research[11], and (4) has responsibility for promoting sanitary conditions in public eating places[12].

States will also have food health laws which will vary from state to state but will be in compliance with federal statutes.

School systems must abide with both federal and state health laws. In addition local governmental food health units will have a great impact upon school food service operations. Local governmental health departments are usually very specific and direct in informing schools of the manner in which food preparation units must function.

Typical food health areas covered by a local departments of health could possibly be[13]:

1. Care of food supplies.
2. Food service personnel.
3. Food equipment and utensils.
   a. Material makeup.
   b. Design and fabrication.
   c. Installation and location.
4. Cleaning and sanitization of equipment and utensils.
5. Storage procedures for equipment and utensils.
6. Sanitary control of the food service facility.
7. Construction and maintenance requirements of the food service area.
8. Inspection procedures.
9. Examination and condemnation of foodstuffs.
10. Regulation enforcement.

The previous factors indicate that specificity of food health laws becomes more dominant at the local level of government. Local health departments have a closer relationship with school food service operations than state or federal agencies.

Local school districts will have even more specific policies concerning the operation of the food service mechanism. These policies will be in addition to the dictates of local, state and federal food and health units. Typical areas concerning health and sanitary measures in school food service areas brought forth by local board of education policy may include[14]:

1. Abiding with all federal, state and county regulations and practices regarding school food services.

2. Employee abidance with and the following of suggestions for the improvement of all school food services (made by the food service manager, the county, and state supervisors).

3. Proper personal appearance and cleanliness of food service personnel.

4. The nonwearing of jewelry in the food preparation area (jewelry can be a safety hazard).

5. The putting up of long hair, the spraying of short hair, and the wearing of hair nets on all hairstyles.

6. The wearing of a fresh clean uniform each day.

7. Forbiddance of unsanitary long fingernails and the wearing of colored nail polish.

8. Only food service employees should have access to food preparation area (unless external personnel have business in the area).

9. Observance of the United States Department of Agriculture regulations regarding the use and care of government foods.

10. To make food as wholesome and attractive as possible.

11. To promote nutrition education.

12. To furnish the food service manager with an annual doctor's statement of each employee's physical health.

13. To report all personal injuries to the food service managers.

14. The wearing of required white, nonskid sole shoes.

It was previously state that the building administrator usually does not have direct control over the food service operation. However, since the food service operation takes place within the confines of the building (in which the principal has authority and responsibility), there is a need for obtaining a knowledge of food and health laws, policies, and regulations. Negative situations such as closure by governmental health authorities, or a mass case of food poisoning will cast a shadow upon the building leader.

H. POLICY AND PUPIL TRANSPORTATION

Pupil transportation is governed by federal and state laws plus the policies of the local board of education. The central office director of transportation should closely follow the procedures dictated by governmental bodies.

Building level operations are involved with the task of pupil transportation, but not in a direct manner. A principal will most likely coordinate with the central office transportation director concerning policies relating to:

1. Time schedules to and from the school setting.
2. Passenger pickup points within the individual school zone.
3. Specific school bus routes within the school's zone.
4. Safety procedures while riding, mounting or dismounting the buses.
5. Pupil discipline and control on board the buses.
6. Safety procedures in the individual school's mounting and dismounting area.
7. Driver-principal relations.
8. Special provisions for the physically handicapped.

In addition to local school district policies in the area of pupil transportation, the principal may desire to construct additional policies (within the framework of the school district) to specifically fit the needs of the building. This may involve procedures such as:

1. School bus safety training of pupils.
2. A reporting system for school bus safety and control violations by pupils.
3. The establishment of principal-driver-pupil-parent conferences concerning pupil rule violations.
4. Disciplinary procedures for pupil violators of passenger policies.
5. Supervision of pupil holding, mounting and dismounting areas.

The principal's legal thrust into the task of pupil transportation will again involve mainly central office policy and the policy constructed to fit the needs at building level.

Federal and state laws are basically pointing at school bus operation, driver standards and training, special vehicles for transporting the handicapped, school bus specifications, and school bus inspections. These items are of more concern to the central office transportation director than the building principal.

I. DUE PROCESS AS IT CONCERNS
BOTH STAFF AND PUPIL PERSONNEL

The schoolhouse is a microcosm of society with both the staff and student body acting as true representatives. As long as organizations contain the human element, there is bound to be intervals of negativism within standard operational procedures. This negativism can be classified from pettiness to power struggles, to disruption, onto that of extreme chaos. The principal as manager of the building must exercise his/her authority to keep a smooth and synchronized functioning of the educational program. Continuous satisfactory (or more than satisfactory) operation of the school's educational program will allow for every segment of the building (instructional and logistical) to meet their various objectives. The accomplishing of the various segmented objectives will allow a smooth flow into the building's primary objective—Educating the children of the community.

Administrative involvement with a conglomeration of personalities both in the staff as well as the student body usually is the springboard to various types of problems with staff and student personnel. Nonadherence to policy, rules, regulations and statutes may lead to the principal's request (to central office and the local board of education) that a staff member or student be removed from the organization (the individual school and the school system).

Prior to the principal's action of proceeding to request dismissed in a teacher or a student, consideration must be made concerning the individual (teacher's or student's) constitutional rights which are provided through due process of the law. Due process or one's constitutional rights acquired as a citizen have their foundation in the fifth and fourteenth amendments of the United States Constitution.

The following segment of the Fifth Amendment to the federal constitution gives a vivid statement concerning the rights of the individual[15]:

> "...nor shall any person be subject for the same offense to be twice put in jeopardy of life or limb; nor shall be compelled in any criminal case to be a witness against himself, nor be deprived of life, liberty, or property, without due process of law..."

The fifth amendment gives direction toward totally encompassing due process throughout the nation. However, section one of the Fourteenth Amendment makes the distinction of further and explicitly delegating due process of the law to the states[16]:

> "All persons born or naturalized in the United States and subject to the jurisdiction thereof, are citizens of the United States and of the State wherein they reside. No state shall make or enforce any law which shall abridge the privileges or immunities of citizens of the United States; nor shall any State deprive any person of life, liberty, or property, without due process of law; nor deny to any person within its jurisdiction the equal protection of the laws ... "

Due process itself can be classified two areas of through. They are substantive due process and procedural due process. Substantive due process is concerned with sum and substance of laws, policies, rules, regulations and procedures of those officers of the public domain and their fairness applied in these situations. Substantive due process opens the door to judicial review of the works of officers of the public.

Procedural due process handily fits itself to personnel situations. This particular classification of due process of the law shapes or conforms laws, rules, regulations, and policies to be carried out in all fairness. Personnel actions involving suspensions or terminations must follow the procedures such as:

1. A statement of the charges.
2. One's right to a hearing.
3. One's right to counsel.
4. One's right to have witnesses.

School systems in their tasks involving staff and student personnel will usually have a system constructed to work with the procedural due process element. Since the building level is in immediate contact with the community, its pupils and its teachers, it is imperative the principals exercise procedural due process in their dealings with both staff and pupil personnel decisions.

Dismissal of nontenured personnel at the end of the contract period may in some states may not require procedural due process. However dismissal during the contract period may require procedural due process in some states. Both tenured and nontenured teachers may select the right of litigation after dismissal by the local board of education. Principals should always be "before the fact" and follow board policy and state statutes to the letter in dismissing or suspending both tenured and nontenured teaching personnel.

McCarty and Cambron make the following statement concerning guidelines that should be used in the assessment of a tenured teacher's due process rights[17]:

1. A teacher is entitled to due process of law prior to dismissal when a property or liberty interest exist.

2. A property interest is created through tenure, implied tenure, or contract.

3. A liberty interest may arise if the dismissal action imposes a stigma or damages the teacher's reputation.

4. At a minimum due process requires that the teacher be provided with notice specifying reasons for dismissal and an opportunity for a hearing at which to present evidence and confront witnesses.

5. All procedures specified by statute or contract must be followed in the dismissal process.

Presentation is also made by McCarty and Cambron concerning the due process procedures that the nontenured teacher may use in support if dismissal threatens[18]:

1. A hearing is required if the school board and its representatives create a stigma that might "foreclose future employment" opportunities.

2. The school board may create a de facto tenure policy, giving rise to "an expectancy of reemployment."

3. Expectancy of reemployment can be based on state statute or contract.

Student suspension and expulsion procedures may vary from state to state and somewhat from school district to school district. Suspensions are less severe and usually cover a short time period to resolve or serve punishment for fracturing or noncompliance with a rule. Teachers and administrators both have the right to commence expulsion proceedings. Both teachers and principals are given the authority to maintain control in the school setting, however, the local board of education has the final word. Statutes, rules, regulations and policies give both the teacher and the building administrator a reference point from which to exercise the authority associated with control of the student body. McCarty and Cambron are of the opinion that the judicial bench has given recognition to the following constitutional safeguards which are concerned with the element of procedural due process[19]:

1. Written notice of the charges, the intention to expel, and the place, time, and circumstances of the hearing, with sufficient time for a defense to be prepared;

2. A full and fair hearing before an impartial adjudicator;

3. The right to legal counsel or some other adult representation;
4. The opportunity to present witnesses or evidence;
5. The opportunity to cross-examine opposing witnesses; and
6. Some type of written record demonstrating that the decision was based on the evidence presented at the hearing.

In using the fifth and fourteenth amendments as the foundation for due process of law, similar actions are involved in dismissal and suspension of both teaching and student personnel. The building level administrator stands at the helm of control over both staff and students. If dismissal or suspension actions are to be taken, policy (building level and local board of education) rules, regulations and statutes must be adhered to. If any legal question arises the principal may wish to consult with his/her immediate superior and/or the local board's legal counsel.

J. SUMMARY

Building level law is found in the building policy book which be formulated by the principal and/or his/her administrative team. A key point that should be kept in mind is that all building level policy has to conform with local board policy, state rules, regulations and statutes, and the federal constitution. All building level policy should be periodically reviewed and evaluated for conformity with daily building operations. Policy that is obsolete should be terminated or altered to fit those requirements that are currently in demand.

Proper management of the building's maintenance and custodial operations programs will reduce safety and health hazards. Reductions in these two areas will help to remove those problems which could result in tort liability situations. The two best defenses against tort liability are:

1. Liability insurance, and
2. To be in the position of—"before the fact."

The principal needs to concentrate mainly on "being before the fact" in terminating all known and possible avenues of approach to safety hazards within the building and on its grounds. Adequate supervision of a more than satisfactory maintenance and custodial operations program is mandatory.

The safety program which is connected with building maintenance and operations has been discussed, however safety (as a deterent to tort liability) goes beyond building care. Areas of concern here may involve safety hazards in classroom instruction, field trips, extracurricular activities, etc.

Security procedures that are properly carried out and supervised by the principal and his/her staff can reduce legal problems such as: (1) tort liability; (2) theft; (3) illegal use of the building and its grounds; and (4) other criminal activities which could spawn at the building scene.

Field trips should be properly planned and coordinated between the principal, the instructional staff and those concerned units at central office (such as instruction, transportation and food service). The field trip tasks will involve the principal and his/her staff to be "before the fact" in planning proper supervision of students and the needed logistical support for the trip. Extracurricular activities will also require proper coordination, supervision, and logistical support in order to avoid foreknown problems and possible tort situations.

Clerical and guidance personnel plus the principal are considered to be the stewards of the school's records and sources of privileged communications. Policy needs to be enforced by the principal to the clerical and guidance staffs that record contents are to be considered confidential. Information that is to be released must be done so by the recommended guidelines of policies, rules, regulations, state and federal statutes.

Policy rules, regulations, and statutes will determine the procedures and guidelines concerning the task of financial management at the building level. The principal must strictly adhere to these directives in order not to cast any shadow of suspicion upon himself/herself and his/her professional career. Strict security measures must also be taken in the handling of the school's funds.

Operation of the building's food service program is mainly a central office effort. However, the food service unit operates within the principal's domain. The principal does bear overall responsibility for this endeavor and needs to have a knowledge of the health laws and other legal procedures involved in the preparation and serving of food to the public.

Pupil transportation is primarily a central office function, however, the principal needs to be familiar with board policy, rules, regulations, and statutes concerned with: (1) transportation safety, (2) passenger control and discipline, (3) scheduling, (4) pickup points, and (5) principal-driver coordination. Building level policy needs to be synchronized with the above items concerning: (1) campus bus parking, (2) mounting and dismounting areas, (3) procedures for transportation related disciplinary problems, (4) pupil transportation safety training, (5) driver coordination, and (6) coordination of the timing of the building's education program with bus time schedules.

Due process procedures as they are concerned with the dismissal of students and staff personnel must be followed absolutely to the letter. A nonchalant attitude by the principal in this area could lead to possible tort situations. The principal has only the right to recommend dismissal of a student or teacher. Only the local board of education can officially terminate a teacher or student from the school system.

When dismissal situations arise, the principal should follow to the letter: (1) local board policy, (2) state rules and regulations, (3) state statutes, and (4) the Fifth and Fourteenth Amendments of the United States Constitution.

REFERENCES

[1]United States Constitution, Amendment X.

[2]Ibid., Preamble.

[3]Johnston, A. M., and Harris, G. "Field Trips and Liability." *Tennessee Teachers* Volume XLII, December, 1974, pp. 5–7.

[4]Jenson, T. J., and Stollar, D. H. *Legal Terms and Phrases Encountered in School Administration.* Columbus, Ohio: The Ohio State University Center for Educational Administration, 1961, p. 12.

[5]Kemerer, F. R., and Deutsch, K. L. *Constitutional Rights and Student Life: Value Conflict in Law and Education.* St. Paul, Minnesota: West Publishing Co., 1979, pp. 680–681.

[6]Ibid., pp. 682–683.

[7]Tennessee State Department of Education. *Tennessee Internal School Financial Management Manual.* Nashville, Tennessee: State of Tennessee, 1977, p. 21.

[8]Tennessee State Board of Education. *Rules, Regulations and Minimum Standards for the Governance of Public Schools in the State of Tennessee.* Nashville, Tennessee: State of Tennessee, 1985, p. 159.

[9]Ibid., pp. 160–170.

[10]World Book, Inc. *The World Book Encyclopedia, Volume 15.* Chicago, Illinois: Scott Fetzer Co., 1985, pp. 801–802.

[11]Ibid., p. 803.

[12]World Book, Inc. *The World Book Encyclopedia, Volume 7.* Chicago, Illinois: Scott Fetzer Co., 1985, p. 302.

[13]Knox County (Tennessee) Health Department. *Regulations Governing Food Service Establishments.* Knoxville, Tennessee: Knox County (Tennessee), 1986, pp. 1–20.

[14]Knox County (Tennessee) Public Schools. *Knox County Food Service Employment Objectives.* Knoxville, Tennessee: Office of School Food Service, 1986.

[15]United States Constitution. Fifth Amendment, 1791.

[16]United States Constitution. Fourteenth Amendment, 1868.
[17]McCarty, M. M. and Cambron, N. H. *Public School Law: Teachers- and Students- Rights.* Boston: Allyn & Bacon, 1981, pp. 114.
[18]Ibid., p. 118.
[19]Ibid., p. 288.

CHAPTER III

THE PRINCIPALSHIP AND
THE SCHOOL COMMUNITY

A. THE SCHOOL—A COMMUNITY'S FOCAL POINT

The individual public school serves its immediate community (a designated segment of the total school district) to which it has been officially assigned by the local board of education. A local school district which represents the local community may be a county, a township, a city or a metropolitan government. A school principal is definitely in need of a knowledge of the entire community, but his/her primary focus should be with the individual school's community. This particular area is the provider of the students that are served by his/her (the principal's) building. The principal is charged with supervising a particular phase (elementary, middle, or secondary education) of education, to the children of the designated community.

A school community along with the overall local community is a part of the state community to which the primary process of public education is charged. Our states in turn make up our national community whose philosophies and ideals are perpetuated through the educational process in the individual school community. A principal is the key managerial hub in overseeing the school's instructional obligation to its community.

In taking a more precise observation of the individual school community, there is another community to which the schoolhouse has a very direct association—the family community. Currently our nation is facing a crisis in the breakdown of the American family. Divorce, separation, one parent families, and the introduction of the "latch key" child is placing additional pressures upon the individual school. These actions are also calling upon the school for innovative programs to assist the child who has been beleaguered by the ills of society. There are occasions when the school should interact and coordinate with external agency activities (within the community) to assist with various social problems. These other agencies could involve:

1. Churches of various denominations.
2. Social service agencies.
3. Local and state governments.
4. Recreational organizations and activities.
5. Organizations promoting the arts.
6. Defensive agencies such as law enforcement and fire prevention and protection.

The school is needed to train the child to be a solid member of society in his/her community. A school needs to work with its community and each family community represented. There is a need for liaison and coordination with community members concerning the cultural maturation of each child according to:

1. Developing socially accepted behavior.
2. Acquiring socially accepted system of values.
3. Responsibility to his/her self and society.
4. Obtaining knowledge and knowing how to apply such knowledge in a practical manner.
5. Proper citizenship.
6. Proper all-around development as an individual.
7. Developing an understanding of society's subsystems and their mores.

Socioeconomic status of the individual school community has a heavy influence upon the goals and the direction of the school. Even though the general and overall goal of the public school is to educate the community's children, the end result may be achieved along a variety of avenues. Higher level socioeconomic groups (if they are in the majority or maintain the balance of power) tend to place considerable pressure upon the local board and the individual schools for quality (and the maintenance of quality) of educational programs. In lower socioeconomic situations one may witness a less intensive effort by the community in general. However, this is not always the case. Many parents within the lower socioeconomic sphere desire the opportunity of their children to engage in an upward movement of the ladder of social class and the future reaping of the economic rewards associated with mobility.

The principal who is conscientious of providing the best of instruction, the opportunity for improvement and advancement for all students (regardless of socioeconomic status) will be properly contributing to the American community as a whole. All Americans need the opportunity for upward mobility.

In making the school a community focal point, effort must be brought forth by both the principal and members of the community. Being the manager of the building, the principal needs to orient both his/her instructional and logistical staffs and liaison officers that frequently interact with the school neighborhood. Action in this area will involve individual and organized efforts by the school staff to take part in or work with specified school and nonschool activities such as:

1. Churches
2. Social organizations
3. Community organizations
4. Community activities
5. Educational-community activities
6. Professional organizations
7. Various community clubs

In some school communities, the principal and his/her staff may find it difficult to formulate liaison and coordination with the surrounding community. Situations of this type should be countered with the enlisted aid of:

1. The building administrative team
2. The instructional staff
3. The clerical staff
4. The custodial staff
5. The food service staff
6. The students
7. Those parental and community persons or organizations that have a positive interest in the school.

An ad hoc committee of the above groups is needed to plan strategy plus methods of obtaining community interest and contributions to the individual school effort. The principal should approve all plans before they are implemented in order to stay within the policy perimeters of the local board of education and directives of the central office. Some planning may be unorthodox and may have the potential for attracting the enlistment of community members, however, it must be legitimate.

The individual school is a microcosm of American society and needs to be regarded as such. It (the school) is the community's focal point and its center for learning. A school is also the nucleus for disseminating knowledge to youth and preparing them (to the best of the individual's ability) to contribute to and be a part of society. A typical community supports the school with finances, personnel, materiel, and services in order that the task of education can be carried out. The school in turn trains and equips the children of the community to be responsible citizens. Such citizens are needed to carry on the philosophical foundations of the nation. A school is indeed the focal point of the community — from a local, state, national and global viewpoint.

B. COMMUNITY ORGANIZATIONS AND ACTIVITIES

Direct involvement with community organizations and their activities will provide bonus points for the school district and the individual school. Tasks of this nature will provide a school system and its individual units an excellent opportunity to obtain and maintain a positive image in the eyes of the public.

Community groups through interaction with school personnel have the opportunity to become acquainted with individuals that are responsible for the daily operation of the public schools.

Before embarking upon a program of school personnel involvement with community organizations, there is a requirement for considering certain foundational factors. Such as:

1. Overall evaluations of the organization.
2. Examination of the organization's philosophy and purpose.
3. A critical study of the possible benefits that the school system can derive through intergroup coordination and task accomplishment.
4. A construction of an organizational study scheme and selection procedures.

In addition to the above mentioned criterion the school district and the individual school will be in need of formulating policy concerning the interaction of public school personnel within community organizational groups. Items that are in need of coverage by policy should be in the following areas:

1. The philosophy of the organization must be in line with that of the school system.
2. Population coverage of the organization.
3. A critical examination of the organization's goals.
4. Interaction procedures between school personnel and organizational personnel.
5. Determining whether the organization has external ties with other units.

6. Establishment of a central office administrator as having direct responsibility for participatory program involvement.
7. Appraisal of the participatory program.

A typical community will most likely offer a diversity of community organizations. Different organizations represent different philosophies, objectives, and an attraction to various segments of the population. Kindred, Bagin, and Gallagher[1] developed the following classification of general community groups which can fit into the public school situation:

1. Cultural groups
2. Principal economic groups
3. Fraternal groups
4. County, state, and national governmental groups
5. American patriotic groups
6. Political groups encompassing American ideals
7. Professional groups
8. Religious groups
9. Retired groups
10. Welfare agency groups
11. Youth organizations

Care, caution, and the following of school district and building policies should be exercised when selecting or working with any of the above groups classifications. The principal needs to bring to mind that he/she carries the overall responsibility of the building, and the professional activities of its personnel on or off site.

The active participation of school personnel with community organizational activities can provide for a more than adequate standard of goodwill between the school and its area. However, there is need for policy development, policy adherence, organizational study, and caution to be exercised if the optimum of balance is to be achieved between school, organization, and community.

C. COMMUNITY PARTICIPATION
IN THE EDUCATIONAL PROGRAM

During the 1960s and early 1970s the American public school system witnessed a significant amount of movement toward the community controlled school system. The late 1960s Ocean Hill-Brownsville confrontation between a neighborhood community and the New York City School System brought forth a classic example of active and direct community input and school control to the nation. Such direct and overt control of the educational program by lay persons can place the public school system on an azimuth toward chaos and destruction. If directions of this nature cannot be properly channeled, the educational process as we currently know it can be drastically altered.

The principal must take caution when proceeding to include community involvement in the school's program. Careful study and planning needs to be taken respecting the (1) extent, (2) type, (3) direction, and (4) objectives of community participation in the individual's school's educational program. A principal must take into account that he/she will be wholly responsible for the instructional task of the building. Accountability will place a true bearing against the building administrator and the instructional staff.

A typical or a more status quo blend of community involvement with the school's educational program currently exists in a number of schools. This can be viewed through community representation within the local board of education. Membership on the local board is not concrete and there are democratic influenced procedures (through the voting process) which allow for the community's desired changes. Changes within a particular community concerning societal thought, values, controlled and uncontrolled inducements will generate the act of board replacement with individual of like opinions.

Each segment of the community will send forth its champion to: (1) enact policy, (2) alter or maintain school district philosophy, (3) adopt and establish budget priorities (as it concerns the overall educational program), (4) acquire, evaluate, and train both instructional and logistical support personnel, and (5) to sit in judgment of personnel concerning infractions of board policy, plus state and federal states, rules, and regulations.

Each individual board member brings not only his/her representation of a particular community, but also a personality which will allow for a particular variety of reciprocal actions with other board members. As board members change so will the previously mentioned actions.

As the social chemistry of the board becomes different so will those policies enacted concerning the school's educational program. This action involves a normal or status quo influence brought about by the input of the community. Though one might find this method somewhat indirect, yet it follows a democratic pattern which involves popular vote and representation of the community.

The principal needs to realize that community involvement in the education program may be classified into three groups. They are:

1. Invited—This particular classification comes as a result of the building's administration and staff opening the doors to community input uncertain program segments. An action of this type is taken after considerable effort in study and planning (on the part of the individual school's administration and staff) has taken place. A task of this nature usually allows for controlled community input.

2. Anticipated—Community involvement of this nature may come as a result of some school action or policy prompts community awareness and concern. Community input of this type may be negative and induce the formation of pressure groups demanding change. Involvement of this type may also lead to community litigation in the courts. Administrators should be familiar enough with the pulse of the community to know when there is a possibility of an anticipated reaction by the lay public. It needs to be noted that some anticipated community actions are positive and their reciprocated actions are favorable.

3. Impromptu—When a community resorts to an impromptu fashioned input of the educational program, the administration and its staff is totally unaware and often is caught off balance. Community input of this type may be planned or unplanned, however, the effort upon the school administration and staff will be the same.

In order to have adequate control over community program input (at the building level) there is need for school district policy and central office coordination. Such policy and coordination should reflect the principal's right to establish a community advisory committee. This should be a standing committee with bylaws which allow for periodic membership changes, goal construction, tasks development, task orientation, task implementation, and evaluation. Administrative team members and instructional staff members should be tactfully orientated as not to allow community persons to gain control of school operation. The school's advisory committee and the education program.

Committee membership should be constructed from:

1. A proper cross section of the school's community.
2. Teachers
3. Logistical staff members
4. Administrative team members

The principal should stand ex-officio concerning committee work actions, however, he/she should have final approval of all committee proposals before they are considered for enactment and as a part of the school's program. All approved committee proposals must be in line with local board and building level policy. All community input should be definitely under the control of the principal and his/her administrative team.

Working guidelines for the building community advisory committee could be in the following areas:

1. Definition of the role of the individual committee member and how it will be played.
2. Definition of the tasks of various subcommittees as they are formulated and the expectations of each subcommittee.
3. Committee size should not be less than ten and no more than twenty-five (depending upon grade level and enrollment of the individual school).
4. Construction, review, evaluation, alteration, and/or termination of bylaws.
5. Assessing the community and the school's desires and needs.
6. Goal construction, achievement, and evaluation.
7. Problem solving.
8. Decision making.
9. Crisis management.
10. Community cooperation.
11. Coordination with community business, industry, and organizations.

Community involvement with the school's program of education needs to be under close scrutiny by the principal and his/her administrative team. Again, care must be taken as not to allow community representatives to overtake administrative authority. An action of this nature would be a boon for the community, but a blemish to the carrying out the task of administrative responsibility.

Community advisory committee proposals need final approval by the building administrator before being enacted. These proposals need to be in line with local board and building level policies. An added caution at this point is that the advisory committee's program needs to reflect the community's social and economical climate.

D. COMMUNITY INFLUENCE AND PRESSURE GROUPS

Some experts in the field of educational administration are of the belief that the doors of the school should be open to the public at large.

Since the public school's foundation has its roots in public ownership, such a thought appears to be plausible and furthermore it is legally correct. However, when a local school board hires: (1) a superintendent, (2) a central office administrative team, (3) the building principal, (4) the building level administrative teams (if building size and demands warrant such a team), (5) instructional support personnel, and (6) the instructional staff, a burden of responsibility is placed upon each of the above sections of the district and school's curricular machine.

Community participation should be welcomed, but yet accepted only to a point of limitation. If the community's thrust goes beyond such boundaries, administrators and other school personnel create the possibility of losing a grip on accountability, authority, and responsibility. In other words there is a strong possibility that the community could become the dominant force with administrators and teachers being no more than programmed robots.

Community participation should be welcomed, but not to the point of direct takeover of the local school district's overall function.

Public schools have been established by the state for the purpose of educating children of the populace. This task is financed through the public tax. However, administrators instructions support personnel, teachers, and logistical workers are given responsibility by the state to perform their duties (which are directed at the overall goal of providing a free public education to all).

Communities should not be shutout of the school's business, but their penetration into the school's business needs to be controlled in a discreet manner. Administrative actions that are discreet in nature can possibly pave the way to positive contributions by the community when the increasing of taxes are needed for school operations or capital outlay. The bridge between school and community must never be burned.

Communities are centers of power and this must be recognized and respected by school personnel. Power represents a nucleus of control by one person or a grouping of persons. Through the medium of control, a particular direction is set in motion towards a certain selected outcome or a series of outcomes. The element of control (by one or more persons) provides for a persuasion of others, not within the nucleus of control, to comply in the power source's attempt to reach a certain selected outcome. The occupant(s) within the center of control become the decision makers, however, the certain selected outcome(s) cannot be guaranteed. If the strength of the power nucleus (of control) has reached a point of absolute greatness, many times the nonreaching of a goals is discarded for new and possibly altered attempts for the same or new goals.

Community power over the school system (as was previously mentioned) comes normally through representation on the local board of education and a variety of facets within the community such as:

1. Families and family groups.
2. Government and governmental organizations.
3. A variety of public and private organizations.
4. Ethnic groupings.
5. Socioeconomic groupings.
6. The Democratic and Republican political parties.
7. Religious denominations and interreligious organizations.
8. Business and industry.
9. The Chamber of Commerce.
10. Labor unions.
11. Cultural groups.
12. Mental health organizations.
13. Medical and dental organizations.
14. Public health organizations.
15. Social welfare organizations.
16. Splinter groups.
17. Formal groups.
18. Informal groups.
19. Professional education groups.

A collective and channeled use of power leads to the formation of the process called influence. Influence is the end result of collected and channeled power. These actions can produce certain types of effects. The principal needs to be aware of both power and its by-product influence in his/her school's community (and the overall school district community). Realization of a two-way process must also be taken into account by the building administrator. A school will have influence upon the community and society in general. Schools will point the direction and prepare individuals to be ready for society. Schools also influence society from the view of how it (the individual school and the school system) process certain aspects of authority upon the community in its (the school's) daily operational process. Items such as the following must be taken into account:

1. Policies.
2. Student discipline.

3. Curriculum guides and programs.
4. Administration of instructional and logistical personnel.
5. Logistical programs.
6. Evaluations.
7. Extracurricular programs.
8. The carrying of state and federal directives.

Community influence upon the school and school system has become more intense and more demanding. This is due to the fact that the community (as a whole or segmented) can greatly contribute to change through:

1. Direct force by demand(s)
2. The ballot box (local, state and federal officials)
3. Referendum
4. Recall
5. The courts

A principal needs to be skillful and tactful when working with the school community. These two factors (skill and tact) can be used to the point that community will have reasonable input into some areas of: (1) problem solving, (2) decision making, (3) planning, and (4) appraising. Care needs to be taken for a more complete control by the principal which would not reduce his/her authority. Neither would there be a desire for a porous construction of the overall building responsibility that has been assigned to the principal.

A more specific segment of the community which can challenge the principal for power is that of the pressure group. Members of these groups are united for some particular objective accomplishment. In order to obtain a programmed achievement of some type, a campaign is waged to gain additional supporters (or a majority or near majority of general community assistance). A majority or slightly less than majority support can have a great impact upon boards of education and other elected officials. This is especially true if these public officials have a fear of the constituency.

School principals need to establish and maintain a system of two way communication (overt and convert) into the territory served by the school. This will enable the building administrator to gain knowledge concerning the feelings and actions of the community. For example:

1. Social climate
2. Activity
3. Projections

4. Community leadership and leadership characteristics
5. Method(s) of persuasion being used currently, or projected for future use
6. Target(s) of influence
7. Strengths and weaknesses

Pressure groups can be small insignificant groups, but through the processes of superbly constructed scheme and programs of influence they can become formidable giants filled with a great determination. The principal (along with the central office staff) should try to cooperate and work with such groups concerning issues and problems. A power struggle with the individual school or overall school community should (if possible) be avoided. The victims of such confrontations are the students. Principals and central office administrators must remember that the schools and the school systems belong to the people. Administrators are charged with the task of operating the community's educational machine. The principal needs to work within the established system in order to coordinate or counteract with community pressure groups.

E. THE SCHOOL AND PUBLIC RELATIONS

The school principal is responsible for and must maintain a program of public relations. A building administrator also has the authority to delegate the task to a member of his/her building administrative team. However, the principal still carries the obligation of program responsibility which opens the door to a need for program supervision.

Public relations activities are a communications tool between the school and its immediate community. This tool allows the school to present itself and its program to the people. Public relations also provides a vehicle for community response toward the school and its program.

The principal needs to consider a number of factors when launching out towards a suitable public relations effort in his/her school's community. The factors to be concerned are as follows:

1. The establishment of a school public relations committee (consisting of administration, instructional staff, and the logistical staff).

2. Target identification of community areas (organizational and the general public) to be reached by the public relations program.

3. The construction of viable and stable projections concerning a public relations program for the school by the public relations committee.

4. Identification of overt and covert fashions of the power structure.

5. Evaluation and approval of a public relations program by the principal (and central office if mandated by policy).

6. Coordination by the principal and his/her subordinates between the school, the public relations program, and the targeted community.

7. Selection of media type (television, radio, the printed word, presentations, events, membership in community, organizations, etc.).

8. Establishment of a collection system for reverse flow communications (community to school).

9. Investigation and appraisal of community feedback.

10. Maintenance of a liaison (using school personnel) between school and community.

11. Maintenance of a troubleshooting mechanism (using school personnel and coordination with central office personnel).

12. Periodic evaluation of the total school public relations effort.

A more than adequate school public relations program will depend greatly upon the leadership and direction provided by the principal. The building's administrative team, the instructional staff, and the logistical staff can assist in the building's effort to carry out an effective program. The fostering and maintaining of positive relations with the community and its various segments is worth more than gold to the school and the school district. Goodwill can produce dividends for the entire school district.

F. SUMMARY

In viewing the individual school one will find that there is a dual representation. That is, the school represents the community and the community represents the school. Administrators, teachers, and logistical workers can be classified as officers and agents assigned to perform certain tasks within the school setting. However, these tasks are utilized into a combined effort which results in the school's daily operational function.

The public school system (except for the District of Columbia) is under the ownership of the state. One then must realize that the people are the state. A careful observation of state government will indicate that the state (except for Hawaii) in turn allows for the creation of the local school district and its policy making group—the local board of education. However, all governing acts of the board and property of the board are given by delegated authority and prime ownership to the state. Community representation at the local school district level comes with the power of the ballot box in the voting board of education members into office.

Within a given community the building administrator must recognize: (1) the influence of overt and covert power structures; (2) formal and informal pressure groups; and (3) other splintered and segmented associations that can have an effect upon the operation of the school.

A key question comes forth when the principal assesses the possibility of community input is—*How extensive should community participation be in our school's educational program?* Before responding, a series of certain items should be kept in mind. They are:

1. The maintenance of an effective public relations program.

2. A constant two-way communications system between school and community.

3. A superior system of coordination between the school, community, community organizations, and the power structure.

4. Heavy supervision of the community's participation with and input to the school's program.

5. Total remembrance of the principal's overall responsibility for the school's educational program.

Positive relations with the school's community should be one of the prime objectives of the principal's leadership thrusts. Positive relations are not given to the administrator. He/she must earn respect by the school's community.

CHAPTER IV

LEADERSHIP OF THE BUILDING LEVEL INSTRUCTIONAL PROGRAM

A. BUILDING LEVEL SUPERVISION AND INSTRUCTIONAL IMPROVEMENT

Instructional Leadership at the Building Level

The process of instruction constructs three primary factors within the school building's curricular atmosphere. They are:

1. *Instruction* is the school's primary purpose.
2. *Instruction* is the vehicle upon which the school achieves its primary goal—EDUCATING THE POPULACE.
3. The principal is the school building's *Instructional Leader.*

Leadership that is provided by the principal in the area of instruction determines (1) the buildings curricular climate, (2) the philosophy of the building administrative team, (3) the instructional staff outlook, and (3) the students' pattern of instructional undertaking. Instructional struggles and objectives can be won or lost by the curricular leadership of the building administrator.

In order to be a:

1. Pacemaker,
2. Innovator,
3. Troubleshooter,
4. One who provides orientation,
5. Taskmaster/taskmistress,
6. Communications transmitter and receiver,
7. Instructional Logistician (providing services and support),
8. Personnel manager (staff and students),
9. Training officer,
10. Space manager, and
11. Appraiser

of the building's instructional program there is need for the principal to set a course of direction. Demand will indicate a series of tasks that the building administrator should set to accomplish. They are:

1. Coordinating with the central office instructional unit's individual grade level and/or subject area's instructional format. This will involve:

   a. Grade level and/or subject area primary and secondary goals (which will also include those various intermittent goals along the yearly academic time line).

   b. Central office's procedures for attaining all instructional goals (primary and secondary).

   c. The central office plan for estimating those requirements for the building's students, and the projection for the level of student achievement.

   d. Central office's plans, procedures, and desired outcomes for teacher orientation and inservice training.

   e. Coordination with the central office units for instruction and personnel for staff recruiting, transferring, and replacement.

   f. Coordination with the central office instructional supervisory unit, and the determination of expected instructional goals by the teaching staff.

   g. Determining and coordinating plans for teacher assistance in instructional presentation and improvement.

   h. Coordinating the plans for actual teacher appraisal.

   i. Coordinating the plans (through standardized teaching procedures) for student appraisal.

2. Constructing, planning and determining the refining of the central office instructional program to meet the needs of the individual building through:

   a. Determining primary and secondary goals of instructional programs (subject area and/or grade levels). This phase should involve intensive combined efforts of subject departmental chairpersons and/or grade level leaders along with teaching staff members.

   b. To provide training for the instructional staff concerning:

      (1) Program alterations
      (2) New programs
      (3) New staff members
      (4) Probationary personnel (nontenured)
      (5) Refresher programs for tenured personnel

   c. Administering the individual building's appraisal of each subject matter and/or grade level instructional program to determine if:

    (1) Overall and secondary instructional programs are being met in regard to:
        (a) Student achievement
        (b) Teacher accountability
        (c) Chronographical achievement
        (d) Building achievement
        (e) The accomplishment of public or community expectations

  d. Providing for instructional support services such as:
    (1) An adequate school library and research center
    (2) Instructional aids and resources
    (3) Electronic instructional assistance
        (a) Audiovisual aids
        (b) Computers
        (c) Robots
    (4) Guidance and counseling
    (5) Psychological services
    (6) School services
    (7) Attendance surveillance
    (8) General pupil personnel management

3. Teacher personnel administration through:
  a. Coordination with central office personnel administration
  b. Teacher recruitment and selection
  c. Supervision of teacher instructional activities
  d. Scheduling and class assignments
  e. Teacher evaluation
  f. Teacher transfer
  g. Promotion of teacher personnel
  h. Teacher dismissal
  i. Training

5. Space management of the building to fit:
  a. Student requirements
  b. Instructional program requirements
  c. Teacher workload
  d. Building synchronization

6. Constructing and maintaining a public relations program concern-

ing the school's instructional format with the school's immediate community.

7. Providing for logistical services which support the instructional program such as:
    a. Clerical and office management
    b. Computer management
    c. Food services
    d. Building maintenance and operations
    e. Transportation coordination
    f. Financial management

8. Establishing and maintaining two-way communications lines with central office and the community.

Instructional leadership at the building level requires a supreme effort by the principal and his/her administrative team. There is also a need for assistance from instructional support personnel such as guidance counselors, librarians, etc. A principal must never forget that instructional leadership is his/her primary task. The typical instructional leader will work with his/her administrative team, instructional upport team, and the instructional staff in the following manner:

1. Keeping personnel aware of all situations concerning the instructional effort.
2. Setting the example by determining the pace which concerns attitude, philosophy, work ethic, and making the effort to go beyond minimal expectations.
3. A proper carrying out of administrative tact and bearing.
4. Being fair but firm with all personnel.

B. INSTRUCTIONAL IMPROVEMENT AND CURRICULUM SUPERVISION AT THE BUILDING LEVEL

Society's quest for knowledge, its need to perpetuate and sustain itself, its need for advancement, its need to repeat some ancient rite, rule or some pattern of a generation or two ago, and those whimsical jolts that place an uneasiness within the souls of mankind all have an influence on the school's curriculum.

Modernistic society will place its burden of alterations upon education. Pedagogy has been the tool for altering the status quo among youth who are preparing for placement and contribution to society. The principal, being a line administrator is in constant contact with the community, and must set the pace for instructional improvement with his/her instructional staff. This pace making feature also needs to include the school's community which is a segment of society within proximity of the school itself.

Prior to reaching the individual school, societal demands usually commence operation with a worldwide, or yet more specifically a national requisition or exigency. This alarm system usually moves down to the primary public education seat of power—the state. State legislatures, state boards of education, and state departments of education will often-times dictate curricular alterations to local boards of education and local level central offices. Central office administration will follow state guide-lines and formulate programmatic alterations for the school district as a whole. It is the duty of the building principal (in accordance with state and central office guidelines) to adjust the curriculum through involve-ment with:

1. The building level instructional program.
2. The community.
3. The students.
4. The instructional staff.

The Building Level Instructional Program:
Planning and Implementation

An individual school's overall instructional program will consist of a variety of subject matter patterned for various grade levels (K–12). By pinpointing any subject at its particular grade level, one will find a series of secondary and primary objectives (which are to be achieved along a projected time line). An instructional time line represents the academic year. The format for the instructional program will be forwarded from the state office of education—to the local board and its central office team—and lastly (from an administrative point of view) to the building principal. A building level administrator must hone the local school district's program to, meet the needs of the school. In meeting the instructional needs of the building, there are three prime factors to con-sider: (1) the community, (2) the students, and (3) the instructional staff.

The Community

In launching the planning phase for the individual building's instructional program, a very critical observation should be made of the community and its children. Input needs to have been made by various school-community groups such as PTA, mothers' clubs, booster clubs, community education programs, school district wide organizations, and special ad hoc school-community committees. Upon the receipt of information regarding the curriculum from the above mentioned groups, the principal, his/her administrative team, department heads, or grade level leaders should go through the process of evaluation. Once the community data is appraised, categorized, prioritized it should compared with the state and local board of education objectives for each specific subject matter area.

If discrepancy exists and their is a possibility for elasticity the school district goals and the school community needs should incorporated (within state law and local board policy limits). However, if there is no room for elasticity between community, state, and school district instructional goals, it will be up to the community and/or educational professional organization to request change. Actions of this nature would be through state legislative units and local boards of education.

A principal's observance of the character of his/her community can assist in shaping the instructional program to meet community needs. Items such as the following factors can provide assistance:

1. Identification of the dominant socioeconomic group.

2. Identification of the less than dominant socioeconomic group(s).

3. What are the instructional program needs of each socioeconomic group?

4. What are the instructional program needs which would allow the less than dominant socioeconomic groups to compete on a level with the dominant socioeconomic group?

5. Identification of the instructional needs required to assist the community's children to compete and function with comparable students in the region, the state and the nation.

6. What are the instructional needs of the community's students to function as responsible American citizens?

Once community information has been processed by the principal and his/her team and the above listed issues have been properly responded to, the second series of processing is ready to commence operations. This second division concerns the students which attend classes at the individual school.

The Students

Students within a particular school are usually broken down into subgroups according to their abilities and levels of achievement (as witnessed by test scores and their grades). These subgroups are further divided into individual classes and class patterns. For example, some schools may further divide students into homogeneous groups (students that are similar according to ability and achievement), or into heterogeneous groups (in which students are not similar or are rather mixed according to ability and achievement). One needs to remember that no matter how grouping is arranged, the individual child's needs should be met.

Instructional program concerns for the individual child should be studied according to:

1. Motivation
    a. Methods of motivation
    b. Time consumed to motivate
2. Achievement of learning objectives
    a. Time consumption involved
    b. Breadth and depth of achievement
3. Manner of acquiring knowledge
    a. Use of the instructional program methods
    b. Use of the student's own methods
    c. Use of supplementary methods outside the standard instructional program

Information concerning the above mentioned three points can be gained from testing, reviewing records, and members of the instructional staff. Data of this nature needs to be processed in order to offer an instructional program within the grasp of all children within a standard instructional unit.

After the principal, the building administrative team, and the instructional leadership team (department heads, and grade level leaders) have received and processed input from the school's community and its students, the school district instructional program should be modified (within legal limits) to meet the building's objectives. Evaluation of the building's objectives can be gained through student achievement scores during the forthcoming academic year.

Elasticity is a must if building objectives are to coincide with school district goals. Socioeconomic standing can have a powerful influence achievement and aptitude testing. Instructional program emphasis can assist in the possibilities of correcting such deficiencies. Program elasticity has the contingency for allowing the principal (in his/her construction of the building's curricular program) to construct variations possibly in:

1. Selecting textbooks and curricular programs that better meet the needs of the students.

2. Seeking and obtaining curricular specialists (exceptional teaching personnel) (in various areas) to assist the mediocre, the less than mediocre, and the gifted students in reaching attainable program goals.

3. Providing three dimensional and "hands on" experiences for the student-learner through educational media services.

4. Seeking and obtaining resource persons, organizations, and task operations for student observation and/or participation in cooperative ventures.

5. Acquainting all students (that are physically and mentally able) to use and work with word processing and computer equipment.

6. Providing each student with the ability to read, comprehend, write, and converse in not only English (the mother tongue), but Spanish (a growing influence in American society) and another language as an elective of the student or his/her parents. Language opportunities should be offered in grades K–12. The schools need to prepare our future citizens to meet future language requirements that are cultivating within our national boundaries.

The building level instructional program should be designed to meet state, local school district, the community, national, and most of all the students' requirements. Students must be trained to be a part of and to work within the American society.

The Instructional Staff

A building unit's instructional staff is charged with the responsibility of carrying out the curricular program. This is accomplished through a medium called the learning process. Any instructional staff member must be guided as to: (1) the curricular program to be presented, (2) how the program will be presented, (3) the time period to be covered by the overall program area, plus the secondary segments of the program area, (4) primary and secondary goals to be attained during the instructional period(s), (5) the method and type of pupil evaluation systems to be used, and (6) measurement procedures to be used concerning instructional accountability.

The principal *must* plan, organize, provide, and administer periodic professional training for his/her instructional staff. The instructional segment of the building's staff must be acquainted with, plus have full knowledge of the area(s) they are to engage in the instructional process. It must be kept in mind that the typical principal may not have been trained in all of the subject areas in a particular school, but he/she needs to have a knowledge of the goals that have been established in each area. Another point which needs to be emphasized is the principal has overall responsibility for the various instructional programs being carried out within the school.

When a principal is faced with program or grade level areas which are unfamiliar, he/she has the opportunity to call on specialists from central office, textbook companies, and/or university settings for assistance. These experts can assist the building leader in providing professional training for the teaching staff.

Building level professional or inservice training supports the principal in carrying out not only the state and local school district instructional programs, but those adaptations that have been made to further meet the needs of the building community and its students.

Professional curricular training should be carried out according to state, local board and building requirements. The needs of the students should be placed in forefront of all proceedings. Inservice programs should be well planned for with the following points kept in mind:

1. Description of the teacher groups that is to be involved in the training session.
2. Identification of the need for professional training.
3. What are the primary and secondary goals to be reached in the professional training session?
4. What is the time period to be allotted for professional training, and the announcement procedures thereof?
5. Is there a need to use resource persons? If so, from what organization will they be attained?
6. Identification of kinds and methods of activities to be used and

how it will assist in solving the problem or need identified in items 1 and 2.

7. Selection of the method for evaluating the professional training activity.
8. A thorough study of the professional training appraisal data, and how further inservice activities can be improved.

With professional training completed and the teaching faculty oriented (not only to state and school district instructional requirements, but also that of the building as well) to the instructional phase, the learning process should commence operation. Responsibility is placed upon the principal's shoulder to measure the effectiveness of individual members of the instructional staff. Supervision of instruction falls mainly upon the shoulders of the building administrator. Some school systems allow for additional supervisory input by building level curriculum coordinators, department chairpersons, grade level leaders and/or from central office instructional units, however, the "buck" usually stops with the building principal. The format for teacher evaluations are most likely to be constructed at the central office level. These forms usually consist of some kind of numerical scale of teacher performance at various levels along with a grand total mark which will give the teacher an overall rating. Typical areas that are placed under evaluation are:

1. Classroom learning climate.
2. Teacher knowledge of the area of instruction.
3. Ability to function with and understand of various student types.
4. Proper communicative exchanges between teacher and the pupil(s).
5. Instructional motivation techniques.
6. Teacher ambition.
7. Overall teacher performance.
8. Proper classroom management (pupil, instructional and noninstructional matters).
9. Mental stability.
10. Proper interaction with parents, community, school-community organizations.
11. Oral delivery.
12. Personal grooming.
13. Character.
14. Assessment and/or identification of problems in teacher performance.
15. Recommendation(s) for solving problems.

16. Teacher input.

17. Teacher and principal approval by signature.

There are other means of evaluating the instructional effectiveness of the teacher other than the usual principal-teacher and supervisor-teacher methods. Other options that available are: (1) student-teacher and (2) teacher-teacher evaluations. Regardless of the method of operation, the principal should have the final decision concerning the outcome of teacher evaluations. These decisions may concern teacher dismissal, tenure appointment, promotion, or merit pay increases.

Principals should assist teachers in methods of correcting faults in instructional performance and classroom management once they are identified. There is also the need for teacher feedback in these situations. Teacher performance may be thwarted by items such as:

1. Pupils with extreme disciplinary problems.
2. Lack of proper teaching aids or materials.
3. Improper pupil grouping.
4. Pupils with extreme learning problems.

Principal interaction with classroom instruction should involve the observation and evaluation of both nontenured and tenured teaching personnel. All members of the instructional staff must meet the instructional goals that have been placed upon the school. The school setting does not fabricate some type of tangible product to place on the market. A school building provides a place in which young minds are trained to perform in society. The community and the nation evaluates the educational profession by the performance of the student once he/she leaves the school environment.

C. ADHERENCE TO CENTRAL OFFICE
CURRICULUM GUIDES AND GOALS

Curriculum formats, guidelines, and goals for building level operations are constructed at central office and are within those formats, guidelines and goals that are expressed in state law, by the state board of education, and the state department of education. Instructional construction and alteration procedures for the local school district are broad and meet those general needs of the school district population. Building adaptation of the curriculum (as previously stated) more specifically meets the needs of the individual building community area of attendance and those students involved.

Curriculum is primarily administratively controlled by the superintendent and the assistant superintendent or director of instruction.

Smaller school districts may (due to size and lack of the ability to remunerate top level administrative specialists) place all of these curricular tasks upon the superintendent and possibly an administrative assistant or two to provide managerial support.

In providing for the school district's curriculum program, the superintendent should provide district leadership and set the example concerning:

1. Financial management of the instructional program which includes budgeting, accounting, and auditing of instructional funds.

2. Personnel administration of the instructional team, the administrative corps (central office and line level (building administrators) involved in the instructional process).

3. Developing, arranging and supporting a program of instructional supervision and the personnel needed in this particular task.

4. Providing for guidance and counseling support of the instructional program.

5. Fostering the development and constructional design of the school district's curriculum.

6. Providing for instruction of the handicapped and gifted child.

7. Overall supervision of social services, psychological services, attendance monitoring, audiovisual services, teaching aid services, library and computerized research services, and paraprofessional instructional assistance personnel.

8. Use of an appraisal system (or systems) to determine whether the curriculum program and its services are meeting the prescribed objectives of the school district.

9. Continuous monitoring of the instructional program to determine if appraisals and observations warrant program termination or alteration.

Another key central office figure in the area of curriculum is the assistant superintendent of curriculum or the director of curriculum (depending upon school district size and organization). In medium to large school systems, the assistant superintendent of curriculum's unit may be further broken down into directorships. For example:

1. Director of elementary education.

2. Director of middle school instruction.

3. Director of secondary education.

4. Director of special and gifted education.

5. Director of vocational education.

Within his/her unit, the assistant superintendent of curriculum should provide leadership concerning:

1. Central office team assistance to the superintendent concerning matters of instruction.
2. Overall instructional evaluation.
3. Instructional improvement programs and procedures.
4. Teacher supervision procedures and the supervisory staff.
5. Program development.
6. Program monitoring.
8. Instructional staff training and improvement.
9. Pupil classification, grouping, and grade reporting.
10. Determining instructional and administrative personnel needs for the school district's curriculum effort.

A primary group which is part of the assistant superintendent of curriculum's unit is that of the instructional supervisors. Supervisors may be segmented according to grade level and/or subject matter. Size, organization, and financial ability of the school district will determine the type of scope of supervisory practice and staff size. Experts within the field of supervision operate from a variety of supervisory practices, however, a firm foundation concerning the supervisor's actions should include:

1. A thorough knowledge of the area in which one will supervise.
2. A thorough knowledge of classroom management procedures.
3. Familiarity with the various socioeconomic foundations of each school within the school district.
4. A thorough study of the academic preparation, personality, tact, bearing, character, and other background information of each teacher to be supervised.
5. Being able to coordinate and communicate (two-way) with building level administrators concerning curriculum procedures, curriculum goals, appraisal procedures, and the monitoring teacher instructional methods.
6. Being able to plan and carryout professional training programs.
7. Helping instructional staff members to:
   a. Project instructional units in time frames concerning:
      (1) Daily
      (2) Weekly
      (3) Monthly
      (4) The grading period

(5) Quarterly, and

(6) The academic year

8. Fostering the conceptual skills of teachers.

9. Assistance in the teacher's technical skills of instruction.

10. Identifying problem areas.

11. Constructing a plan to assist the teacher in removing problem areas.

12. Creating a two-way communications flow between the teacher and the supervisor.

13. Monitoring the instructional goal accomplishments of the teacher and the students.

14. The use of tact in handling negative situations including recommendations for probation extension or teacher dismissal.

15. Assist teachers in improving instructional and classroom management skills.

16. Assist the teacher in constructing testing procedures and other methods of evaluating student work.

17. Being able to conduct teacher group discussions and improvement seminars.

18. Keeping teachers aware of following school district curriculum guides.

Coordination between central office supervisory personnel and the building principals is a must. Central office curriculum guides and goals represent perimeters and accomplishments that are needed to make the building's instructional endeavor a success. Principals need to take time for classroom observation, supervision, and assistance. This gives the principal professional leverage and proof of an instructional staff member's ability or nonability to carry out required teaching duties. Principal monitoring of the classroom also provides evidence as to whether the teacher is staying within school district curricular guidelines. Indication is also brought forth as to whether both the student and the teacher are attaining their prescribed goals. Actions of this type will allow the principal and the central office supervisor to compare findings concerning teacher personnel. Another benefit of this process if that information obtained can be used in considering a teacher for tenure or promotion. Tenured personnel also need to be monitored to assure that the school district's instructional obligations are being met.

D. MANAGING INSTRUCTIONAL SERVICES

Each school building will require that certain instructional services are needed to support the various instructional programs. In providing for these instructional services there is need for school principals to engage in proper and adequate managerial procedures. Building level administrators involved in overseeing the school's instructional services activities should maintain a leadership role in the areas of:

1. Projecting the instructional services program for the forthcoming academic year.

2. Coordinating instructional services with individual instructional programs.

3. Establishing and enforcing policy concerning instructional services within the school building.

4. Appraisal of the school's instructional services program.

5. Alteration of the school's instructional program (from appraisal findings) to meet the more-than-adequate standards required in instructional program assistance.

The instructional services indicated at this point concerns those services that are directly involved with the instructional program. These services are not concerned with pupil personnel, but have a direct influence upon each instructional offering within the school. Duties that are of concern in this area are:

1. School library services.

2. Computerized instructional assistance.

3. Educational media services.

School Library Services

Every public school district in the United States needs to strive for an adequate (or more-than-adequate) library center in each of the schools (whether an elementary, middle, or senior high school setting). Today's learning requirements at all grade levels require that the student be given the opportunity for supplemental study and research opportunities. Students at all grade levels need to be instructed in the library's system of operations, service offering, and research opportunities. Also, pupils should be made aware of library policies, book and materials lending procedures and control, plus other library service offerings. Library skills should be introduced to children during the primary years.

The principal, school librarian and the classroom teachers should enforce school library policy concerning:

1. Care of books and other library materials.

2. Library loaning and returning procedures.

3. The arrangement and classification of books in the card catalog and on the shelf.

4. The Library of Congress Cataloging System for identification of various classifications of book offerings.

5. The proper training of students in proper use of library devices such as copying machines, microfiche, computerized library systems, etc.

6. Students should be oriented in basic (elementary years), intermediate (middle school), and advanced (high school years) research procedures.

There is a need for serious planning by the principal, the school librarian, department chairpersons or grade level leaders, and teachers concerning book and periodical collection and development of the school's library. Great care and serious thought should be carried out during this phase. Reference also needs to be made toward recent court cases across the land concerning parental disapproval of school library offerings and textbook usage within the school. The previously mentioned group could be formed into a committee with parental appointments. These lay persons would be representative of the community and have an active part in library collection and development proceedings.

Computerized Instructional Services

Administrative planning, policy, coordinating and evaluation is also required here just as well as any of the instructional services. Here again a close relationship between the principal, departmental chairpersons, grade level leaders, and teachers must take place. Additional coordination and training may be required with central office computer and instructional personnel concerning computer operation plus program offerings in various areas of the instructional format.

Computer assisted instruction will require a training program to acquaint the student with computer operation and learning assistance programs offered for computer use. Students should also be trained to use the computer as a research supplemental informational tool.

Computers can be programmed to reach the various learning levels of the children involved. It (the computer) can also be used as a device to challenge the premium student. Child motivation can at times be easier gained through the use of computerized instruction. Administrators and teachers need to realize that computerized instruction has a dual approach to the learning process. It (computerized learning) can be constructed within the individual instructional program and be a part of various segmented offerings of the unit itself. The computer can be an additional force to assist instruction that has been given in a role that may be remedial and/or accelerated. In addition to the previously described basic avenues of approach to computer usage in instruction, the computer can also be used as a high speed research tool. As a research instrument, the student is given the key to an electronic explosion of knowledge which has no elemental man-made depth or breadth. The student must be trained to select only those bursts of knowledge that apply to his/her current quest.

Computers in the learning process create a dual kinship between the student and the machine. Though inanimate, the computer allows for the student to become better aware of a systematic portion of the curriculum, or it can be said that the student is given the opportunity to explore beyond that which has been constructed by instructional specialists for a particular point within the academic time period.

Before students can be given the liberty of remedial opportunities or acceleration beyond the norm, the teacher must be trained and competent in the use plus knowledge of computer operations and program offerings. Building administrators should allow for teachers to gain this knowledge through college or university course offerings and/or inservice training.

Educational Media Services

If one is to provide a more panoramic view to the instructional process, there is a need to use a variety of learner assistance tools called educational media. Educational media can assist the teacher as well as the student in the conquering of instructional unit goals. Landers and Meyers define educational media as[1]:

"... a broad term referring to all tools for teaching and all approaches to learning. It encompasses such long used media as the following: books and other printed materials, maps, globes, pictures, models, realia, graphics, displays, dioramas, community resources, field trips, and plays; as well as audio-visual materials and equipment, teaching machines, computers, television (also VCR's), dial access information systems and student-response systems."

All of the items and their uses as previously mentioned must be supervised by the building administrator or delegated by his/her to responsible administrative or instructional personnel within the building. Use of these items must be coordinated with the various instructional units (grades and/or subject offerings) within the building. Policy should cover time period usage, the coinciding of media use with planned instruction, and its position on the instructional time line. There should also be an adequate inventory of various media items in order to prevent instructional bottlenecks with teachers of the same grade or subject area. Inventory procedures and identification system are needed for administrative property accounting procedures.

Administrators, department heads or grade level leaders, plus central office media and instructional personnel need to keep teaching personnel aware of the instructional media materials at their disposal. This task can be accomplished through inservice meetings, workshops, and catalog offerings and services. Some school districts have media centers that are open to all teachers within the school district along with media counselors ready to offer assistance.

The principal needs to have knowledge of the media offered and requested by the instructional staff, the system (whether central office and/or building constructed) for teachers acquiring and returning media (whether assigned from a media center or central office). If media items are located at building level administration is needed not only for loan and return procedures, but also for storage, storage space, and security.

E. SUMMARY

Building level instruction has its foundation in state law, state board of education dictates, state department of education rules and standards, and the curriculum program as established by the board of education to meet the school district's needs. The principal is situated with another dimension in that he/she must take the school district instructional program and fit it to meet the needs of the individual school community. The school community is a microcosm of the overall local school district. A building administrator along with his/her administrative and instructional leadership teams (along with community input) must form in the curriculum building task together. This particular venture is needed to fit the instructional program to meet the needs of the children.

In order to gain evidence that the school's instructional program is being carried out and meeting the goals of the school district and the state, the principal must supervise the instruction taking place within the building. This task is performed through classroom observations and evaluation of tenured and nontenured teaching personnel. Teachers that are having difficulties should be assisted in various methods of instructional improvement.

When curricular programs are somewhat adjusted to meet the building's needs (for its students and community) adherence to central office directives is a must. Central office instructional personnel many times will assist building instructional staffs in staff development through inservice training, workshops, and other types of exercises. The central office instructional office usually will employ a supervisory staff to monitor instruction within the district's schools. Here again, the theme should be to assist teachers in instructional improvement. Central office supervision will also observe instructional staff members to determine if curriculum guides are being adhered to and that curriculum goals are being accomplished.

The building principal has not only been charged with being responsible for the overall instructional program within the school, but also with the proper management of instructional services. Services such as the building library, computerized instruction, and instructional media must be properly administered if it is to be effective in instructional program assistance. The policies governing the various instructional services are the key to proper administrative control and synchronized program assistance for both the teacher and the student.

REFERENCES

[1]Landers, Thomas J., and Myers, Judith G. *Essentials of School Management.* Philadelphia: W. B. Saunders Co., 1977, p. 265.

PART TWO

MANAGERIAL AND LOGISTICAL THEORY
AT BUILDING LEVEL

CHAPTER V

LEADERSHIP AND PLANNING

A. THE PRINCIPAL—CHIEF EXECUTIVE OFFICER OF THE SCHOOL BUILDING COMPLEX

School Building Organization

Organizational patterns of individual school buildings vary between school districts and within the school district. General school district differentiation may result due to the following factors:

1. Geographical size of the school district.
2. Pupil population size.
3. Philosophy of the school district.
4. Financial status of the school district.
5. Overall school district goals.
6. Overall school district needs.

Intradistrict or building diversification may be the result of:

1. Needs (instructional and logistical) of the individual school.
2. Grade level programs of the school (elementary, middle, or senior high school).
3. Instructional objectives of the school.
4. Logistical objectives of the school.
5. School plant size, construction, and design.
6. Budgetary latitudes and limitations.
7. Building level philosophy.

School district and building level factors influence the selection and maintaining of an organizational pattern within the building. There is a need to break down the term organization and obtain a critical view of the mechanics that are responsible for its operation. The key factor in building level organization—is that of personnel and position placement. Individuals involved in the organizational pattern can be categorized into four major groups which are:

1. Administrational—Building leaders that are involved with those

tasks that directly have an effect upon the personnel of a given building. Such as the instructional and instructional support efforts.

2. Managerial—Building leaders that are involved with certain tasks that place an indirect influence upon the building's personnel. For example, logistical services (such as clerical support, building maintenance, and operations, etc.).

The principal will find himself/herself involved with both administrative and managerial duties. He/she (the principal) will be held responsible for task performance and achievement in both of these areas.

3. The third category of personnel involved in the building organizational pattern are the educational specialists. These individuals are staff members that serve as curriculum coordinators, department chairpersons or grade level leaders, guidance and counseling personnel, librarians, educational media and resource persons, and school community relations personnel (such as attendance officers, social workers, etc.).

4. Logistical staff members form the last category of personnel involved in the school's organizational pattern. Individuals that are assigned the responsibility for clerical services, food services, etc. Personnel in this category provide service and support to the building operation.

Organization of the school building should allow for the principle of unity. The foundation for the need of unity within the building's organizational pattern would be that the labor effort by all building personnel would be entwined. This entwinement would also serve the purpose of assisting the school to achieve its overall goal of educating the public.

Prime building leaders (principals and assistant principals) and secondary leaders (such as department chairpersons or grade level leaders, head custodians, senior secretaries, cafeteria managers, etc.) should be connected with their subordinates through established two way communications networks. The communication network would assist leaders and subordinate in problem identification, problem solving and decision making. It must be kept in mind that school building size and population will have a great influence upon the number of administrators and subordinate leaders within the organizational pattern. In smaller buildings one will possibly find a number of positions assigned to the principal and individual members of the school's organization. In other words a variety of tasks are placed upon each key individual rather than an individual for each task (as witnessed by a larger building's administrative team and other secondary leaders.

The Principal As Chief Executive Officer

As the person who has been assigned overall responsibility for the building, its operation, and its personnel, the principal also has the role of chief executive. As for the principal's involvement within the school's business matters, the famous adage of former President Harry S. Truman applies — "The buck stops here." Chains of command at building level will vary according to the makeup which has been prescribed by the board of education. Figure 2 illustrates the line and staff operation with the principal as the chief executive officer (CEO) for the typical medium to large sized elementary, middle, or secondary school. The principal maintains a direct chain of command with the assistant principal(s) department chairpersons or grade level leaders and teachers (concerning instructional matters). Staff input to both the principal and the building administrative team is provided by three distinct units along with their representatives. They are the instructional services, pupil personnel services, and logistical support service units. Staff personnel do not have the privilege of a direct command upon the instructional program and as personnel. Their (the staff) input is presented to the CEO or principal for consideration and approval to incorporate within the school's operational scheme. Depending upon school district organizational patterns, representatives from ibrary, psychological, health, food, and custodial services may be assigned directly from central office. If this procedure is used, there will be need for the maintenance of coordination between these individuals and the building CEO (principal). Figure 2 easily applies to the CEO and his/her line and staff operations at either the elementary, middle, or high school.

To summarize the principal's position as building leader notice should be given to the many functions that are an integral part of the chief building level administrative position. These functions are:

1. The chief executive officer (CEO) of the school
2. The school-community relations expert.
3. A curriculum expert and instructional leader within the building.
4. A human relations expert (both staff and students).
5. The primary communicator who is involved with both transmission and reception.
6. Receives, seeks, and acts on program alteration.
7. An educational projector.
8. A program constructionist and taskmaster.
9. An appraiser of programs and personnel.

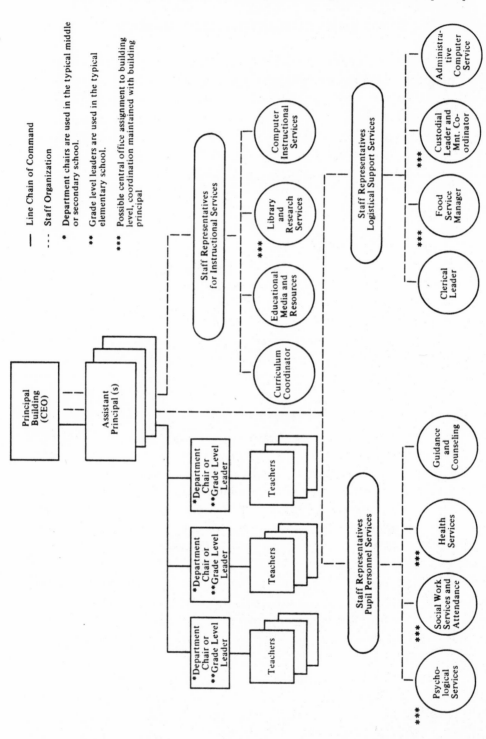

Figure 2. A Typical Medium to Large Sized Elementary, Middle or Secondary School Line and Staff Organizational Chart.

B. SCHOOL BUILDING LEADERSHIP

A leader can be described as one that provides authoritative control through the art of organizational philosophy, activities, and individuals. Leadership in the individual school building incompasses direction by the principal regarding:

1. The promotion of school district and building philosophy as it influences the educational process and the educational profession.
2. The staff, students and school community.
3. Those activities (instructional and logistical) that are integral parts of the school operation (see Figure 3).

In observing building level leadership, a penetrating view of philosophical direction needs to be taken. Prime organizational philosophy at the local level will be constructed by the nation, the state, and the community through its elected boards of education. Additional philosophical foundations of a lesser degree will be provided by the local school superintendent and his/her administrative team, the central office staff, and the building principal. An individual school building is a segment of school district society, and it possesses those qualities which are unique to its being and its place within the overall community. The principal first sets the pace of leadership within the school through a predetermined philosophical direction. Predetermination as previously stated comes through social and governmental levels ranging beyond the school. A principal's personal philosophical contribution should conform to the needs of his/her school and its community. Philosophical direction comes with a daily promoting process which involves the building staff, the student body and the building community with certain societal demands such as:

1. Those proper truths, concepts, and principles of existence.
2. Promoting need for wisdom and control of life's activities.

These factors are needed to properly influence the school's staff, student body, building level programs, and the community to the direction of education within our society.

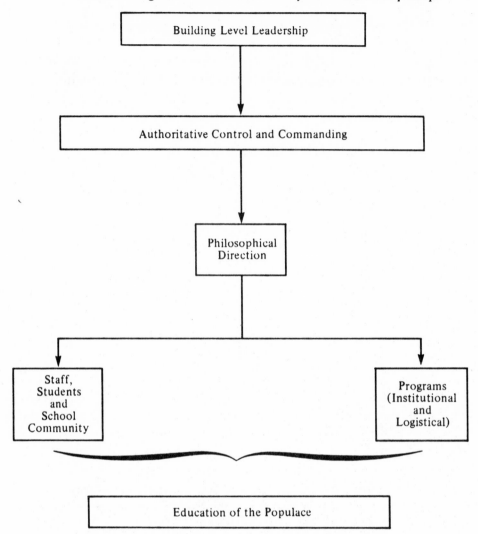

Figure 3. Leadership of the Individual School Building.

Leadership and Individuals

Individuals that are guided by the leadership of the school principal can be grouped into three categories. The first group to be discussed is the overall school staff. This group involves both the instructional, instructional support, and the logistical services teams within the building. These teams are involved with: (1) needs planning, (2) goal construction, (3) goal accomplishment, (4) task assignments, (5) task procedures, (6) problem identification, (7) problem solving, (8) decision making, plus

(9) building policy establishment and enforcement. The teams are also involved in providing administrative procedures which are necessary for satisfactory school operation. The principal should establish and maintain two-way communication lines with the building staff and other individuals (internal or external) that are involved within his/her zone of leadership.

The second category of persons that are within the principal's sphere of leadership is that of the student body. To the student the principal represents a person of leadership in the areas of:

1. Program offerings
2. Class scheduling
3. School student policy
4. Student discipline and control
5. Extracurricular activities
6. Student personnel administration
7. Student services
8. Grade reporting procedures
9. Student-parent-school relationships
10. References and recommendations
11. School promotion and tradition
12. Pupil transportation coordinator and controller
13. Breakfast and lunch scheduling
14. Control of breakfast and lunch areas.

The third and final category of individuals that are involved with leadership actions of the school principal is that of the school community. A school's community observes its principal as leading the community's instructional program offered by the school. He/she (the principal) is also considered the link between community and the building's instructional staff. A typical community will most likely observe the principal as the person that also provides the school with direction concerning extracurricular activities. Often community members will use the principal as their champion concerning building-central office matters.

Program Leadership

Program leadership involves two major areas at building levels. They are the instructional and the logistical. Instructional program leadership concerns may involve:

1. The various program offerings

2. Program construction
3. Program alteration
4. Program deletion
5. Program monitoring, supervision, and evaluation
6. Program assistance
7. Administration of all personnel involved in the instructional program

Within the instructional program format there is another segment which is in need of direction. This area can be identified by the term instructional services. The principal needs to exercise control over educational media and learning resources within the building. For those media and resources services that are external to the building (provided by central office) coordination is also needed concerning time consumption and assigned cost factors. Media and resources need to be established within the educational program in order to eliminate conflicts, bottlenecks. Provision is also needed for a synchronized operation in conjunction with standard educational program offerings. Logistical program leadership will be brought forth in later units of the book.

Style of Leadership

The style of leadership carried out by an individual principal will be unique according to:

1. Individual character.
2. One's personal perception of social and work ethics.
3. Methods of task assigning and task accomplishment.
4. Methods of goal determination and goal accomplishment.
5. One's concept of appraisal techniques.

By moving away from the personality of a given leader, entry should be made to yet another dimension. This dimension can be identified by conditions that are external to the building environment. For example: (1) Federal laws and directives, (2) state laws and directives, (3) board of education policies, (4) central office rules and regulations, (5) community pressures, (6) organizational (laypersons, professional societies, employee unions, etc.) pressures. External groups of this nature can have a heavy influence upon the leadership style and techniques of a building administrator.

Another avenue of approach which can influence a principal's style and technique of leadership, is that of internal pressures (within the building environment). Abilities and attitudes of subordinate staff members (the building administrative team, the instructional staff, the logistical support team) can possibly be a barometer to the principal's intensity of administrative power. Mostly positive subordinate groups will usually require less administrative prodding than mostly negative subordinate groups. Antiadministrative attitudes of subordinate personnel have the possibility of existing in numerous types of groups. However, if there is a high representation of antiadministrative followers within a given group, then a more stern approach and display of administrative power may be required of the principal (if he/she is to survive). In any setting (whether mostly positive or negative), antiadministration groups should be systematically neutralized. Actions of this nature need to be carried out if the principal's standard of leadership is to survive, and the school's goals are to be accomplished.

C. CENTRAL OFFICE DICTATES AND BUILDING LEVEL MANAGEMENT

The direction of various programs to the building level will represent board policies riding on the vehicle of central office administrative team dictates. The superintendent and his/her central office administrative team will construct and provide direction for the flow of building level programs (both instructional and logistical). A central office command post looks upon the various instructional and logistical programs mainly as a district-wide procedure. The central office format is more panoramic in scope than that of the building. However, one may find that the central office team may provide for specific programs within specific schools.

The Superintendent

In order to examine the area of central office dictates to the individual school, one should view the superintendent and the central office administrative team. The typical superintendent's team in a medium to large sized school district will most likely cover the areas of:
1. Curriculum
2. Logistical services
3. Personnel management
4. Pupil personnel services

5. Buildings and grounds management
6. Community affairs

First, let's look into the areas where a typical school superintendent can undertake tasks which will influence the building level. A typical superintendent should be in the process of reviewing and evaluating current policies for maintaining, altering, or terminating. Needs assessments should be made at the superintendent's level to determine if new policy should be built. All altered, terminated, and newly constructed policies needs to be administratively packaged and presented to the local board for review and possible passage into legal operating form. Once passed and placed into the board of education minutes, the policy becomes legal and binding on its date of implementation. Altered, terminated, or new policy is then dictated to the central office team and then to administrators at the building level. More complex policy procedures may require inservice training periods for principals, assistant principals, and staff members.

Instructional, logistical, and other nonacademic functions within the school system are given direction and guidance by the office of the superintendent. Overall support can be provided to activities such as:

1. Budgeting and financial management
2. Personnel needs and labor-management relations
3. Public relations
4. Support needs and services
5. Legal affairs
6. Computer services
7. Research matters, and
8. Plant management and upkeep

will have directives from the superintendent to respective members of the central office team, that will in turn forward specific directions to the building principals. The school building represents the lowest level administrative unit within the school district organizational format. Principals are in the position to further disseminate central office directives to their various building units.

The Assistant Superintendent of Curriculum

Central office team influence upon building level administration will come from the six previously mentioned team areas. Let's first take a look at the position of assistant superintendent of curriculum. This particular team member is in the position to indicate task flow and provide building level administrative personnel with assistance in the areas of:

1. Instructional planning and coordinating.
2. Instructional support services.
3. Teacher supervision and evaluation.
4. Instructional improvement.
5. Instructional training.

The Assistant Superintendent of Logistical Services

The assistant superintendent of logistical services covers the building level principal in those matters of providing that service support which is needed to keep the instructional program operational. Input coming from the central office logistical unit to the building principal will most likely involve the area of:

1. Financial management
2. Supply management
3. Equipment management
4. Storage management and procedures
5. Computer services
6. Food services
7. Transportation services
8. Risk management
9. Logistical services evaluations
10. Clerical support services

The Assistant Superintendent of Personnel

A key segment of the central office team in which a great influence is placed upon the principal and his/her building level operation, is the office of assistant superintendent of personnel. Various school systems will usually offer a variety of organizational patterns concerning personnel administration. In some school systems the administration of teacher personnel may come under the authority of the central office instructional unit. Logistical workers in some school districts may be administered out of the logistical management unit. Some school systems may place both instructional and logistical personnel under the assistant superintendent of logistical services. Using the approach of a unit headed by an assistant superintendent of personnel places the staff needs (both instructional and logistical) under one roof.

Principals are given guidance and the work format concerning personnel administration (instructional and logistical) in the areas of:

1. Recruiting
2. Selection
3. Appointment and Assignment
4. Training
5. Evaluation
6. Leaves and Terminations
7. Transfer
8. Promotions
9. Demotions
10. Labor-management relations
11. Grievances
12. Contract negotiations
13. Psychological and Counseling services (including drug, alcohol, and mental health matters)
14. Salary administration
15. Payroll procedures

Assistant Superintendent of Pupil Personnel

A well established system of coordination, assistance and delegated authority is needed by building level from central office involving the area of pupil personnel. The assistant superintendent of pupil personnel should realize that a proper relationship between his/her office and the principal's office is vital. Task procedures involving this particular area of concern are:

1. Health services
2. Guidance and counseling
3. Psychological services
4. Attendance monitoring
5. Social work services
6. Gifted and special education instructional programs and services

Assistant Superintendent of Buildings and Grounds

The assistant superintendent of buildings and grounds should have close contact with principals concerning procedures for building needs, operations, and maintenance. Building needs may require the constructing of additions to existing structures due to program or enrollment needs. In the area of needs there may requirements for building modifications (due again to program or enrollment needs). Building maintenance will require those items concerning the building, building equipment and surrounding grounds according to repair, replacing and servicing procedures. Operational activities at the building level will involve custodial services such as housekeeping, groundskeeping, and those minor repairs needed to keep the building functional on a daily basis.

The Assistant Superintendent of Community Affairs

Directives to the principal from the assistant superintendent of community affairs are also of prime importance. The individual school being the school district is smallest administrative unit plus the organization which is closest to the community. An individual school automatically becomes the central office representative to a community as well as a springboard for public relations activities within the community. The public school can be used to disseminate a variety of media devices such as bulletins, announcements, newsletters, etc. School-community programs such as those provided by school-community organizations, community education, etc., can serve to assist the school district in its public relations endeavors. The principal and his/her school staff can assist the school district in campaigning for public school issues that have been placed upon the ballot. Central office public affairs personnel need to have and keep a close relationship with building principal. The principal and his/her staff are in a position to obtain dividends for the local public school system.

In summary, presentation has been brought forth that supports the fact that the typical building administrator is in need of direction, guidance and pronounced zones of operational limitations. The key to such support is the superintendent and the central office administrative team. The superintendent and the team should likewise be in support of the principal being granted those rights to direct central office authority to his/her staff.

D. THE PRINCIPAL AND GOAL CONSTRUCTION

The organizational pattern that applies to any individual school automatically opens the door to the planning or projection process. Climactic results achieved at the end of the planning process are labeled as goals. Goals are categorized as those which are primary, general or overall in nature, and those goals that are secondary. The secondary goal is vital in the promoting the possibility of achieving the primary goal. Secondary goals are similar to the mass of clocklike synchronized gear work which assists in the primary role of time indication. The overall primary goal of any school (whether elementary, middle, or high school) is the proper education and training of its students. If the school's operational procedures are going to be sound and effective in the daily performance of various task areas, an appropriate construction of goals is necessary.

Building administrators and key members of the building staff need to take part in the construction of primary and secondary goals. This action should assist those preparations for the school as a whole and the various subordinate units within the school. The principal needs to obtain input from the school staff in the following areas:

1. Building level administrative team (assistant principals)
2. Department chairpersons or grade level leaders
3. Custodial staff leaders
4. Clerical staff leader
5. Cafeteria manager
6. Guidance and counseling leader.
7. School librarian
8. Educational media coordinator.
9. Building paraprofessional leader.

Participation by the above groups should bring together specific, but yet a marbled assortment of goals needed (both primary and secondary) that are in the various task areas which a part of the total building organization.

Each member of the building staff (along with the building administrators) should: (1) first take an assessment of the needs of their respective units, (2) establish a brainstorming technique to identify methods that could be employed in meeting the needs of the school an respective subordinate units, (3) the brainstorming list should then be reduced to only those items that are the most direct in meeting unit needs, and

(4) identification of the desired outcome of the method of meeting the needs of the unit (the school and its subunits) which are appropriate. Once the desired outcome or goals are established for accomplishing a series of needs (primary and secondary) for a particular building, an appraisal of the each individual goal is in order.

A series of appraisal points could be:

1. That there is a possibility that the goal can be attained.
2. That the goal can be attained within the period specified.
3. That there is room for subordinate leaders to innovate and operate through their own abilities to initiate action.
4. That all constructed goals have the ability to blend into the schools overall or primary goals.
5. That all constructed goals are approved by the principal before commencing the implementation process.
6. That all constructed goals allow for a two-way communication process for all individuals concerned.
7. That all goals constructed and implemented are appraised for success or failure.

By the principal using his/her staff leaders in needs assessments, goal determination, design, and construction, goal selection, task performance, and total evaluation, a delegation of authority is realized. Subordinate leaders have the opportunity to identify their unit's primary and secondary goals. Subordinate leaders can also assist their personnel in those tasks which lead to goal accomplishment.

The principal should obtain the staff's various goal construction information and formulate it into the building master plan. A building master plan would include the school's overall goals (which the principal and the administrative team have formulated. A master plan should outline the pattern into which the school's various instructional and logistical goals are blended into the school's general goal system.

E. BUILDING LEVEL PLANNING PROJECTIONS

The previous chapter division presented goal construction procedures within the building setting with great emphasis contributions of the building staff. At this point the principal and his/her administrative team's procedures should concern the fusing of staff input with overall administrative input.

After goals or objectives have been constructed, established, and revised for implementation, the principal needs to coordinate his/her administrative team to undertake the following tasks which will be a segment of the goals to be accomplished.

1. Outlining the various instructional and noninstructional programs, procedures, and objectives.

2. Keeping instructional media available, in readiness, and coordinated with the instructional time line.

3. Obtaining needed supplies and equipment.

4. Obtaining budgetary funds and the accounting system to be used in financial management procedures.

5. Having both the logistical and instructional personnel needed for the academic and fiscal periods being considered in the planning stages.

6. Providing for the time to be consumed in the building's instructional and logistical effort.

The above functions place the finishing touch to the goals that established for the individual school. The previous actions point to the meshing of theory with fact.

Building level administrative members should also engage in the following procedures when formulating building planning projections:

1. Identify the plan(s) by title and code.

2. Indicate the avenue of approach and the purpose of the overall planning projection.

3. Make a detailed analysis of the major objective to be achieved.

4. Identify all alternative solutions presented by the principal and his/her team.

5. Project the possible outcomes of each alternative.

6. Selection of the primary planning projection scheme.

7. Selection of the secondary planning projection scheme (as an emergency backup).

8. Evaluation of the planning projection after implementation and projection termination point.

9. Record detailed study of the evaluation data and recommendations for refinement of further planning procedures (whether or not the goal of the planning projection goal is attained or not).

Principals need to provide adequate leadership in the building level planning process. He/she (the principal) needs to enlist the aid of the building administrative team and other key members of the building staff in goal construction, planning projections, and goal achievement.

F. TIME MANAGEMENT AND BUILDING LEADERSHIP

With immortals (as presented in various religious ideologies) there is an absence of time while mere mortals are confronted with a certain chronological block called the lifespan. Within the lifespan which involves the animate and the inanimate, time must be accounted for. Time is readily being consumed within the chronological framework. The zone of limitations within this framework are conception and termination. This principle also applies to various planned programs, fiscal periods, academic periods, grading periods, the calendar year, quarterly periods, semiannual periods, five year plans, ten year plans, etc.

In a managerial sense, time needs to be examined from three dimensions which are[1]:

1. The elapsed dimension
2. The current dimension, and
3. The projected dimension

Within each of these dimensions organizations or schools have been or are currently involved with, the managing of various blocks of time. Mention should also be presented here to indicate that there may be an overlapping within the various time frames. These acts have been committed in order to present a quasiperpetual state of being.

The school administrator needs to place the process of time management into the construction of planning projections. Managing of time as it concerns the elapsed division is an impossibility, because one cannot recover that which has past. However, the elapsed dimension can provide historical information which can assist operations in the current and projected phases. By allowing for time management to be used to its greatest potential, focus needs to be made in planning for projected periods of activity. Entering time management procedures during the current dimension can be effective, however, maximum effectiveness cannot be achieved. Maximum effectiveness is usually reduced, due to the fusing of time management procedures with an ongoing program activity. Gaining familiarity during the fusing period can create additional loss of time. Personnel, procedures, supply usage, equipment operation, etc., must establish a new pattern of working within the established pattern of operation.

Previous discussions presented earlier in this chapter lend themselves to the management of time by the school principal.

1. First, there needs to be the identification of the goal(s) that are to

be achieved. Identification also needs to be made of the personnel and various units (internal and external to the building) that will be involved.

2. A time analysis needs to be made concerning past time consumption periods involved with similar programs. If a new program is being planned for, a detailed projection is needed.

The administrator needs to determine the total number of activities that will be involved in a particular future program. Once this task is completed, a projected and panoramic picture of program conception and the point of termination is realized. This will give the administrator a view of the time which is projected to be consumed by the program.

3. Time management procedures should allow for the identification of possible program obstacles and their removal. Estimated time for this action must also be considered from a time consumption point of view.

4. An estimated figure for additional time consumption involved with possible unforeseen circumstances (for example, supply and equipment shortages, personnel problems, financial problems, etc.).

5. Time allowance needed for fusing with existing practices, or making complete changeovers should be considered in determining program time consumption.

6. Once the time management schedule is in operation synchronization must be gained and maintained.

7. All time management procedures must allow for two-way communication action for all individuals involved.

8. Evaluation of the time management program.

9. Analysis of the evaluation results.

10. Modification of time management procedures if necessary.

11. Development of time management standards for the school building.

Planning projections at the building level need to be incorporated within some type of time management scheme. The waste of time within the building setting can be detrimental to its operation and purpose. Time loss features present within the building setting should be identified and eliminated through the principal's leadership.

G. SUMMARY

As the chief executive officer (CEO) of the school, the principal needs to obtain maximum use of his/her administrative team; the instructional leadership team, the instructional staff, the instructional service group, and the logistical staff. Input by the subordinate leaders within the building can provide assistance for its proper operation.

Through adequate leadership within the building, the principal can exercise authoritative control practices, provide philosophical direction to his/her staff, students, and community, plus philosophical direction to the instructional and logistical programs. Leadership style also plays a significant part in working with subordinates and achieving the building's objectives.

Central office delegates authority and also provides both instructional and logistical program direction to the individual school. Central office also places zones of limitations for the building to abide by. Principals and their staffs must adhere to the dictates of central office if program flow is to be steady along with the accomplishing of prescribed goals.

Both building administrative and staff personnel should have input in the principal's task of building goal construction. These various staff members should be thoroughly acquainted with the needs and the goals (both primary and secondary) that are necessary for achievement within the building organization. Principal coordination of those activities relating to goal construction plays a very influential role in construction of the building's planning projections and the accompanying use of time management. Time management will provide for the proper gear meshing of the planning machine.

REFERENCES

[1]Harris, George W., Jr., *Management of the Public School Logistical System.* Springfield, Illinois: Charles C Thomas, Publisher, 1985, pp. 7–10.

CHAPTER VI

DECISION MAKING AND PROBLEM SOLVING AT THE LINE ADMINISTRATIVE LEVEL

A. RESPONSIBILITY, AUTHORITY AND DELEGATION

Responsibility

A school building and its staff form the smallest administrative unit within the school district. A school can also be considered an administrative line unit due to its proximity to the community. A typical school building has not only daily contact with the community's children, but it (the school) also maintains a constant influence within its area of attendance. Citizens of the community are the financial foundation of the public school district (through the process of taxation). The provision of public financial support builds within the community structure a monitoring and evaluation system to determine if their monies are: (1) providing a competent instructional program for their children, and (2) the proper maintenance of the responsibility factor by administrative personnel in funding plus operating the community's educational program. A community may press the two previous issues toward a local board of education and the superintendent in demanding accountability for school district. However, the community's observation of daily educational operations at the individual building level are more vivid and open to closer scrutiny. The principal through his/her position becomes the central office administrative representative in the field, and he/she is duly charged with the responsibility of carrying out board policy and central office directives. A concerned public observes and also comprehends the fact that the principal is the administrative focal point. By being officially assigned as the building's leader, the principal becomes accountable for educational related actions within the school, its environs and wherever there is any undertaking officially involving the school's name.

Greenwood[1] makes the following statement concerning responsibility:

"Responsibility is the counterpart of authority. As there is a comparable duty corresponding to every right of individuals in society, there is also a corresponding responsibility for every defined area of authority for management. From the standpoint of the management process, responsibility is achieved through establishment of accountability procedures. These procedures spell out in detail the method, time, and place for reporting on, accounting for, the use of delegated authority."

The building level administrator being placed in a school setting has been officially delegated a certain segment of authority (by virtue of his/her position as principal). This delegation allows for the principal to act as an agent of the board and central office. Within the delegation of authority and the administrative coverage of the individual school setting, there has also been assigned a zone of responsibility. Within the responsibility zone authority is practiced as a means of assurance that: (1) the various assignments are carried out, (2) goals are achieved, and (3) policies and directives are enforced and adhered to. If neither assignments, goals, nor the rules are carried out in the building setting, then irresponsibility takes over from that of responsibility.

In viewing irresponsibility, or the negative side of following proper courses of action, Roe and Drake[2] present the following:

". . . Each social group, including the school, must determine the behavior necessary for the successful operation of that group. The more numbers of the group involved in determining what the proper behavior is and the penalty for unacceptable behavior, the more goodwill there will be in following the rules and accepting the consequences if they break them. For everyone will recognize the rules are for the good of the group and therefore the good of the individual. In other words, 'We have rules and penalties because we care about the group and therefore we care about the individual.' However, once the feeling prevails that rules are punitive and not group centered and their enforcement implies the school does not care for the individual then battle lines are drawn."

The above statement made by Roe and Drake indicates that the leader is responsible for the group and its successful operation, however, tact needs to be considered in enforcement procedures. School staffs and student bodies are in need of a more vivid plus panoramic picture that policies, rules, etc., are for the good of the school and not as a means of punishment.

Authority and delegation will be presented later in the chapter, however, it is necessary at this point to present the relationship between responsibility delegation and authority. Previous statements brought out the fact that the position of principal carries with it certain obligations that are tagged with responsibility. From a general point of view the principal is responsible for the entire building program. There are also segmented responsibilities (which in total constitute the overall program). For example, this fact can be observed in instruction, instructional support, logistics, extracurricular activities, etc. A principal is held accountable for the attainment of the objectives assigned to him/her. The previous sentence illustrates an important fact in that the principal and the principal alone is responsible for his/her school, its program, its staff, and its students. He/she (the principal) cannot delegate this act of trustworthiness to another. However, the principal can delegate his/her authority, or a portion of authority to another staff member. This act gives another the right to act with authority (and its invested power) to operate in the place of the principal and as a representative of the principal. Clarity is needed at this point to show that the principal's overall responsibility is still present regardless of the actions of authority entrusted to a subordinate. In observing the directional flow of superior-subordinate actions, one will find that authority has a downward flow (superior to subordinate) while responsibility flows upward (subordinate to superior). An administrator never breaks the hold of responsibility to his/her superiors.

Authority

Authority is usually formally invested in a position of leadership. The right of authority has most likely been granted through some type of legislative arrangement or coercion or even more severely—terror tactics and forced takeovers. School administration will hopefully exclude coercion and terror tactics.

Administrative personnel need to realize that the negative uses of coercion or terror tactics will provide an invitation to future disaster which in turn can eliminate the achievement of predetermined goals. Authority should be handled in a firm but fair manner. An action of this nature is required in order to obtain the desired, or more favorably the maximum, productive output of subordinate personnel. The school organization is in need of a systematic logical order of authority if it is to function positively and survive.

Greenwood gives two excellent points concerning authority[3]:

"One major proposition of the transactional view of authority is that it is reciprocal. This idea stems in part from the psychological theory of perception which tells us that reality is not some fixed entity, but is defined by each individual's perception . . ."

Here Greenwood is looking upon the fact of how subordinates sense that authority may well indicate their characters and their philosophies (personal and organizational). This indication may be positive, negative, or neutral in the mind of the subordinate which in turn can influence productivity and goal achievement.

Greenwood's second point is that:

"Authority, too, is not a static, immutable quality that some people have while others do not. Rather, it is a subtle interrelationship whose consequences are defined by everyone concerned. The process is reciprocal, because each actor tries to anticipate the reaction of all participants before he acts . . ."

Superiors over a period of time will construct a mental dossier of each immediate subordinate concerning his/her individual personality and reactions to various types of problems or situations. Personal interests, opportunities, survival mechanisms and tactics have a great influence concerning the types of reactions expected by both superiors and subordinates in organizational authority game playing.

In addition to reciprocity and anticipation, another passenger on the vehicle of authority is that of influence. Through authority a superior may possibly modify the personal aspects of a subordinate in such areas as attitudes, philosophy, behavior, perceptions, etc.

Authority also serves as a carrier for power. Power can be labeled as the force which brings forth influence on subordinate personnel. Subordinates are aware of the power available to a superior and his/her prerogative to bring it to bear upon those in lesser positions. Subordinates also realize the rewards and penalties which can result from the power of a superior.

Roe and Drake make an excellent summary in focusing on authority and power within the realm of the building principal[4]:

". . . Without control little progress is made but hierarchical control can evolve into rigid authoritarianism and decentralized diffused control can degenerate into chaos. Thus a dilemma! One has further concern when analyzing the legitimate power base of the principal for it will be discovered that it is really quite small when compared to the usual concept of an administrator's power.

Our analysis of the power base of the typical principal shows that much of the old-fashioned legitimate power of the principal is more imagined than real. Looking at the dwindling of his (her) power from this viewpoint a typical principal might be very jealous of the power he (she) has left and guard it with fervor."

Teacher and logistical employee unions and associations over the years have somewhat weakened the authority of the principalship. The subordinate power of the grievance has partially caused a "walking on eggshells" effect upon principals. The central office usually looks in disdain upon building administrators that are frequently attacked through grievance procedures. Acts of this nature have the possibility of placing the principal on thin ice in his/her attempt to operate the building.

Delegation

Delegation can be termed as the entrusting (by a superior) of authority (along with power and influence) to a subordinate to act as one's representative. The subordinate, as one who has received delegation, takes on (as an agent) all authority which is contained within the zone authorized. For example, the school district superintendent delegates all of his/her authority concerning logistical support and services to the logistical or business manager of the central office team. However, the superintendent still has overall responsibility for the logistical endeavor. Responsibility has not been delegated, but the authority to manage (by the logistical manager) the logistical program has. For example, a logistical or business manager acquires a zone of responsibility (for school district logistics) that is innate to his/her position along with the authority to operate from the superintendent. Delegation and its relationship to authority and responsibility was mentioned earlier in this chapter.

A more demanding observation of delegation indicates that:

1. There is need for a legal foundation such as a statute, policy, job description, etc., to allow for superiors to delegate and subordinates to be delegated to.

2. The act of delegation should always be formal and written out in vivid and concise terms. Accordance with this procedure will avoid varied interpretations and confusion.

3. When the subordinate receives a writ of delegation from his/her superior, there is a need for formal acceptance and comprehension. Here again formality can reduce misunderstandings and potential bottlenecks in daily operations.

4. Delegation creates a new zone of responsibility to the subordinate. However, overall responsibility still belongs to the superior. The subordinate is accountable for his/her actions as a result of the original delegation.

5. The subordinate can possibly be the superior within his/her assigned unit. He/she should follow the previous four factors when delegating to those leaders within his/her unit that are subordinate to him/her.

In looking at the preceding five steps one can find that the act of delegating has the possibility of being prevalent within a given organization. Here again this action will depend upon the legislation of the organization.

There are times when administrators may hesitate or refuse to delegate authority to their subordinate leaders. Three prime categories are usually at the foundation concerning actions of this nature. They are:

1. Fear
    a. Fear of outstanding subordinates.
    b. Fear of losing one's position of authority.
    c. Fear of superiors.
2. Marginal or nonproductive subordinates
3. Untrustworthy subordinates

If any of the above three problems exist steps must be taken to rectify the situation, or disaster may result from managerial overloading and the nonachievement of objectives.

B. PROBLEM AWARENESS AND IDENTIFICATION

During the daily operational process of the school organization there will be periods of time when goals (both primary and secondary) are not being met. This may be due to: (1) personnel conflicts, (2) disturbances or stoppages in the logistical service and support, (3) governmental or judicial issues, (4) administrative issues, etc. In fact the list could go on and on. All of the previous items give an indication to the fact that there is question which has been brought forth for inquiry, consideration, or resolution. In further identification of the negative situation (which has disturbed normal operations within the organization) one can go beyond that of which is readily visible. The obstacle or quandary may be situational, it may be of the physical world, or there may be human involvement (direct or indirect).

When synchronization and normal flow are retarded or terminated, there is notice that some type of problem or problems exist within the organization. Objectives either are not met or the accomplishment takes place beyond the projected time line. At this point the administrator should be able to recognize that these signs indicating there are serious disturbances influencing task performance. Analysis needs to take place to determine what is the cause of the symptoms taking place. Is it due to:

1. Human error, misunderstanding attitude, incompetence, etc.
2. Logistical services and support.
3. Instructional programs and support.
4. Central office dictates.
5. Board policy.
6. Governmental and/or judicial directives.
7. Accountability questions.
8. Quality control.
9. Quality assurance.
10. Employee unions and organizations.
11. Other internal sources.
12. External sources.

Once the administrator is aware of the problem, then he/she should analyze the symptoms, and finally extract the cause which has produced the symptoms. These actions will place the problem(s) into the target area for identification. Identification of the problem then should go into another phase promoting further study with questions along the following lines:

1. Has this problem been identified in previous operations?
2. Were the same or similar individuals, issues, logistical services or items; and instructional programs or services involved in previous incidents?
3. Is the problem entirely new in nature?
4. What were the administration's previous actions in similar matters of the past?
5. Is it probable to find or construct a solution within the school unit involved?
6. Is it probable to find or construct a solution within the school district organization?
7. Does this problem indicate that external assistance is needed for resolution?
8. Is it likely that this problem will appear again in the future?

Once all of the above questions have been answered, the administrator should be able to classify the problem and then proceed constructing and studying alternatives to solutions for solving procedures.

C. PROBLEM STUDY, ALTERNATIVES, AND SOLVING PROCEDURES

Once the problem has been identified and classified, a study is needed by the administrator to determine the route to solution. Varied methods of solving the problem may be determined, but a detailed study of the probable outcomes should also take place. The principal cannot identify all possible outcomes to specific situations, because unforeseen circumstances remain a probability. However, if the building administrator has invited staff input into consideration of possible alternatives to a particular solution, a much wider or panoramic view can be constructed for a more in-depth study.

All alternatives brought forth (by the principal with or without staff input) need to be appraised to determine if feasibility exists. Determination of feasibility includes the study of probable outcomes. A question can be asked as to what will be the results of a projected outcome? Will the results be positive or negative to the school organization or those individuals which are part of the organization? Or could there be future probable negative or positive consequences? Probable outcomes should be taken into account before a final decision is made. Staff input rather than sole administrative input to the study and appraisal of alternatives gives the principal more latitude for consideration before making the final decision.

Some alternative solutions may be discarded even before the study or appraisal period commences. The principal and/or central office administration may already be involved in current situations or operations that will present certain alternatives from being explored. For example:
1. Shortage or nonavailability of personnel.
2. Shortage or nonavailability of needed supplies and equipment.
3. Fiscally unaffordable.
4. Logistical support and services not available.
5. Conflicts with projected time lines.
6. Space management and other facility problems.
7. Constraints by building and central office administration.

After a thorough period of study or appraisal of alternatives, the administrator (and possibly his/her staff) are ready for a decision. The decision making process should result in identifying the route that is felt to be the most appropriate solution to the problem(s) at hand. Once that decision is made, the key administrator must adhere to it. A major factor in this issue is that whether the principal uses staff input in obtaining the final decision, or acts in a solo fashion, he/she is responsible for the alternative taken.

Alternative decisions need to follow a pattern of providing a cushion for security and convenience. This can be achieved through determining both a primary and secondary alternatives to solve the problem. If the primary route is blocked through some unforeseen circumstance, then the administrator has a secondary alternative ready for implementation.

D. THE MULTILEVEL DECISION MAKING PROCESS AT BUILDING LEVEL

Decision making is the ultimate act of administrative power. Problems are (1) recognized, (2) identified and studied, (3) alternatives are constructed and studied, and (4) decisions are made as to method of solving the situation. The act of deciding the method for solving a particular issue can rest solely within the power realm of the principal, or he/she can share the power of decision with the:

1. Building level administrative team (assistant principals)
2. Subject departmental chairpersons (middle and secondary schools)
3. Grade level leaders (elementary schools)
4. Educational resources staff persons
5. Guidance and counseling staff members
6. Teaching faculty
7. Logistical staff members
8. Student body
9. Community

Depending upon the type of issues concerned and magnitude of the problem at hand, segments or the entire above listing can be involved with the final decision.

The use of a multilevel (only those parties concerned with a specific problem) decision making process allows for:

1. Greater input.
2. Gives each individual a sense of self worth as a member of the school team.

3. Provides for greater cooperation between staff members, students and community.
4. It gives all parties a 360° observation of the initial problem, alternative decisions, the primary decision and a view of the school's operational phase.
5. It also indicates to each individual his/her position within the school environment, and the level of individual importance involved in the process.
6. Calls for a greater span of innovation provided by the school staff.
7. Collected motivation is provided by the staff rather than a singular administrative endeavor.
8. Multilevel decision making provides for a more panoramic appraisal during the predecision and postdecision phases.

Problems are solved as a team effort and not that of an authoritarian administrative thrust. However, some principals may look upon multilevel decision making as a device which threatens his/her building leadership. Negative points of multilevel decision making may be:

1. Excessive time consumption (especially in extremely critical situations).
2. Staff input may not be of a serious nature, due to fear of school administration and security of employment.
3. Allowing for the opportunity of political dealings and power plays.
4. The principal's overall responsibility for the decision regardless of multilevel input.

It is the option of the principal and/or central office to promote and carryout a multilevel decision making process at building level. Some school systems may desire the interaction of subordinate building staff members into the decision making process while others may discourage it. Some school districts may promote a more principal-centered slant toward the building's decision making format. If a decision is made by group input, the principal still bears the responsibility (as previously stated) of the aftereffects (whether positive or negative). In order to maintain a margin of managerial safety, the principal needs to have the option of approval or disapproval on all group constructed decisions.

E. THE PRINCIPAL AS THE SUPREME DECISION MAKER

If the process of decision is to be dealt with solely by the principal, the previous factors brought out earlier in the chapter should have already taken place. Such as:

1. Problem awareness.
2. Problem identification
3. Problem study.
4. Alternative construction.
5. Alternative selection and solving procedures.

Even if staff input is considered, the above five steps need to take place if a practicable decision is to be reached. Once the die of decision is cast, it is then implemented throughout the building organization and those concerned areas external (but within the legal territorial limits) to the building's operations. This phase can be identified as the carrying-out procedure. The following series of steps may assist in this endeavor:

1. Attack the problem with all available power and influence (both the principal and his/her subordinate leaders). This step is definitely useful if time and circumstances are critical.

2. If time and circumstances are not in the critical zone, the carrying out of a decision may involve preplanned systematic maneuvers to overcome explosive or potentially explosive situation(s).

3. Execute administrative penetration to the problem's nucleus.

4. Once the nucleus of the problem has been attacked, exploitation of its outer areas needs to take place.

5. Simultaneous and preplanned systematic neutralization of the problem's nerve center and outer elements should also take place.

6. Once the problem has been defeated, prepare immediately for a counter-attack by the problem causing forces.

7. Neutralize the counter move (through preplanned procedures).

8. Evaluate the decision and its after effects.

9. Record evaluation results for possible future actions.

The results of a particular decision may be positive or negative. Regardless of the outcome, the principal is responsible for the action(s) taken. An administrator has to stand behind the decision actions taken at his/her building. In order to avoid negative situations great care and forethought is needed during the periods of problem awareness, problem identification, and the selection of an alternative as the decision to overcome the problem (see Figure 4).

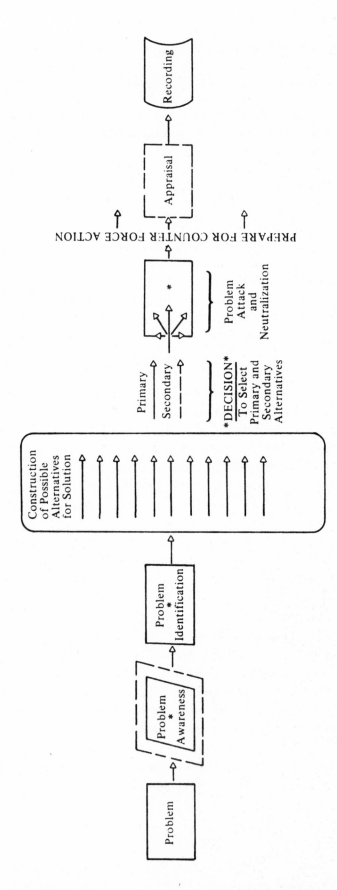

Figure 4. Decision Making and Problem Solving.

F. SUMMARY

The managerial position of principal covers an area of responsibility for all functions with the building and its area. Principal responsibility cannot be moved or delegated to another subordinate leader, but the principal's authority (or power) is allowed to do so. The subordinate to which the principal has delegated his/her authority has been given the right to act in place of the building leader.

Uncertainties, difficulties, and doubts caused by individuals or inanimate objects can be defined as an issue or a problem. Problems occur in many organizations and must be dealt with by administrative personnel. Ignoring a problem will not remove it, but place the organization within a zone of possible jeopardy. A danger zone of this type can lead to the organization's loss of effectiveness and the nonachieving of planned objectives. The staff should be oriented to be aware of problems and be able to identify and determine their causes.

Once a problem is identified, study should be made by the principal and/or his/her staff (which can provide a multilevel contribution) of alternatives to problem solution. The next step would be the principal's (with or without group input) to select the proper alternative (through decision) to solve the issue at hand. The decision may be multilevel in nature (including the input of the building staff) or it may be a supreme decision selected solely by the principal himself/herself. Central office or individual principal discretion may determine whether staff input is to be entered concerning building level decisions. Regardless of the selection of the type of decision making format, the principal has overall responsibility for the action taken. If the multilevel approach is taken, the principal needs to have the option provide final approval or disapproval to staff decisional input.

REFERENCES

[1]Greenwood, William T. *Management in Organizational Behavior Theories: An Interdisciplinary Approach.* Cincinnati: Southwestern Publishing Co., 1965, p. 447.

[2]Roe, William H., and Drake, Thelbert L. *The Principalship, Second Edition.* New York: Macmillan Publishing Co., Inc., 1980, p. 315.

[3]Greenwood, Ibid., p. 515.

[4]Roe and Drake, Ibid., p. 98.

CHAPTER VII

LOGISTICAL FOUNDATIONS AND
THE BUILDING MANAGER

A. BUILDING—CENTRAL OFFICE
LOGISTICAL COORDINATION

The nerve center for a school district's logistical program is the office of the logistical or business manager. Staff leaders assigned to the logistical or business manager's team (in medium to large-sized school districts) will supervise the areas of:

1. Transportation
2. Food Service
3. Facility Planning and Capital Outlay
4. Building Maintenance and Operations
5. Personnel Management
6. Financial Management
7. Equipment Purchasing
8. Supply Purchasing
9. Computer Management
10. Safety
11. Security
12. Public Relations
13. Warehouse Management
14. Clerical Services

Smaller school districts will usually add the various logistical tasks to personnel already within the organizational format. In extremely small school areas, the superintendent may perform all of the above logistical tasks in addition to the administration of instructional requirements. Whatever the size of the school district, there is a need for logistical coordination with principals at the building level. Logistical services and support comes to the building level by way of the central office direction (see Figure 5).

Logistical coordination between central office and the individual school

121

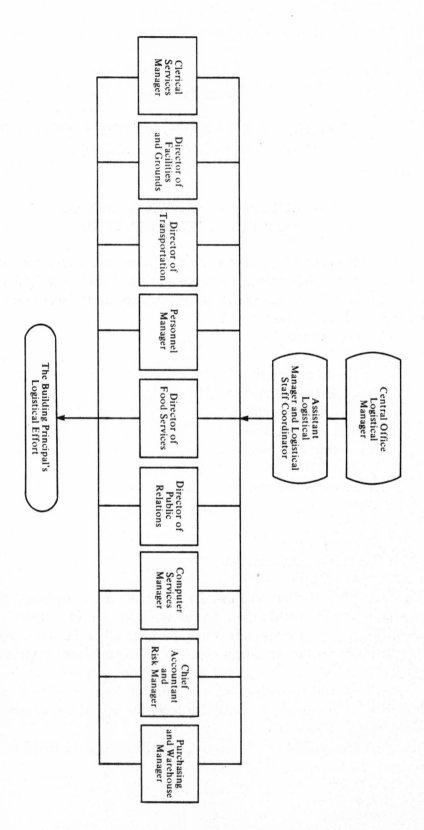

Figure 5. Central Office-Building Level Logistical Coordination for the Typical Medium to Large Sized School District.

building has within it a vital thrust of providing support and services to the building's instructional program. Building level requirements for support and service will be directly or indirectly brought forth in the fourteen previously mentioned areas. Explanation is required to illustrate a connection between the logistical staff support programs and the individual building logistical program. A desired outcome of this connection is the synchronization of uninterrupted logistical assistance to the school's daily operation.

In order to achieve uninterrupted logistical continuity between central office and the building level, there must be careful and concise planning projections, guidance and supervision of all logistical operational activities, continuous appraisal, and the proper recording of appraisal results for future endeavors.

Central office logistical operations will construct policy and guidelines for building level logistical procedures. The principal should adhere strictly to these directives. In spite of central office directives there is need of elasticity (at the building level) to allow the principal to fit central office logistical requirements to that individual uniqueness which is applicable to each building. Building level logistical and logistical staff requirements may vary due to building size, enrollment, and organization. In some school systems, the principal is given latitude in establishing the organizational format for his/her building. An action of this nature may result in a variety of organizational patterns for the building level logistical staff.

Another important point which is vital to the coordination of logistical support and services between the central office logistical team and the principal is that of communications. The communications system between the central office logistical unit and the building level logistical unit should be two-way. Two-way communications link-ups provide for upward or downward flow from superior to subordinate and from subordinate to superior. Knowledge concerning logistical flow is needed at both levels of operation. The same factors will apply to the superior-subordinate pattern between the principal and his/her building logistical team.

True logistical coordination between the logistical manager (plus his/her team) and the building logistical manager (the principal) will be evident in the adequate or more than adequate support and servicing of the building instructional program. Smooth operations and positive appraisals will indicate that the logistical machine is properly functioning through careful planning projections by central office and building management.

Certain features of the building logistical program such as the following factors will indicate positive logistical operations:

1. An excellent food service program.
2. Proper bus scheduling and pupil discipline coordination.
3. Adequate building level clerical support.
4. A satisfactory custodial operations program.
5. Timely central office honoring of building level maintenance requests.
6. Proper budgeting, accounting, and auditing procedures.
7. Adequate and timely purchasing and delivery procedures.
8. Satisfactory building level storage management.
9. Adequate central office assistance concerning personnel administration and employee relations.
10. Supply and equipment inventory procedures.
11. Satisfactory computer operations (within the building and with central office).
12. Adequate safety and security measures.
13. Periodically scheduled and emergency groundskeeping (lawn cutting, snow and ice removal, tree trimming, etc.) activities.
14. Public relations guidance and procedures.

There are some considerations which need to be made by central office logistics in determining a logistical program for building level situations. Within the typical school districts there are schools which are in close proximity to the central office, warehouse installations, centralized food preparation centers, transportation centers, etc. In addition there are those building units that are located in remote areas far from logistical centers of activity. Individual school units also serve a variety of clientele such as:

1. Various socioeconomic groups.
2. Various ethnic groups.
3. Industry, business or governmental employee groups (within the community setting).
4. College bound students.
5. Vocational education students.
6. Special education students.
7. Gifted students.

Coordination between the central office logistical arm and the building logistical support and services is dependent upon central office recognition of the logistical needs of every building unit within the school district. Additional variables that should be considered by the central office logistical manager and his/her staff are:

1. The total number of school buildings within the district.
2. The specific number of secondary schools.
3. The specific number of middle schools.
4. The specific number of elementary schools.
5. Program classifications and location of secondary, middle, and elementary schools.
6. Location and size of the centralized food preparation center (if applicable).
7. Location and size of each regional food preparation center (if applicable).
8. Location and size of school decentralized (intrabuilding unit) food preparation centers (if applicable).
9. Location and size of satellite food service centers (intrabuilding food preparation units which provide food services to nearby schools).
10. Type of meal service (breakfast, lunch, and possibly evening meals for children in after school "latchkey" programs).
11. Location and size of central warehouse and delivery unit.
12. Location and size of regionalized warehouse and delivery units (if applicable).
13. Size of individual school storage units.
14. Total number of school buses owned or contracted with private owners.
15. Location and size of transportation center (if buses are board owned).
16. Total number of pupils riding buses and the location of *each* bus stop.
17. Location and description of each bus route.
18. Magnitude of school district and individual building computer systems.
19. Total number of employees (certificated and noncertificated), job classifications, job descriptions, and building assignments or contacts.
20. School district and building level communications network.
21. Total and individual building custodial operations programs.
22. Building maintenance programs (total and individual plus scheduled and probable needs.

23. Programmed grounds care for each building unit.
24. Overall and individual building clerical needs.
25. Computerized supply and equipment instant inventory situations.
26. Budget construction schedule, format, and administration for the school district and each individual school.
27. Financial reporting system for all building units.
28. Accounting and auditing procedures for all buildings.
29. Warehouse delivery schedules and routes to all schools.
30. Public relations guidelines and procedures concerning the media, school election issues (excluding school board elections).
31. Assure adequate coverage of each building and its concerns through a proper risk management program.
32. Elasticity to service those unique and individual building logistical needs.

Once the logistical manager has accounted for the above mentioned factors he/she has the information to serve the needs of each principal within the school district. However, the central office logistical manager should have enough flexibility within the logistical program to meet the special needs of any particular building. Cooperation and coordination should be carried out by the logistical manager to adequately serve and assist the needs of each school building.

B. THE PRINCIPAL AND LOGISTICAL SYSTEMS OF SUPPORT

Within a school building's organization, the principal will be involved with coordinating the logistical thrust from central office. This action is carried out to meet the needs of an individual school. The school's instructional program must be supported and serviced logistically if it is to survive. A principal needs to involve himself/herself with the *Logistical Systems of Support* in a true effort to provide the instructional phase with adequate service and support. Within the *Logistical Systems of Support* the school principal will be concerned with[1]:

1. **Measured Intervals or Time** — Logistical tasks highly dependent upon measured intervals that are planned to be consumed. Time periods are established to commence at a particular point and then terminating at another. Building level managers (principals) of logistics must concern themselves with chronographic dimensions from three points of view which are:

a. *Consumed or elapsed time periods* in which certain logistical operations have taken place in supporting and servicing the instructional program. Past logistical ventures can provide highly important information which can be used in current or future operations. Logistical trends have the possibility of being somewhat determined by a careful study of past records. The term somewhat is used here due to the fact that the study of the past leads way to probability and not that of certainty.

b. *Current time periods* will provide the principal with the logistical action which is presently being engaged within the school. At this juncture, the principal and his/her building logistical team (clerical and computer staff, custodial staff, food service staff, and any other auxiliary employees) can determine whether logistical goals are being met and whether the instructional program is being properly assisted. Obstacles, bottlenecks, and other trouble signs will reveal themselves during the current phase of logistical operations. The principal as the school's logistical manager has the opportunity during the current dimension to direct and assist his/her logistical subordinate leaders to take measures to solve any logistical problems that may arise. Successful and unsuccessful troubleshooting methods should be placed in the records for elapsed time periods. Such information could be helpful in future situations.

c. *Future or projected time periods* are of significance to the principal's logistical format. Planning operations will take place during current periods with elapsed time periods providing a record of vital information which can assist in the attempt to eliminate known and probable risks, obstacles plus impeding actions. Projected time periods that are important to the principal in establishing the school's logistical program are:

1. The school district budget or fiscal year.
2. The state fiscal year.
3. The federal fiscal year.
4. The calendar year.
5. The academic year.
6. Academic evaluation periods.
7. Personnel evaluation periods.
8. Program evaluation periods.

2. **Financial Management.** Money must be provided in order to operate the building's instructional program. Depending upon the school

district's policies toward the principal's direct or indirect involvement in the school's budgetary affairs, the factor of stewardship of public monies remains. Monies flow throughout the school and its main office on a daily basis involving such items as:

    a. Extracurricular affairs

    b. School petty cash

    c. Fines and breakage expense

    d. Fund raising

    e. Food services

    f. Purchases (school and student)

    g. Student and organizational projects

In some school systems, principals are placed in charge of handling the school building's entire budget for the fiscal period. While in other districts usually the above seven items will comprise of the building level financial management endeavor along with:

    a. Approved accounting procedures

    b. Auditing (local, state and federal)

    c. Periodic financial reporting (local, state and federal).

    3. **Personnel Management.** People of various skills are needed to operate both the instructional and logistical programs within a given building. Certain managerial features regarding building personnel needs to be carried out such as:

    a. Recruiting

    b. Hiring

    c. Initial and inservice training

    d. Assignments

    e. Evaluations

    f. Transfers

    g. Leaves

    h. Substituting

    i. Daily accounting

    j. Payroll coordination with central office

    k. Grievances

    l. Labor-management relations

    m. Suspensions

    n. Terminations

    o. Attrition monitoring

    4. **Supply and Equipment Storage.** Supply and equipment items are usually planned during the budget construction period and are many

times delivered during the beginning of the new fiscal period. School logisticians will usually attempt to program delivery of such items before the academic year commences. However, there are times during the academic year that additional supply and equipment items need to be purchased to meet building demand. Note is taken at this point to indicate that supply items are consumable in feature and are used in order to assist a particular purpose, for example: soap, chalk, erasure, paper, wax, pencils, paper products, etc. Equipment items are usually fixed (and not consumable) and depreciate with age and use. Such objects as water heaters, furnaces, audiovisual gear, air conditioners, drinking fountains, chairs, desks, etc.

Storage space within the school building must be managed by the building principal to assure safe and secure area or areas for the placement of supplies and equipment items not in use. The storage area should be secure from unauthorized entry. A storage area needs to maintain a systematic accounting procedure (for items entering and leaving the storage area) through a hand-operated or computerized inventory operation. Supply and equipment items represent monies that are applied to the school's budget for a particular fiscal period. Principals should also take steps to prevent hoarding schemes by segments of the staff which may deprive others of their supply and equipment needs. The same feature will hold true for service and support staff members within the building.

5. **Computer Management.** Some school districts have completely computerized their school buildings while others are partially computerized, and yet still others are still working with outdated manual methods. Outdated methods still in use may be due to school district affordability, or school board denial to leave the status quo. Schools that are computerized and especially buildings that are linked with computers at central office are at a great advantage over those districts which have not given way to the electronic age. Building level computer systems need to be managed directly by the principal or his/her designee. However, the principal will have overall responsibility for the building's computer service system. A computer system can assist both the logistical and instructional tasks in the building's daily operations. Computerized and other electronic functions will demand precision management at the school office level. Some of the logistical services assisted by the computer could be: (a) financial management, (2) food service, (3) personnel management, (4) record keeping, (5) supply and equipment inventories,

(6) planning projections, (7) temperature and atmospheric control (heating, ventilating and cooling, (8) fire safety, (9) electronic security and surveillance, (10) building upkeep and maintenance, etc.

6. **Support Services.** Those services that are within the school and assist the instructional operation are task areas that should be included within the principal's area of managerial responsibility. These particular logistical operations take place within the confines of the building. A principal is in need of direct knowledge of; needs to coordinate with; and take surveillance of endeavors such as:

   a. Food Service
      (1) Feeding schedules
      (2) Health environment of food preparation and service areas.
      (3) Student lunchroom conduct
      (4) Menu planning
      (5) Financial accounting
      (6) Food preparation periods (The bakers' late night and early morning preparations; the cooks' early morning preparations. Coordination will be needed for building entry regarding food service personnel.)
      (7) Storage of foodstuffs
   b. Transportation
      (1) On campus student mounting and dismounting areas.
      (2) Coordinating school and bus schedules.
      (3) Coordinating with drivers and parents regarding pupil conduct on buses.
      (4) Having knowledge of bus routes and stops (regarding passengers attending the school).
      (5) Coordinating with central office pupil transportation director regarding bus use for extracurricular activities.
   c. Building Maintenance
      Coordinating with central office facilities management regarding repair, replacement, and service tasks involving the upkeep of the building. Some maintenance may be periodic—such as painting, electrical rewiring, furnace servicing and cleaning, etc. Other maintenance requirements are impromptu in nature and require immediate attention. For example, wind damage to a roof; glass breakage; sewer stoppage; water line breakage, etc.

d. Building Operations

The principal should oversee (on a daily basis) those building operational tasks by the custodial staff. Custodial services assist in keeping the building open and ready for instruction. Custodial personnel are usually responsible for:

(1) Housekeeping
(2) User maintenance of equipment
(3) Storage of supplies and equipment
*(4) Groundskeeping
*(5) Ice and snow removal
(6) Sanitation procedures
(7) Refuse removal from building and grounds
(8) Operation of heating, cooling, and ventilating equipment
(9) Custodial computer operating and monitoring.

(*In some school systems the central office building and grounds unit will operate groundskeeping, snow and ice removal services.)

3. Office Management and Clerical Services

Although the principal is responsible for overall office management and its clerical services, there is most likely a delegation of duties to the building secretary or office manager (if the school is large enough to require a secretarial staff). The senior secretary or office manager is a key person in seeing that clerical, and computer services are accomplished along with being the initial contact person with parents, community person, or other visitors to the school.

The typical building principal is heavily involved with the *Logistical Systems of Support* which heavily influences the instructional operations within the building. Time must be divided by the principal between his/her instructional duties, staff and student personnel procedures, and the logistical requirements of the school. In larger buildings the principal will most likely have an administrative team of assistant principals. Authority is usually delegated to the building administrative team which in turn take charge of logistics, instruction, student plus staff personnel, and educational resources. Regardless of the delegation procedures, the principal must still bear overall responsibility. Building level business or logistical services cannot be downplayed and must monitored to assure adequate instructional assistance.

C. THE INSTRUCTIONAL-LOGISTICAL BLEND

The principal's primary task within the building is to provide leadership to the instructional program. Another task which is secondary to instruction is the principal's responsibility for providing logistical support and service to the instructional program. Building level instructional administration is *direct* toward the responsible member(s) of the building administrative team (depending upon building organizational construction); the guidance staff; department chairpersons or grade level leaders; educational resources personnel; the teaching staff and the students involved in the learning process. Logistical management tasks of the principalship are indirect to the instructional segment of the above mentioned individuals. This circuitousness is due to the logistical role being *in support of and service to* those involved in instruction. However, building management of logistics directly influences members of the building's logistical staff. The dual approach is due to subordinate logistical personnel being charged with the support and service blending with the instruction program. This mix or blend is preplanned to coordinate with instructional timing and thrusts. More information concerning this particular point will be brought forth later in the chapter.

A more critical perspective of building level instructional leadership is in order for discussion. The principal should look upon his/her instructional program as meeting:

1. Demands of American society
2. State requirements
3. Local school district requirements
4. Community (building and district wide) needs
5. And the needs of the individual child attending his/her school.

The above demands, requirements, and needs should be formulated into goals to be achieved by building administration, staff, and students. In order to keep the instructional task in operation, constructed goals are the results of planned instructional programs in various subject areas. If action is taken to place the instructional or learning program in operation, there is a need for staff and learning resources. Staff involvement in the instructional process will include: (1) inservice training for the teaching staff, (2) supervision of the instructional process in various subject and/or grade level areas, (3) assistance to teaching staff members in instructional methodology, (4) evaluation of teachers, department chairs or grade level leaders, and subordinate administrators involved directly with the curriculum process, (5) educational resources such as library services, educational media, teaching aids, field trips, computerized instruction, etc., should be planned, supervised and evaluated for program effectiveness, (6) student evaluations according to instructional progress and achievement, and (7) program evaluation (subject matter and/or grade level) according to progress and achievement by both students and teacher.

One may ask the question: How does the building level logistical scheme fit into the instructional offering? The proper response could be through careful planning projections and a proper mix or blending with the instructional program at the appropriate time. A principal along with his/her administrative team, the guidance staff, the educational resources team, department chairs or grade level leaders and building logistical supervisors need to construct their planning projections well in advance of the forthcoming fiscal period and academic year. Logistical plans should also be included within budgetary preparations for a forthcoming fiscal period.

Teacher input to department chairs or grade level leaders along with other subordinate members of both instructional and logistical units (within the building) will provide for better logistical-instructional blending. Direction will be required in planning logistics according to:

1. Obtaining the monies through previously planned budgeting for building logistical support.

2. Requesting, purchasing, receiving, and storing all supply and equipment items needed for the forthcoming academic year.

3. Requesting, purchasing, receiving, and storing all textbooks, educational resources materials, library acquisitions of printed and nonprinted materials to be required during the new school year.

4. Employing proper space management procedures for the building's instructional and logistical needs according to the academic year's grading periods.

5. Establishment of the building's financial accounting system for the fiscal period along with financial reporting and auditing preparations.

6. Determining personnel needs (instructional and logistical) for the fiscal and academic periods. Keeping into account terminations, transfers, leaves, and resignations of the prior period. Student instructional and/or logistical program alterations can require increases or decreases concerning personnel requirements.

7. Analyses of various time periods such as:

    a. The academic year
    b. The fiscal year
    c. Seasonal periods
    d. Testing and grading periods
    e. Extracurricular event periods to determine demand of logistical support and service needs.

8. Normal and peak periods for clerical support needs. For example:
    a. Schedule constructions
    b. Accounting, auditing, and financial reporting periods
    c. Peak computer usage periods
    d. Inventories
    e. Public relations projects
    f. Personnel and program evaluations
    g. Special fund raising events
    h. Student programs
    i. Graduation planning
    j. Parental conferences and visits

9. Coordinating with the central office transportation office (before the academic year) to coordinate:
    a. School operation hours with bus arrivals and departures.
    b. Bus schedules, routes, and stops within the building's zone of attendance.
    c. Methods for instructing students concerning school bus safety procedures and rules.
    d. Passenger disciplinary procedures between the driver, the school, and parents.

10. Preparing for the upkeep of the facility through maintenance needs and building custodial tasks. Custodial duties should be planned for the fiscal and the academic periods in regard to:
    a. Requesting, purchasing, receiving, and storing of all custodial supply and equipment items.
    b. Construction of programs for housekeeping, sanitizing and other custodial task requirements according to the following periods:
        (1) Daily
        (2) Weekly
        (3) Monthly
        (4) Quarterly
        (5) Semiannually
        (6) Annually

(7) Seasonally

(8) Emergencies

(9) Various building events

(10) Instructional program requirements

Planned supervision of heating, cooling, ventilating and groundskeeping requirements according to periodic needs.

11. Food preparation, service and management according to:

    a. Meal programs—breakfast, lunch, and special events.

    b. Master menu preparation.

    c. Advanced weekly or monthly menu notices to students and parents.

    d. Peak and low dining periods.

    e. Requests, purchasing, receiving, and storage of food service supplies and equipment.

    f. Waste removal and temporary outside storage. Also coordination with garbage pickup services.

    g. Cleaning and sanitary measures.

    h. Food service personnel requirements (health and administrative).

    i. Periodic requests, purchasing, receiving, and storage of foodstuffs to meet the master menu schedule.

All of the factors which were previously mentioned must be coordinated with the fiscal and academic time periods in order to accurately blend with instructional requirements. Principal and staff (instructional and logistical) planning is the key to the timely logistical support and service to the instructional program. Other factors that are needed to provide a proper logistical and instructional mix is that of the principal's delegation of authority to subordinate instructional and logistical leaders within the building. Another important factor is that of the principal having a two-way communication system between his/her office and subordinate logistical and instructional leaders. In addition a two-way communications network is needed between *all* subordinate leaders in order to achieve clarity of purpose and efficiency of task operations.

D. LOGISTICAL SUPPORT FACTORS AT THE BUILDING LEVEL

Logistical functions of the typical school building are dependent upon a variety of conditions. These conditions may be internal or external to the school's total area of operations. Factors such as:

1. Federal, state and local laws,
2. Board of education policies,
3. Central office directives,
4. Staff size and requirements,
5. Student population and requirements,
6. Instructional program requirements,
7. Logistical program requirements,
8. Community demands, and
9. Financial direction, priorities, and restraints.

These factors can alter the building's logistical objectives and the degree to which there is adequate support of the instructional arm. In taking a closer observation of the above nine points, the principal and his/her logistical team will have to construct a plan indicating barriers, selecting priorities, establishing a series of plans for the removal of barriers, deciding a course of action, and evaluation of the results of logistical services and support.

Activities of the building logistical team can involve the general tasks of:

1. Constructing planning projections which blend and synchronize with instructional undertakings.

2. Having a thorough knowledge of the building's instructional program.

3. Obtaining needed services and materiel.

4. Use of proper storage and inventory procedures.

5. Being able to meet instructional needs within a planned and specific time frame.

6. Being able to adequately handle logistical troubleshooting procedures.

7. Solving logistical problems.

The prime key to a successful blend of logistical and instructional efforts within a building setting is the above mentioned factor of planning projections. Logistical-instructional planning projections should be carried out by the principal and his/her logistical prior to the forthcoming fiscal and academic periods. An advanced knowledge of the building's financial status (as presented in the annual budget construction ask) will allow the principal and the school's logistical leaders to diagram the school's logistical program. Quantity and quality can be determined concerning the building's logistical outlook during the fiscal and academic working periods.

E. LOGISTICAL SUBORDINATE LEADERS
AT BUILDING LEVEL

Logistical leaders assigned to the school can be termed as the building level logistical team. These individuals (the school's logistical leaders) are usually in charge of those units which provide essential building services. The building administrator is in a position to act as logistical team leader and to coordinate with each member of the team (representing a particular logistical service or support feature of the school's operation). Logistical leaders operating within the confines of the building are involved with two major categories of task assignments. They are:

1. The building and instructional support service category. Tasks within this classification are concerned with that assistance which is involved with overall logistical assistance to the building's program such as:

    a. Specific unit time allocations and planning.
    b. Program evaluations of the individual logistical unit.
    c. Program alterations of the individual logistical unit.
    d. Unit goal construction.
    e. Unit goal achievement.
    f. Troubleshooting.
    g. Alternative construction to problem solving.
    h. Alternative selection to unit problem solving.
    i. Results of problem solving attempts.
    j. Coordinating with other logistical leaders at the building level.
    k. Coordinating with the principal.
    l. Coordinating with the central office logistical team.
    m. Coordinating with the school's instructional staff.
    n. Two-way communications systems between the principal and the building logistical units.

Since this classification deals directly with instruction, a greater emphasis will be placed upon the following category which is indirect in its support effort.

2. Internal unit category. Each logistical unit leader within the building is assigned to administer his/her logistical section within the building sector. He/she will be in charge of certain areas within their respective logistical units, such as:

    a. Unit personnel management, training, and evaluations.
    b. Supply and equipment requisitions and purchases.

    c. Unit inventory procedures and storage management.

    d. Equipment servicing and maintenance.

    e. Priority establishment.

    f. Establishment and maintenance of a two way communications network between the logistical unit leader, his/her unit staff, the teaching staff, the educational resources staff, and the principal.

    g. Unit authority and delegation procedures.

    h. Unit accountability.

The building level logistical unit leader is in charge of a microcosmic section of the central office logistical program. His/her (the unit leader) is concerned with and responsible for a particular logistical phase of operation within the building setting. A unit logistical leader must synchronize his/her segment of the logistical program with the building's total logistical and instructional efforts.

Logistical leaders that make up the building logistical team are (see Figure 6):

1. *The Office Manager or Senior Secretary* —the person assigned to this position supervises the clerical and administrative computer operations within the building.

2. *Food Service Manager* — Provides for the management of mass feeding of the school's students and staff.

3. *Building Operations and Maintenance Coordinator* —Supervises all building custodial operations necessary to keep the school plant functional. The operations and maintenance coordinator will also alert the logistical team leader (the principal) concerning any needs involving the request for maintenance services (from central office).

4. *Transportation Coordinator* —This logistical position may involve a teacher, administrative team member, or the principal (depending upon school organization and size). The transportation coordinator is needed to assure proper procedures between bus schedules, student passengers, and school schedules.

The previously mentioned personnel are the school's prime logistical leaders. Their specific duties (which will be emphasized in the next chapter unit) bring forth a broader logistical net within the building.

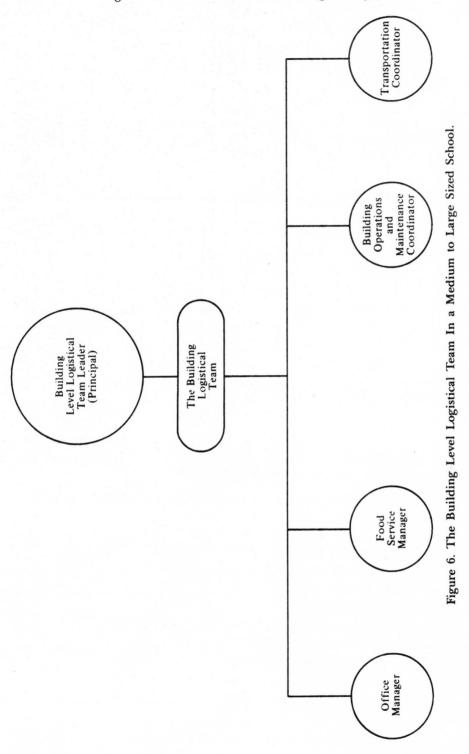

Figure 6. The Building Level Logistical Team In a Medium to Large Sized School.

F. LOGISTICAL SUPPORT AREAS AT BUILDING LEVEL

The logistical subordinate leaders assigned to the school building level will usually cover the task areas of (1) office management, (2) food service management, (3) building operations and maintenance, and (4) transportation coordination. School building size, pupil population size, and building organizational plan will determine the allocation and placement of logistical personnel in the four major areas mentioned. Regardless of size or organizational scheme these four major task areas should be carried out in order to support the building educational program. One will also discover that there may be an overlapping of support and services within these four areas. However, those features of overlapping will usually apply to more than one of the major task areas. For example computer services could apply to several points of the logistical program along with inventory procedures.

A sharp focus is needed in analyzing each of the building's four major logistical areas. Within this breakdown there will be a revealing of the central office logistical effort as it is incorporated into the building level administrative organization.

1. **The Office Manager or Senior Secretary**
    a. Logistical tasks performed under the supervision of this position are:
        (1) Financial Management
        (2) Staff Personnel Management
        (3) Pupil Personnel Management
        (4) Purchasing Procedures
        (5) Receiving Procedures for Purchases
        (6) Supply and Equipment Distribution and Inventory Procedures
        (7) Storage Management
        (8) Space Management
        (9) Reporting
        (10) Formal Maintenance Requests (to Central Office)
        (11) Logistical and Administrative Computer Management
        (12) Clerical Services
        (13) Safety Program Management
        (14) Security Program Management
        (15) Building Level Public Relations Program Management
        (16) Planning Projection Assistance

(17) Inservice
2. **Food Service Manager**
   a. Building logistical tasks of the head of school cafeteria services would be in the areas of:
      (1) Food Service Personnel Management
      (2) Financial Management
      (3) Foodstuff Requests and Purchasing Procedures
      (4) Food Center Supply/Equipment Requests and Purchasing
      (5) Food Stuff Storage
      (6) Supply and Equipment Storage
      (7) Equipment Maintenance
      (8) Menu Planning and Coordination
      (9) Cleaning, Sanitizing and Safety Procedures
      (10) Food Security Procedures
      (11) Food Preparation (cooking and baking) Procedures
      (12) Inservice Training
      (13) Recipe Management and Coordination
      (14) Computer Management
3. **Building Operations and Maintenance Coordinator**
   a. Supervisory personnel assigned to this particular position need to be involved with the following duties:
      (1) Housekeeping
      (2) Building Sanitization
      (3) Groundskeeping
      (4) Thermostatic and Atmospheric Control (Heating, Cooling and Ventilating)
      (5) Maintenance Awareness, Identification, and Correction Requests Procedures
      (6) User Maintenance and Servicing of Equipment
      (7) Supply and Equipment Storage
      (8) Inventory Procedures
      (9) Waste Removal and Control
      (10) Inservice Training
      (11) Computer Management
4. **Transportation Coordinator**
   a. The building logistical leader in this area should have involvement in the following task concerning building synchronization with the central office pupil transportation office:

(1) Direct Involvement with Central Office Transportation Operations for the Building
(2) Daily Contact with all Driver Personnel
(3) Management of Pupil Control and Disciplinary Procedures
(4) Awareness of Bus Routes, Schedules, and Stops
(5) Transportation Coordination for Special Events (Field Trips and Extracurricular Activities)
(6) Pupil-Bus Assignments
(7) Supervision of Pupil Holding Areas, Transfer Points, Mounting and Dismounting Areas
(8) Information Gathering Concerning Danger Areas on Bus Routes and at Bus Stops
(9) Building Weather Information Officer

Subordinate building logistical leaders and their support areas are of vital importance to the building. The building logistical team needs to be well informed coordinated within the building scene. It is up to the principal to properly use his/her logistical team and to integrate it with the instructional staff and administrative team. The building principal needs also to act as logistical team leader and to direct his/her logistical staff towards the achievement of team goals and overall building goals.

G. SUMMARY

A building administrator should be knowledgeable of the central office logistical effort and how this effort is coordinated within the building level logistical arm. Logistical systems of support will contain the features of time, finances, personnel, supplies, equipment, storage, computer management, and support services which will flow from central office to the individual school setting.

Logistics are carried out for the specific function of assisting and providing instruction with a base from which to operate. Building instructional and logistical functions must be carefully planned in order to provide for a perfect blend. A satisfactory blend has the capability to allow for the accomplishment of the building's objectives.

Logistical support areas of the individual school building are supervised and maintained by logistical leaders that are subordinate of the principal. These individuals form a building logistical team with the principal serving as team leader. The logistical team leader (the principal) needs to include his/her logistical team in the building's planning projections. There is also necessity for involvement with the building's administrative team and instructional staff in order to provide for a better synchronization of logistical and instructional efforts.

REFERENCES

[1]Harris, George W., Jr. *Management of the Public School Logistical System.* Springfield, Illinois: Charles C Thomas, Publisher, 1985, pp. 7–13.

PART THREE

MANAGING A MOST CRITICAL COMMODITY: HUMAN RESOURCES

CHAPTER VIII

INTRODUCTION AND INNOVATIONS
FOR MODERN HUMAN RESOURCES MANAGEMENT

A. ESTABLISHING AND MAINTAINING THE
HUMAN RESOURCES MANAGEMENT PROGRAM

The American worker has been the driving force behind the nation's development and success. The role of America's worker has evolved over the past 100 years. The industrial revolution worker was faced with long working hours, oftentimes hazardous working conditions and child labor abuses. The emergence of labor legislation and labor unions forced business magnates to view the worker in a different light—that of a person who was a vital and integral part of the organization. Many experts have stated that worker productivity is enhanced when management shows an interest in the workers, be it changes to the physical plant or worker incentives. Special interest in the worker since the late 1970s has prompted personnel specialists to look into the management practices of other countries to get indicators of how they achieve productivity and employee pride and satisfaction as mutual by-products. In fact, the growing interest in the American worker has prompted changes in personnel departmental operations and services. Personnel departments have expanded into human resources departments in a great number of businesses and public entities today.

B. HUMAN RELATIONS AND
HUMAN RESOURCES MANAGEMENT

The human resources department addresses a multiplicity of employee related functions including the traditional personnel department functions such as recruitment, the classification and compensation systems, employee records, labor relations, safety and training, and benefits administration. New additions to human resources are likely to be employee training and development programs, employee assistance programs, and human relations programs.

The emergence of human resources management indicate that businesses recognize the American workers as a most valuable commodity in the organization. The public school system is no different from the private sector when it comes to placing value upon its workers. Each worker from groundskeeper to the district superintendent has an impact on American youths.

Realizing that the school system's personnel functions are centralized and managed by school administrators, the school principal occupies a unique position in administrating a number of programs as an immediate supervisor and head of the individual school.

Chapters 8, 9, and 10, respectively, will discuss recent innovations for modern human resources management, investigate the highly specialized functions of a proposed human resources management program and finally, examine human relations as a separate, but integral part of human resources management.

C. LEGAL ISSUES AND INNOVATIONS FOR MODERN HUMAN RESOURCES MANAGEMENT: AN UPDATE

The establishment of the Equal Employment Opportunity (EEO) Act and eventually the Equal Employment Opportunity Commission (EEOC) changed the hiring practices in virtually every industry since 1977. The EEO Act prohibits discrimination against persons based on race, color, sex, national origin, handicap status, and age. Hiring entities have been required to maintain records of applicants pertaining to the factors being monitored. EEOC, in its *Uniform Guidelines* specified that fair hiring would be accomplished through the four-fifths rule. Hiring for minority group members as specified was to be equal to at least 80 percent of the hiring rate for majority group members. The guidelines go farther to dictate the type and outcomes of selection screening devices as they pertain to the identified minority group members. Selection screening devices are required to examine enabling skills or simulated exercises of the actual job both of which must pertain to the knowledge, skills, and abilities required in order to perform the job. These guidelines require employers to check their screening devices (particularly written, oral, or physical agility examinations) for adverse impact. Adverse impact occurs when an element of the screening device eliminates a particular group. Employers are required to assess the portion of the screening device causing the problem and to determine another means of screening the same trait that does not eliminate certain persons.

Affirmative Action plans and goals have also been required of employers in seeing that they adhere to fair hiring practices. Such goals and records have enabled employers to monitor their own hiring practices. The EEOC remains the watchdog of hiring practices having local and regional hearings on thousands of cases each year.

The Equal Pay Act of 1963 required employers to compensate employees equally for the same work performed. In principle, the act prohibits paying a male worker more than a female worker who performs the same job duties. It goes further to prohibit employers from assigning particular group members to low paying unskilled jobs.

The EEO and Equal Pay Acts in many cases caused human resources managers to reorganize and add specialized personnel to their departments in order to monitor the organization's progress in keeping with the new laws. The remedial efforts of the EEO and Equal Pay Acts have made it possible for many well-qualified personnel who may have been filtered out of the hiring process to now be included in the workforce.

Comparable worth is considered the most recent legal issue affecting human resources management. Comparable worth goes a step beyond equal pay for equal work. It compares jobs traditionally held by males and females and considers the worth of both jobs to the organization in terms of compensation. For example, the position of secretary (a traditionally female dominated job paying $12,500 yearly) compared to a pest control worker (traditionally a male dominated job paying $14,000 yearly). Comparable worth was one of the most feared legal issues as the 1980s came into being. The fear was coupled with the following three extremely difficult questions:

1. What traits would be examined to determine the worth of a job?
2. What instrument could be devised to accurately measure the worth of a job?
3. How could such an extensive study be undertaken and maintained?

Taking on such an overwhelming job of realigning jobs in accordance to their value to the organization was sure to cause even more confusion in setting pay ranges. Different organizations would be sure to have different values attributed to the same jobs. Salary comparisons would be impossible.

Comparable Worth continues to be an issue, however, some of the fears of human resources managers have been quieted since a 1985 ruling by the EEOC. The commission refused to act on the behalf of women claiming pay discrimination on the basis of comparable worth. The nearly 300 cases pending the hearing by EEOC would not have to go to the courts. The EEOC, in an unanimous ruling determined that there is no legal basis whereby the federal government must determine and establish a standard for wages in different female and male dominated jobs. The premise effecting the ruling stemmed from the fact that neither sex was barred from entering traditionally male or female-dominated jobs. Furthermore there was a variety of sufficient legislative muscle to assure it[1].

Title VII of the Civil Rights Act of 1964 prohibits discrimination in compensation on the basis of sex, however, the U.S. Civil Rights Commission did not recognize comparable worth in an earlier ruling. Comparable worth still is a concern and will continue to be until men and women enter into professions of their own choosing and those (e.g., female heads of families and older female workers) who have traditionally been forced into low paying jobs will no longer be in the job market. The next century is likely to bring about great changes in the way of traditional male/female jobs.

The means of determining pay equity has also been given new light by the U.S. General Accounting Office (GAO). According to the GAO, economic and job content analyses are both appropriate when examining pay equity and wage disparity by sex. The two analyses are desirable because they provide subjective and objective viewpoints[2].

The economic analysis takes an objective look at the job and characteristics of the incumbent such as education, work experience, the number of women in the position, and related positions and the structure of the position within the organization. The economic analysis provides information on factors influencing pay differentials. The job content analysis, however, looks at the relative value of a job to the employer. The job content approach or sometimes called a job evaluation may be any one of four methods including:

1. Ranking—an ordering of jobs based on their importance to the organization,
2. Grade description—an ordering of jobs by numeric levels reflecting pay,
3. Factor comparison—jobs having similar characteristics that are placed together then separated by importance,
4. Point factor system—a number value given to several job character-

istics and a total or composite score placing the job in the hierarchy of jobs within the organization.

The point factor system is often used in both the private and public sectors in setting wage scales. GAO believes that the job evaluation methodology is also another means of addressing comparable worth simply, because the job evaluation examines a job's worth to the organization regardless of sex.

While laws have shaped the modern human resources department, events taking place within the organization have and continue to prompt even more changes. These primary changes seem to center around the employee.

D. HUMAN INTEREST ANSWERS TO MANAGEMENT PROBLEMS

The 1980s have found the United States looking over its shoulders at the foreign competition, even imposing trade sanctions against its best competitors. Perhaps the reason is because the productivity of our nation's workforce has been waning. Labor unions at the bargaining tables fight for higher wages and improved fringe benefits, but goods produced by the American worker oftentime fall behind foreign goods in quality and cost. Each year thousands of students are graduated who lack basic skills enabling them to secure jobs in the fast-paced high technological society toward which we are moving. Most organizations are top heavy with a high ratio of management to worker. As a result of these concerns, the 1980s have found businesses and public entitled alike, searching for a panacea. The proverbial finger is pointed at upper management from middle managers and workers alike. Many companies have called in professional consultants to carefully examine the malady of sagging productivity and employee disinterest. The professionals' answers have run the gamut from total reorganization to terminating all of the new programs and getting back to basic foundations. Current literature leans toward a humanistic view of people management. The next section will address communication theory, employee programs and finally a few employee-centered approaches for bolstering employee participant.

Communication

Communication can be defined as an exchange of information between two or more parties. It is essential that there be a common point of reference between sender and receiver in order for the message sent to be received and translated. Although the parties communicating may have a common point of reference, other factors such as experience, environment, culture, sex, ethnicity, religion, political persuasion, and emotions can effect how the message is translated. The workplace complicates the reference factor by adding the way in which the worker may view himself/herself within the organization; from whom the message is coming; the circumstances at hand; the intonation of the sender; and persons present witnessing the communiqué. In an organizational setting, communication is usually handled in a top down fashion. Decisions are made at the top and news of the decision is filtered through the upper management, through middle management, supervisors, and eventually the workers. Managers today have begun to consider a bottom up communication model as well. A lot of information from the bottom end of the model provides feedback on the information filtered down plus keen insight from a fresh perspective. All of this can be accomplished through effective listening.

Effective listening, according to Burack and Smith (1982), involves more than hearing what an employee is saying. It involves interpretation or understanding, judgment or a value placed on the information given and finally a response. Some researchers have even cited listening as carrying the larger part of the communication burden. Written communication causes excesses in time and materials by going through the processes of: (1) writing or dictating communication, (2) then typing and disseminating it, and (3) finally separating the communication, reading it, responding plus filing or discarding it. Speaking and listening lead out respectively when it comes to the most effective communication[3].

Listening can be distorted by the listener's inability to concentrate on the message, a tendency to zero in on specific tangential information, having preconceived conclusions and ignoring nonverbal gestures. Nonverbal gestures are displayed naturally and often are a more reliable indicator of communication than are words.

Managers can discourage communication from subordinates when they do not listen properly. Subordinates often interpret poor listening skills as indicators to withdraw and become inhibited. Some managers are overwhelmed with conversing and then failing to let their subordinates enter into a communication exchange. Sometimes managers are not secure enought to experience the exchange of information from subordinates. All of these shortcomings, however, can be overcome if managers examine their listening skills and attempt to improve their situation. The organization stands to gain from communication that flows freely both downwards and upwards.

Communication plays a critical part within any organization specifically when information is to be selectively disseminated throughout the unit. Such information should be disseminated in a controlled or filtered fashion (see Figure 7). Certain matters are made known to only a few at strategic levels and positions throughout the organization. All employees are not privy to all of the information within an organization. To make them so would be wasteful of the organization's resources. Also such action could have damaging effects on the employees who lacked other knowledge or information influencing the decisions to be made.

There are a number of media available to an organization for communication purposes. Memoranda are most often sent throughout an organization usually following a route of key personnel. It is a fast and effective means of communicating vital information and to solicit immediate responses from selected employees when used appropriately. One disadvantage is that so many memoranda can be circulated about until they become ineffective. Generating memoranda is also costly when you consider the amount of time it takes to compose, type, duplicate, mail, sort, route, read, and reply multiplied by the number of employees handling the memoranda.

Newsletters are another means of communicating a variety of topics throughout an organization. Topics can include anything from policy and procedural changes to general information. Employees usually look forward to newsletter issues because their personal interest is often kindled when feature articles zero in on employee concerns. There are, however, some disadvantages of newsletters. Firstly, newsletters are distributed on a scheduled basis (e.g., monthly or even bimonthly). If a particular matter came up and information needed to be communicated immediately, the newsletter would not be helpful. Secondly, because a newsletter is a general publication, the information contained in it must be general information. It becomes impossible for information to be filtered or controlled at certain levels.

Videotaped communiqués are fast becoming an effective medium for

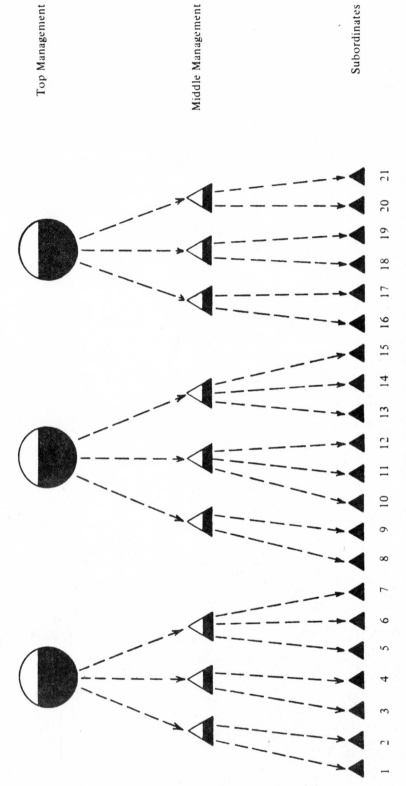

Top Management

Middle Management

Subordinates

Figure 7. The Information Filtering System.

quickly and selectively disseminating information throughout an organization. It provides a personalized touch with tremendous impact. This is particularly so when the videotaped message comes from a high ranking officer within the organization. There is, however, a disadvantage to using videotaped communiqués. The video equipment (camera, videotape players, monitors, duplicating machine and tapes) can be costly. If an organization already has video equipment, and as video equipment costs decline, it could fast become a most viable means of sending information throughout the unit.

Employee Development Programs

A work environment that fosters employees' personal growth is positively viewed by employees. It is for this reason that a number of organizations, both public and private, have established employee development programs. Employee development programs provide professional and middle management employees with periodic meetings, forums, workshops and speakers on a range of topics affecting the employees in their present positions as well as the positions to which they would aspire. Unlike a training and development program (which will be discussed in a later chapter), employee development programs are less formal and are usually part of a social setting. For example, a breakfast or luncheon and can readily solicit input from attendees as to the topics they would like to have presented. Providing such a program to a select group of employees can be an effective means of demonstrating top management's interest in the employees and their personal development. This also provides top management an opportunity to consider such programs as a valuable asset to the organization.

Employee Assistance Programs

Employee assistance programs are another means by which organizations have taken steps to address the personal aspect of their employees. Such programs cover employee needs that directly or indirectly influence them while working. The employee's needs might include relief from alcohol or drug dependence problems, smoking, personal or family crises, personal overweight, etc. Programs could be constructed to work with the previously mentioned items. Some programs may be held in-house while others are handled by specific agencies through referral.

Employee assistance programs have been met with much success. The services should be available to all. Since all employees are aware of the services, supervisors could easily refer their subordinates to a human resources specialist. The human resources specialist then becomes a liaison between the employee and a contracted or public referral agency. Such matters should be handled with the highest discretion. Oftentimes problems that have directly affected employee performance can be worked out to solution via services provided by the employee assistance program. An organization that has taken an interest in every aspect affecting an employee directly or indirectly is held in high esteem. An employee will want to stay where someone cares about his/her and his/her family.

Team Approaches

Organizational problems are often resolved when input from employees at various levels of the organization is given serious consideration. Team approaches are successful when they are formed and operate in their appropriate fashions.

Task forces have been formed by many organizations to address particular problems, however, it is not problem-solving entity. A task force calls for selected employees possessing particular skills from strategically important areas within the organization. A task force has but one objective. Its purpose is usually to generate several viable alternatives to a problem after having conducted a considerable amount of research. The alternatives are taken into consideration by upper and/or middle management. Their decision may or may not incorporate any of the alternatives generated from the task force. After the objective has been reached the task force is disbanded.

Usually there is not training for task force participants. Roles and research assignments are assumed on a voluntary basis. Leadership is held by a person or persons designated by management.

Quality circles[4] serve a purpose quite different from that of a task force. They consist of a group of workers from a specific area who meet on a regularly scheduled basis to carefully identify problems, their causes, and how to determine their solutions. When given the authority by upper management, quality circles can take action by putting the recommended solution to work. Quality circles come into existence when management personnel invite this type of workers participation. In essence, a participative type of management philosophy must be in operation before quality circles can function. Management personnel must also have a positive outlook on the organization's workers, their resourcefulness and their abilities in making things work. Upper management plays a primary role in the quality circle's existence by determining its control system, guidelines, goals, and objectives. A wide cross section of the organization's management needs to participate in the quality circle steering committee on a rotating basis. Before quality circles are in full-fledged operation, considerable training must be conducted by a facilitator or coordinator of the entire program. The first group that meets is considered experimental or a pilot program. The malfunctions of the pilot program quality circle can be untangled through troubleshooting. This action would allow leaders and member participation roles to be refined, therefore giving upper management an indicator of how functional quality circles can function within the organization.

Quality circles require some very specific personality traits from participants. These persons (participants) must possess goal-oriented of results-centered behavior, general considerable enthusiasm, have a balanced perspective of the organization plus upper management's philosophy, and an understanding of the group's section. Most of all, it is critical that quality circle participants believe in upper management's commitment to their operation. Employees where quality circles are in operation can play an active role and have the opportunity to feel that they are very much a part of the organization. Additional dividends will prevail when they (the employees) sense that their contributions are valued.

E. COMPUTER TECHNOLOGY'S IMPACT ON HUMAN RESOURCES MANAGEMENT

The emergence of the computer age has encouraged streamlined and reorganized operations throughout many organizations (both public and private). A number of in-house studies conducted by information processing systems analysts (liaisons between data processing and other departments) have generally identified areas by which a centralized computer system or a main frame could benefit the entire organization's operations and services. First of all, their data bound tasks which were redundant and were being performed by several decentralized units. Such findings led to the beginning of a computer-based Human Resources Information System (HRIS). Today's HRIS can meet a number of needs throughout the typical organization, provided that systems and subsystems are carefully coordinated and functioning interdependently. Systems are identified as groups or the departments within an organization; subsystems are even smaller units such as the sections within a group or department (see Figure 8). When systems and subsystems work interdependently, their access to the same information streamlines and simplifies operations, therefore, eliminating the need for manual record-keeping, and duplicated efforts. Any number of reports can also be generated from given information. The carefully designed program developed by in-house or contracted programmers makes the input and access of information possible. A number of human resources departments also use individual microcomputers with interoffice hook-ups. Several software (prepared program) packages are available on the market which meet human resources needs and are easy to use. Microcomputers provide two added benefits. They permit free usage at any time since they are not tied in to the main frame which must be shared. Microcomputers can restrict access to information and limit usage by others since it is housed within one department (and can have a number of security clearances tied to its use).

The HRIS has made it possible and perhaps necessary to expand the function of human resources. Figure 9 identifies three basic human resources operations and provides examples of how information gathered from such operations when input into a carefully designed human resources program can generate information, making it possible to expand into other areas. These operations and others will be discussed in detail in the subsequent chapter.

A HRIS can do only so much, however. It is limited by environment (what is available) and organizational (what it is permitted to do) factors. Provided that these have been determined, the information input, processed and retrieved can create a highly sophisticated human resources department.

SUMMARY

Human resources management has evolved from an organizational operation esteemed by other "more important" departments as a "necessary evil" to a vital component of the organization. There are more changes on the horizon as we approach a new decade and eventually a new century. Changes in human resources departments and organizations

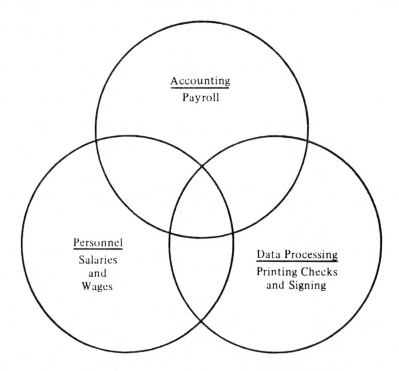

Figure 8. Three Systems Working Interdependently.

have generated advanced planning methods for such measures in a highly specialized area. This area is known as organizational development. Specialists in organizational development are taking their places in the human resources department. They (the specialists) provide much needed input on such matters as strategic planning, manpower planning, employee development, and effective measures for meeting organizational-employee needs. Organizational development specialists will soon be common place within most organizations as they face new challenges.

Accountability is required of businesses both private and public, from auto makers to educators. Consumers or the public wants what it is paying for. Consumer or community advocacy and a rise in the news media's involvement in the quality of goods and services will have great influence on the cost factor. Wages and prices will spiral as more is required of goods, services, and employees.

Job security will be a critical issue as our nation moves from a factory-oriented work force to one of service and high-technology. Employees will be required to shift to other industries. Unless they possess easily assimilated skills and abilities, they (the employees) still face unemploy-

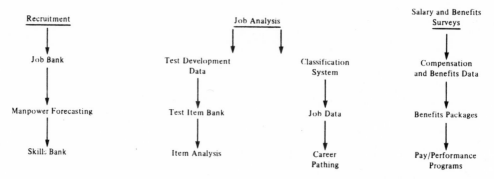

Figure 9. Data Flow and the Three Basic Human Resources Operations.

ment unless they can be retrained in order to reenter the job market. It will continue to be critical that human resources managers keep contact with the pulse of the job market so that changes can be anticipated.

Organizations will most likely continue to generate more employee-centered programs as the quality of work life becomes an issue of growing importance. Employees will need to take a greater role in organizational operations and making decisions affecting the terms of their employment. As the needs of the American worker become more pressing, changes in benefit packages may be necessary. Retirement options will have to be revised as the numbers of older employees increase. Presently benefits comprise over 40 percent of payroll costs. In order to contain costs, more organizations will probably provide a cafeteria style of benefits packages. Such packages allows an employee to use a particular amount of benefit dollars to select and purchase benefits as his/her needs dictate.

The changes that we may expect to see may require human resources management to keep pace with the changes taking place in our society.

REFERENCES

[1]International Personnel Management Association — United States, *IPMA News,* July 1985, pp. 1, 8, Washington, D.C.

[2]International Personnel Management Association — United States, *IPMA News,* April 1985, pp. 4, Washington, D.C.

[3]Burack, Elmer H., and Robert D. Smith, *Personnel Management: A Human Resource Systems Approach,* John Wiley and Sons, Inc., NY, 1982, pp. 379.

[4]Dewar, Donald L. *The Quality Circle Guide to Participation Management,* Under cc by Quality Circle Institute Printed in U.S., Prentice-Hall, Inc., Englewood Cliffs, New Jersey, 1980, pp. 2.

CHAPTER IX

ESTABLISHING AND MAINTAINING A HUMAN RESOURCES MANAGEMENT PROGRAM

The segments of the human resources management program are interrelated. Therefore, it is important that the school principal have an understanding of each segment of human resources (although all segments may not affect the individual school). Chapter IX examines the segments of a proposed human resources program. The chapter begins with an overview of an existing program's effectiveness followed by discussions on the classification system, recruitment, the compensation system, labor relations, training and development, and finally, policy making.

A. EXAMINING THE EXISTING PROGRAM

There are a number of indicators as to how well an existing human resources program is doing. Recruitments in a well-functioning program will most likely provide a pool of well-qualified candidates representing a proportionate cross section of the population. Searches for qualified candidates can be cost effective if they are planned and conducted on a systematic and timely basis.

Internal promotions and transfers of employees show that human resources are being used effectively; that the time and training programs invested in employees are being used throughout the organization. Promotions and transfers serve a position purpose in the interest of employees. Their abilities, skills, and experiences can be developed by promotions and lateral moves throughout an organization.

Job descriptions and class specifications (required training and experience for each job title) should be reviewed on a periodic basis and kept up-to-date. By having current job descriptions it becomes possible for accurate salary studies to be conducted (so that salary ranges are not lagging behind nor exceeding the salaries of persons occupying the same type of jobs in comparable organizations).

161

Up-to-date, competitive salaries are tied to performance via a performance appraisal system. In the efficient human resources program, performance appraisal is based on a merit system, pay for performance or some other specified system. The desired performance parameters are clearly stated and reviewed regularly for the employee's and supervisors' encouraged discussion before and during evaluation periods. The human resources program monitors the timely handling of the performance appraisal system and reviews each one and its supporting documentation assuring the performance appraisal's integrity.

Employee absenteeism and turnover are monitored on a periodic basis by each departmental unit. These data are compared with performance appraisals and exit interviews (by designated human resources personnel) respectively to keep abreast of trends or specific problems. Employee grievances are handled in a prescribed manner. The procedures are readily available to each employee and the efficient human resources manager sees that the prescribed grievance procedures are followed.

The human resources program will require that records on safety training and accidents be kept by a records management section so that goals can be monitored and adjustments be made in training or job assignment (if required). Record keeping is also monitored by a human resources specialist on affirmative action goals, EEOC data and periodic updates on EEOC litigation.

Employees' job satisfaction and morale are studied through the use of professionally developed personnel inventories, because employees are valued in a well-running human resources program. Inventories are used strategically and at appropriate times due to their highly sensitive data. Information generated from job satisfaction and morale studies are used in making management decisions.

B. THE CLASSIFICATION SYSTEM

The job classification system is the backbone of an organization's structure. It has far reaching effects on other segments of the human resources program such as the compensation system, recruitment, and training.

A job classification system consists of: (1) description and class specifications for every job class within the organization with a code number for each job class, (2) a questionnaire or specially designed instrument which provides detailed information on job duties performed by incumbents in job classes, (3) a planned program for a systematic review of all job classes with procedures for realigning and establishing new job classes.

A job class can be described as one or more positions performing relatively similar tasks of equal complexity in a common environment requiring the same knowledge, skills, abilities, training, and experience as enabling abilities to perform the work. An example would be the job class of groundskeeper. Some persons having the title of groundskeeper could work in a stadium area where lawn maintenance would be a primary part of the work performed. Another groundskeeper could be assigned to maintaining hedges, flowers, and snow removal. A job description would include the types of duties performed by both incumbents. Although their job duties might vary, they essentially perform the same work.

At times, however, due to the nature of a changing environment or roles, job duties can change. It is important that job classes be reviewed on a regular basis so that changes can be incorporated in new description revisions or if necessary. The duties and responsibilities performed by an incumbent occupying a given position may call for the position to be reclassified to another existing job class or to a newly created class. Job reviews, if conducted every 18 to 24 months can create a synchronized program. When changes have been made in several jobs throughout a given class it is sometimes necessary for a comprehensive study to be undertaken by human resources specialists.

Comprehensive studies require considerably special care because they generate a lot of attention on the part of the incumbents involved, and may or may not lead to incumbents' expectations. Special comprehensive studies are often performed when examining a job class having multiple levels such as Clerk-Typist I, Clerk-Typist II, and Clerk-Typist III. The job duties are listed by job class and incumbents. Adjustments are then made by placing incumbents under appropriate job classes and revisions are made to the job class descriptions. Sometimes new job classes are created with new names. The names of a job class incorporates something about the job duties or its assignment. Selecting a name can involve some creativity, however, standards for job titles have been uniformly set by the United States Department of Labor. The publication, *Dictionary of Occupational Titles* (D.O.T.) lists virtually every job title that is conceivable by a code number reflecting the industry and its skilled, technical or professional nature. Human resources specialists often refer to the D.O.T. when making changes to the name of a job class. The D.O.T. also gives a thumbnail sketch of the typical duties of a given job title.

The end result of conducting job reviews and special studies is the generation of job description and class specifications. Information contained in incumbents' completed questionnaires is consolidated in the following categories:

General statement of duties — a brief explanation of what duties are typically performed.

Explanation of duties — specific categories of duties are identified along with their expected outcomes, levels of responsibility is described areas where such incumbents work are described along with the identification of the immediate supervising employee.

Illustrative examples — may be included but are not exhaustive of all duties performed by persons occupying the job class.

Required knowledge, skills, abilities, and personal characteristics — are listed as the information one must know, the precision with which one must perform with ability, the learned behaviors one must exhibit, and specific personality traits that an incumbent must possess in order to successfully perform the job at entry level.

Required experience and training — identify the previous exposure to a particular type of work and education are necessary in order to perform successfully at the entry level.

Job descriptions and class specifications are often combined so that filing is not duplicated. Job descriptions and class specifications do not describe incumbents and the traits and experience that they possess. They (job descriptions) rather describe the duties and experience required of the job in order to perform the work satisfactorily and meet prescribed objectives.

The Human Resources Information System (HRIS) lends itself amicably to the classification system. A position control system, a check and balance system for reviewing allocated positions by section, job title, and a coding system can be generated at any time. Word processing capabilities can make revisions to job descriptions and class specification a simple task. Maintaining files of job description and class specification can be eliminated by storage on disc and printing them when necessary.

It is important that employees and supervisors alike know about the have access to job descriptions. The school principal occupies a critical position in seeing firsthand how appropriately personnel within the school are classified and can make requests for positions to be reviewed.

C. THE COMPENSATION SYSTEM

Job evaluation is a means by which job classes are assigned a relative value to one another within an organization as reflected by determining salaries or wages. A specially trained job evaluation committee reviews data and makes critical decisions on the value of selected job classes. There are several methods of job evaluation, all of which fall into two categories: the whole job methods and factor methods.

The whole job methods are easy to devise but generally are lacking in flexibility when it comes to determining changes in wages when there are changes in job content. They also tend to be subjective. Whole job methods include:

Ranking — a comparison of job classes from least important to most important based on a summary of duties performed;

Market Pricing — benchmark or specially selected job classes are given brief descriptions of duties and required experience and traits are used to compare salary ranges in a compensation survey. The benchmark data are put back into the existing pay scale and adjustments are made accordingly.

Factor methods involve some type of compensable variable (or element of the job that has a value) applied to specific factors of job classes.

Narrative Approach — assimilates information contained in the classification questionnaire or listed job task statements into specific pay levels depending upon such predetermined factors as responsibility, knowledge, skill, and working conditions.

General Point Factor Comparison Methods — use factors numerically based and specified standards for evaluating job worth.

Statistical Methods — use highly complex applications such as multiple regression to determine statistical significance of jobs using multiple factors simultaneously.

The factor methods provide more objectivity than whole job methods. They, however, are considerably time consuming, can become highly complex, require specially trained personnel and significant cost in acquiring some methods from private consultants. As changes take place in various industries it is conceivable that human resource programs will be required to substantiate job evaluation decisions by selecting a methodology that meets their ever growing needs. The HRIS can play a vital role in providing the sophisticated technology in making sound management decisions.

Benefits are closely tied in to compensation. Surveys and ingenious thinking help the human resources program to keep abreast of what is available on the benefits market, yet contains costs.

D. LABOR RELATIONS

Unionization has touched virtually every industry, including the public sector. The on-going process of collective bargaining has a tremendous impact on the compensation system as human resources specialists along with union representatives examine fringe benefits and wages. The objective of the human resources program is to provide mutually agreeable and desirable benefits to employees at minimal cost. The bargaining process progresses in a specific fashion and is governed by federal laws. The bargaining process begins with notification to modify or terminate the contract. The Taft-Hartley Act requires that notification be given 60 days prior to the contract's expiration date. It is during this period that human resources and management personnel prepare for negotiation by exploring ways of improving operations, benefits and policies, reviewing the existing contractual agreement, and examining economic factors that can or will determine what they can realistically offer. Union officials, during this time are preparing the proposed changes they wish to have incorporated into a new contract.

It is after notification for collective bargaining is given that union representatives and management, represented by human resources personnel exchange their demands, which specify what they want to gain during the bargaining process. Considerable time is spent in reviewing demands by both union and management persons so that negotiating will proceed as smoothly as possible. Bargaining persons may enter the actual bargaining process with fairly close or distant positions. Bargaining sessions can be likened to a tug of war with heated debates and power plays. Depending on how well the sides have prepared themselves, support and/or opposition from either management or union members can make or break the climate at the bargaining table. It is during this time that outside factors such as public sentiment on a given issue or pressure form political factions can have a tremendous effect on the success of bargaining. Negotiators use a variety of tactics in seeking to get what they want. All during the process small committees from both sides represented carefully examine ways in which to find agreement. Oftentimes, this is where the real bargaining takes place, and where agreements come into being as the smaller informal groups work quietly toward settlement. Legal counsel is invited to participate as the formal settlement is drafted for ratification by union members. Should there be disapproval, the bargaining phase continues.

Labor relations requires highly skilled human resources personnel who are able to examine existing benefits and programs and see how modifications can be made with minimal cost to the organization while satisfying the needs and demands of employees.

E. RECRUITMENT

Finding suitable candidates and filling vacant positions with the best qualified is the objective of recruitment. Having qualified candidate readily available so that lost hours and costly overtime are avoided is indicative of manpower planning. An innovative human resources program utilizes the availability of the HRIS to keep account of interested and qualified persons for specific jobs in what is known as a job bank. It serves the same purpose for entry-level positions as for promotional opportunities.

Recruitment challenges human resource specialists to use their creativity in finding good applicant resources such as private and public job agencies, college job placement offices, and the wise use of media such as professional and technical journals, television, cable, and newspaper advertisements.

Screening employees on their qualifications can be done in any number of ways. The one-on-one interview is familiar to everyone. It can be a cursory screening device or an in-depth interview during which time the interviewer may assume even an antagonist role to screen stress reactions. The session may query applicant experience and training or probe into the applicant's philosophy for "fitting" into the organization. Nearly every job applicant goes through a one-on-one interview before being hired.

Written examinations are often used as a preliminary screening device. They may use multiple choice, matching, fill-in-the-blank, or essay-type questions.

Physical agility examinations are screening devices used to measure an applicant's physical prowess in a work simulated course or an alternative indicator of specific body strengths.

Performance examinations test applicants on their skill in operating specific equipment in a work simulated exercise. Assessment centers are a highly complex work simulation exercise that calls into play a great number of skills and abilities, particularly those found in administrative and professional positions.

The HRIS plays a critical part in maintaining test information by keeping questions in a test item bank, performing item analysis functions thereby purging the bank of poor test items, scoring written examinations, calculating pass points, and storing test data.

The Uniform Guidelines of the EEOC sets the standard for testing job applicants. Tests are to be on job-related subject matters and are to assess skills required of a candidate at entry. Human resources specialists select the testing method that most efficiently assesses enabling skills. Care is taken in considering the ease of a administration, the time taken, and cost containment.

Prior to the final selection, some human resources departments conduct checks into the backgrounds of the seriously considered candidates by contacting previous employers. If the position is one requiring clearance for sensitive or highly confidential information, more extensive background checks can include FBI checks and psychological test batteries.

Human resources personnel conduct employee orientation programs so that newly hired personnel may be acclimated to the organization's policies, benefits, and procedures.

The HRIS can be used to track employees as they become a part of the organization and progress through it. An employee record system can be used to maintain employees' training, experience, continuing education, and career path through the organization. When promotional opportunities arise, it will be easy to access those employees possessing specific backgrounds.

F. TRAINING AND DEVELOPMENT

An organization that realizes its employees are valuable human resources usually has a high opinion of their employees' continued training. Human resources specialists have found that it takes more than one year before a newly hired employee becomes productive (i.e., no long requires orientation to job duties and direct supervision). A considerable amount of time and money is invested in newly hired employees. To lose them to another employer rather than using employees' talents within the organization by furthering their training would be wasteful.

The training and development section of the human resources program can serve two purposes: one in the personal interest of employee's development and the other in meeting organization-wide training needs. Some services of training specialists are referred to experts in the particular field needed. However, some training specialists are able to meet a number of employee needs by providing career counseling, conducting some stand-up training, and selecting trainers for topics on which they are not able to conduct training. Employee concerns and training will be conducted separately.

Employee Development

Training specialists may assist employees in determining what career to pursue or where their strengths or areas of interest like by administering any number of career interest tests. This may also be done on a referral basis to a career counselor. The results of the test are tabulated. During subsequent visits, the employee's interests are compared with his/her training, experience and the possibility of entering into the career choice field. Oftentimes a plan is put together where specific training and/or specific jobs are identified and steps are identified where after having been attained, lead to the chosen career. Identifying specific jobs within an organization that logically and capably prepare employees to enter other jobs in a lateral and progressive zig-zag format is called career pathing. When career pathing has been established and is used by training specialists, employees are encouraged and are likely to follow progression and be of even greater value to the organization.

Organizational Training

The training process begins with information specifying where employees and supervisors feel that instruction is needed or where new procedures of equipment dictate employees' education. Training can result from top management's decision on remedying social issues, safety hazards or employee morale issues. The information gathered by training specialists is known as a needs assessment. Information is usually obtained by departmental units and charted so that common training needs can be noted and specialized needs identified as well.

The amount of training done and the quantity of specialized training has a bearing on the dollars allocated to the training session. Training specialists and other qualified professionals in other areas of the organization's employ can be used as trainers. They might include a risk manager's training on safety procedures, a human resources specialist's training on benefits or special procedures. However, it is often necessary to seek trainers from the professional public market. Training specialists prepare a detailed description of training needs by stating objectives, the degree to which the objective is to be met, specific points of interest, description of participants, length of time, and related information. This is known as a request for proposals and is sent to interested prospective trainers. The proposals received are reviewed, trainers are interviewed by training personnel and a trainer is selected. The end of the training session usually calls for an evaluation of the trainer and course content to ascertain that programs are meeting organizational needs and expectations.

G. POLICY MAKING

The human resources program is largely dependent upon policies as they determine authority and how the program is to be operated. Human resources policies are largely determined by the authority given them from various administration entities. Policy is also sometimes governed by federal laws in such areas as employment (EEOC), compensation (Equal Pay Act) and labor relations (Taft Hartley Act).

Economic situations, political events, and even social issues can make it necessary for alterations in policy. Procedural changes will usually follow. Policy changes are not always popular among employees. Sometime they meet resistance and problems affecting part or all of the organization. Such action has been the experience of a great businesses and has furthered the development of the behavioral sciences until they have now become a part of the human resources program.

H. SUMMARY

Programs regarding the human relations aspect of the organization should be reviewed to determine if adequate recruitment is taking place. This is needed in order to provide a qualified labor pool. The training endeavor also should be examined to determine if both training and organizational goals are being met. Promotions, transfers, job descriptions plus classifications, and comparative salary studies should be studied in order to place the organization in the competitive zone with like organizations.

Labor relations between the organizational administration and employees should be at such a level as to allow for high morale and quality production. Policy should be closely tied to labor or professional organizational relations and the effective operation of the organization.

CHAPTER X

HUMAN RELATIONS, HUMAN BEHAVIOR, AND HUMAN RESOURCES MANAGEMENT

A. ORGANIZATIONAL PHILOSOPHY

Human relations are the interactions between people. Those interactions include both pleasant and unpleasant encounters. People engaged in work form relationships with coworkers, supervisors, subordinates, and others with whom they may interact indirectly. Human relations also refers to two entities with entirely different objectives such as an organization with goals for its employees in career development[5]. Chapter X will first examine some basic components of human relations. Human resources management entails keeping a balance between employees and the organization so that each can realize its goals and operate efficiently. The social sciences, particularly psychology, have been the models on which organizational behavior has been built. Organization behavior will be the second area of focus. Organizational development, its principles and practices will be the final topic of discussion.

Human Relations

Business and other organizations have included human relations in their human resources departments as a means of resolving employee problems. In order for human relations to work, managers have had to realize human problems have factors that are not under human control. For example, the aesthetics of the physical plant in which employees work, the complexity of an organizational structure, or the organizational philosophy can have effects on the views formed by administrators, managers, and employees alike. The multiple factors initiating employee problems are as diverse as the employees themselves. There usually are not simple solutions for complex problems. It usually takes a number of years for problems to surface an takes considerable time to resolve them.

173

There is no one way of resolving employee problems. The solution used at one time may not work a second time.

Communication plays a vital role in human relations. In Chapter VIII, the importance of both downward and upward communication was discussed. A great deal of communication takes place between employees. Informal communication between managers or supervisors and employees at all levels is nearly as important, if not more important than formal communication. Informal communication permits free discussion, sharing of viewpoints and more information exchange than formal communication.

It is through communication that managers can learn a lot about what needs are important to employees and what motivates them. The things that employees want are not necessarily matters that pertain to their work. Past experience has shown that the work environment with such factors as employee recognition, benefits, practices, and equality of opportunity are typical causes of job dissatisfaction.

When there is job dissatisfaction a number of behaviors ensue, some of which are disturbing to the work environment or even disruptive. If the communication avenues between the dissatisfied employee and supervisor are open and functioning, steps can be taken to resolve, diminish or better understand the employee problem. Often just talking about the dissatisfaction with the employee and providing additional information will enlighten the employee and solve the problem. Other times, counseling may be the better alternative.

Counseling can be conducted by supervisors, human resources specialists and professional counselors. Counseling is used when the employee's problem is of an emotional nature and it requires the employee to see his/her own problem. Emotions are just a part of the person as are his/her physical attributes. The employee's self-concept (self-confidence and self-esteem) are often closely associated with the employee's problem. There are several forms in which counseling may be used to have maximum effectiveness for a specific employee problem.

Reassurance is a form of counseling that helps the employee to look at a solution to problems by examining the problems himself/herself and finding the causes. It often helps the employee to learn that he/she is not alone, and that others have had similar problems similar to his/hers. A disadvantage of this particular counseling modality is that it may be a short-lived solution to an even larger problem. An employee with a serious self-esteem problem, for example, may not believe that he/she can face and solve his/her own problems.

Counseling may take the form of advice. In this instance, the counselor makes a judgment about the employee's problem and offers possible solutions. There are instances where advice giving counsel is appropriate. Unfortunately, it has the greatest disadvantage right with its high point, because it encourages employee dependency upon the counselor who provides the advice.

When an employee who has undergone counseling and emerges with a new set of values which are now internalized and operating he/she has successfully reoriented his/her thinking as a result of counseling. This is one of the more difficult forms of counseling. It usually requires professional counseling expertise and considerable time before results are obtained[6].

If employee dissatisfaction has resulted in disruptive or divergent behavior which has violated organizational policy, then disciplinary action may be implemented. Employee discipline does not necessarily have to mean punishment. It is most successful when it gives rise to increased communication and understanding between employee and supervisor and when it encourages the employee to be motivated by more cooperative factors.

Motivation plays an interesting role in human relations. Some managers spend considerable time and effort in attempting to find ways to motivate employees. Incentive programs are established to persuade employees to undertake tasks management's way. This method does not always work. If an employee senses that he/she is viewed disparagingly and feels victimized, the incentives will be seen as manipulative. This "carrot-on-the-stick" approach, regardless of its shortcomings is still one of the most popularly used incentives today[7]. Abraham Maslow's hierarchy of needs provides a possible solution for motivating desirable employee behavior. Maslow's model states that there are physical, social, emotional, and personal growth needs that must be met respectively. Others have elaborated on Maslow's model. The point that they all have in common is this: when an employee's lower level needs such as food, clothing, and shelter are met, he can be motivated only by higher level needs. Rewards such as time off or even money will not necessarily increase production. One must understand what motivates the employee before incentives can be used effectively. Motivators vary as do individuals[8].

Human relations incorporates a multiplicity of disciplines in its theory and applications including that of the social sciences. The following section will examine the organization from a behavioral standpoint.

B. ORGANIZATIONAL BEHAVIOR MANAGEMENT

Organizational behavior may be defined as the study of employee behavior within an organization based on behavioral science theories. Organizational behavior is an explanation of behavior through scientific concepts rather than behavioral approaches to managing people. Knowledge of organizational behavior methods and understanding its concepts can certainly aid managers in examining the organization and its employees; however, it is not a panacea. The organization will still have to function amid some employee dissatisfaction. This is a fact of life.

What makes employees behave as they do? Behaviorists, more specifically purists of behaviorism say that behavior may be explained by operant conditioning. Benjamin Skinner, one of the foremost proponents of behaviorism stated that operant conditioning modifies behavior by changing the reward or aversion associated with a behavior (be it desirable or undesirable). Skinner and other behaviorists believe that through operant conditioning and rewards given at strategic times, behaviors can be learned and repeated through a variety of reinforcement schedules. The more a behavior is rewarded, the more that behavior is reinforced and will appear again. Unfortunately, this applies to undesirable behaviors, too. If they are rewarded, they will be reinforced and will reappear. On the converse, behaviors are extinguished when the reinforcement is discontinued[9].

Hedonistic theorists[10] state that employees behave in accordance to a pleasure principle. Employees may act in certain ways to maximize pleasure and minimize or eliminate uncomfortable events. This theory is the basis for current thought on motivation. According to hedonistic theory, an employee realizes a deficiency of a particular need and becomes sensitive to surrounding stimuli effecting a resolution to the need. The employee searches for something to eliminate a particular need and eventually finds it, even if it is disruptive.

The real answer to the question on behavior is likely to be a combination of the behaviorist and hedonistic theories. Employees are not programmed robots who are not affected by intrinsic needs nor are they so totally self-centered that they are unaffected by external stimuli. Employees' job performance is usually satisfying because a need has been met and has been reinforced in some manner.

Organizational behavior theory provides an interesting account of behaviors such as frustration and aggression. Frustration is the result of a road block to satisfying a critical need. Aggression, on the other hand is explained as a by-product of frustration that is a learned behavior. Aggression is one aspect of frustration that can be directed at others throughout an organization taking on many forms. Aggression can have extremely damaging effects if it is allowed to fester within an organization.

Organizational behavior theory parallels some of the human relations concepts on needs discussed earlier. Work groups largely effect employee behavior, because needs for affiliation, cohesiveness, conformity are satisfied. Work groups can influence behavior to the degree that an employee may even sacrifice another lower level need (e.g., a monetary reward for meritorious performance which would isolate him/her) in order to be an accepted member of a work group.

The total organization is viewed in organizational behavior theory as a series of systems having multiple purposes, including a system which perpetuates the existence of the organization and a power distribution system. Organizational structure is a by-product of the purpose set forth. As organizational purposes and focuses change, so does the rest of the organization.

C. ORGANIZATIONAL DEVELOPMENT

Organizational change can be prompted by economic, societal, or technological factors. Changes are realized through interventions that either change employees from one activity to another, change the work that employees perform or change the interaction patterns between people. Organizational development (OD) is the use of several techniques for interventions affecting the relationships among employees. The primary purposes of OD are to: (1) have a positive effect on the organization climate or the unique atmosphere or climate that one might "feel" in an organization and, (2) improve employee performance.

OD encompasses a number of the theories discussed earlier in the chapter. Specialists in OD intervention first collect data on the flow of interaction between employees in the targeted area. Problems are isolated and OD specialists learn what techniques might best further intervention. Learning takes place as employees are exposed to the inappropriateness of certain behaviors and beliefs and begin to incorporate new ones in their places. This is a difficult and often not totally successful process.

OD techniques include using sensitivity group training (also known as

T-groups) to assist employees in the targeted group in learning. During group sessions, members are given basic guideline and interact, paying close attention to group members' behaviors. Considerable time is spent in providing feedback on interpreted behavior. T-groups are an invaluable tool where behavioral changes are required. They provide a safe environment where participants may feel less inhibited about masking behavior or responses. T-groups, however, require a professionally trained facilitator who is knowledgeable of how the group might need to be steered, particularly if there are participants who are acquainted. OD specialists use team building exercises to further group interaction according to the new, desired behavior. The exercises may call for different types of behavior in generating a group effort. The methods employed by OD specialists to effect change must be used judiciously and appropriately. Otherwise the results could be disastrous[11].

Does OD really work? It is a relatively new field and some controlled studies have been conducted. But the number some major U.S. corporations have used OD in some form or another is approximately 46 percent. OD is most successful when it is used with support of top management and others influencing its success. OD also solicits participation on a voluntary basis and can be applied to the appropriate area. If changes are to be sustained, it is imperative that there be incentives reinforcing the changes made in a positive manner, because change is both imminent and inevitable[12].

D. SUMMARY

The availability of programs depends largely upon what the school district human resources unit wishes to departments (personnel units) offer its employees. However, knowledge of developments in programs that promote employees' personal and professional growth might well be the catalyst for the school principal's taking a stand in helping to initiate change.

The more informed one is on an issue, the better one can respond to the issue and enlighten others as well. The same is true of the school principal who becomes familiar with the workings of the school district's human resources department's programs. The principal is really an extension of the human resources department and can be solely responsible for the programs' success at the school level. When the human resources program is able to be of benefit to employees, they in turn, are better able care for, serve and educate the most valued persons of all, our nation's children.

REFERENCES

[5]Halloran, Jack, *Applied Human Relations: An Organizational Approach*, Prentice-Hall, Inc., Englewood Cliffs, New Jersey, 1978, pp. 5.

[6]Davis, Keith, *Human Behavior at Work: Organizational Behavior*, McGraw Hill, Inc., NY, 1981, pp. 450.

[7]Halloran, Jack, *Applied Human Relations: An Organizational Approach*, Prentice-Hall, Inc., Englewood Cliffs, New Jersey, 1978, pp. 107.

[8]Halloran, Jack, Ibid., pp. 103–4.

[9]Halloran, Jack, Ibid., pp. 118.

[10]Behling, Orlando, and Schriesheim, Chester, *Organizational Behavior, Theory and Application*, Allyn and Bacon, Boston, MA, 1976, pp. 66.

[11]Larwood, Laurie, *Organizational Behavior in Management*, Kent Publishing Co., A Division of Wadsworth, Inc., Boston, MA, 1984, pp. 452.

[12]Larwood, Laurie, Ibid., pp. 452.

PART FOUR

MANAGEMENT OF ESSENTIAL LOGISTICAL ACTIVITIES

CHAPTER XI

FISCAL AND ELECTRONIC SERVICES

A. ACCOUNTING AND AUDITING

The typical elementary or secondary school building can be termed as a business house without a direct profit motive incorporated within its operational format. Use of the expression, direct profit, denotes the objective of an organization to provide a financial return beyond expenses to those in ownership. A school building whose primary mission is that of educating the populace does not involve itself in a direct profit motive action. The school's action is more of an indirect profit motive in those certain cases where goods or services are to provide cash for the school's general operation or specific operations (athletics, clubs, and other activities) within the school body. These profits are indirect in that they are not dispensed to individual owners or stockholders. Profits gained in school activity marketing ventures are used within that particular activities operation, or for specific or general needs within the overall setting. School funds belong to the state (from a legal point of view) and are under the stewardship of the principal.

A school building normally is involved with both an inward and outward flow of funds from various sources. Financial activities of this nature require that some system (or systems) of observation and control be established to monitor financial transactions within the school setting. A school should have two primary observation and control mediums within its daily operational plan. They are:

1. An Established Accounting System

Some states may require that all of its local school districts follow a uniform system of accounting to provide for better management and control. Uniform state accounting systems can also provide for a less restrictive flow of accounting procedures and various financial reports between the principal, central office, plus various state offices of education.

Some school districts within the nation may place greater emphasis on a school district uniform accounting and financial reporting system for the central office and its numerous school building units. Whether a state or local uniform accounting system is used, benefits should be gained at both building level and central office administrative units.

2. The Principal

The principal is the key to accounting and other financial activities necessary for building level operations. The *Tennessee Internal Financial Management Manual* brings forth the following points concerning the accounting and related financial management duties. Emphasis is also made concerning responsibilities and direction that must be followed by building level administrators[1]:

1. To institute and follow rules, regulations, standards, and procedures of the state department of education and other policies as may be adopted by the local board which has jurisdiction over the schools.

2. To provide for the safekeeping and handling of all monies and other tangible property of every character, irrespective of the source of such monies or the purpose for which they were derived (according to state law).

3. To submit financial reports and other materials on time as directed by the local board of education and the state.

4. To deliver to central office all financial records, books, ledgers, reports, etc., as directed by the local superintendent and/or the local board of education.

The previously mentioned areas can generally apply to a number of school buildings operating in the United States. A principal is responsible for his/her building's financial mechanism. He/she (the principal) should adhere to legal guidelines established by state and the local boards of education. States and local boards should lean toward some uniform type of accounting system for building level financial management. Uniformity lessens the chance for inaccuracy in computation and procedures, plus it (uniformity) provides a platform to enhance and greater synchronize computerized accounting functions. School district wide, or better yet statewide uniform accounting procedures allows for convenience in auditing procedures by governmental units. A uniform accounting approach automatically terminates any zealous desire to create and function with some autonomous accounting activity. An independent action of this kind has the possibility to lead a building unit to financial disaster.

Funds Within the School

Funds are sums of money which are set aside for certain financial actions to be carried out within the school. Regardless of the classification or the nature of these funds, they must be accounted for according to the receiving, expending and/or holding (surplus) phases applicable to normal transactional procedures.

Five general and primary classifications of funds concerned with building level financial operations are:

1. *General Fund* — This particular fund is concerned with those revenues and expenditures which are of concern to a school's overall or general population.

2. *Restricted Fund* — Monies in this category are limited for use (revenues and expenditures) of a definite segment (not general) of the school population. For example, the junior class; a certain third grade class; the athletic department; the German Language Club; and other activity functions within the building.

3. *Food Service Fund* — Those schools which receive governmental (state and/or federal) food service monies are required by law to maintain a separate fund for food service operations only. In many school district food service managers take responsibility for supervising and accounting measures in this particular area.

4. *Petty Cash Fund* — There are a number of schools which allow within their daily financial operations a small amount of cash to be used at office level. This fund (or the petty cash fund) may be used to purchase items that are low in value (and within state law and local board policy and which are not in requirement of standard purchasing procedures). The petty cash fund can be used to make change in the school's various transactions. Petty cash can be realized as an item of convenience. Proper accounting procedures need to be used with petty cash just as they are with general, restricted, and food service funds.

Due to its quick access and convenience to thwart time consumption and official red tape, petty cash can become an albatross around the principal's neck if proper accounting procedures are not enforced to indicate outflow and replenishment.

5. *Community-School Funds* — Monies in this category will involve those funds which are received and expended by community or parental groups associated with the school. Such as athletic booster clubs, mothers clubs, parent-teacher organizations, etc. Principal responsibility for the

accounting of such funds will depend upon state law and/or local board of education policy. If the principal is responsible for community-school funds, then he/she must maintain control over revenue generation; fund receipts; the dispensing of funds; and the overall financial and accounting procedures of each community-school organization involved with his/her school.

Principals that are involved with school organizations that are controlled by nonschool personnel need to prepare themselves for possible conflicts (both financial and political) with segments of the organization. There is a need for state law and board policy in this area, however, if such direction does not exist the principal must make policy. A key point to remember is that the organization is most likely using the school's name in the endeavors. Such an action by the organization can in turn place the factor of responsibility upon the building administrator. Administrative responsibility placement will move toward the school building if the school's name is used in a business or fund raising venture. This can be especially true if gross negativism or disaster has taken place within the confines of the community-school organization.

Accounting Procedures

All of the previously listed funds must be accounted for by the use of some type of accounting system. Accounting as it concerns the petty cash fund is usually different from the other four funds which were presented. Accounting for petty cash will involve[2]:

1. The establishment of the petty cash fund by writing a check for petty cash.

2. Individuals drawing from petty cash must always make out and attach a petty cash receipt to the petty cash book.

3. Upon the completion of a purchase through the use of petty cash, the vendor's receipt or invoice should be given to the keeper of petty cash for proof and the justification for further replenishing of the petty cash account.

Discussion is in order to introduce various financial forms within the school building. These items which assist in the school's accounting procedures are:

1. The Prenumbered Receipt Book—This book is used to construct receipts for monies received from school personnel, students, activity organizations, and organizations or individuals external to the school.

Receipt information should be entered daily with the general journal (a book of account which will be mentioned later).

2. Teacher Collection Book—Which is used as a record by the teacher to show indicate monies received by individual students for a particular event or donation. Teacher personnel present the collection book along with the total funds received to the school office. The school office in turn will write a receipt to the teacher.

3. Purchase Request, Order and Receipt Forms—These items are part of the building level purchasing system which will be presented in a later chapter, however, the cost of items purchased by the school must be indicated in its accounting system.

4. Prenumbered Checks—For cash payments from general and restricted accounts. Also the school's checking account will be used to replenish the petty cash account. Monthly bank statements and bank reconciliation statements by school office personnel will indicate further accuracy of the school's financial picture.

Community-school funds and the food service fund will usually maintain their own checking account and books of account.

5. Individual School Activity Fund Financial Record Book—Each school activity needs to maintain a record of its balance at the beginning of the fiscal year (or school year; its cash receipts; its cash payments; and its balance at the end of the fiscal period (or school term).

6. Activity Ticket Record Book—This book indicates (through a prenumbered color coded ticketing system) the total number of tickets sold along with the total monies received for a particular school event. Any discrepancies between total tickets sold a projected ticket receipts will be indicated.

Example of some of the building level's financial reports will be presented later within the chapter.

Key books of account in the building's accounting system are:

1. The General Journal—This book (also known as the book of original entry) is used on a daily basis to record all cash entering or leaving the school. Along with each individual cash figure (coming or going) is the date, time, reason and/or the identification of a supporting document (receipt number, check number, invoice, pay order, etc.) and the accounts concerned with the transaction. This particular element involves the system of double entry accounting which has illustrates the fact that there two involved accounts in the ledger (the book of accounts) one will be gaining funds while the other is losing funds. Or another way to

present this point is that for every account that is debited one must be credited). All accounts have both a debit and credit side for possible entry which depends upon the nature of the transaction.

2. At the end of the school's business day the various entries in the general journal (with the debited and credited accounts indicated) are posted (or placed) to the various indicated accounts of the ledger. The accounts of the ledger are usually balanced at the end of the month. However, an account's balance can be shown at any time by subtracting an account's debit from its credit side, or credit from its debit side (depending on whether the account is a debit or credit balance account.

The three major classifications of school accounts are:

1. The Asset Account—Accounts that indicate ownership.

2. The Liability Account—an account which shows that something is owed.

3. The Fund Balance Account—this account indicates the solvency of the school building.

Asset accounts will most likely have debit balances while liability and fund balance accounts will usually have credit balances.

Audits

Audits are an evaluation of the school's accounting system for accuracy and legality of transaction. In many situations state law and local board policy will require that than an audit be taken of the individual school's accounting procedures. The principal is considered the chief steward of the school's finances and financial management program. He/she (the principal) is held accountable for financial transactions and accounting procedures that have taken place during a given fiscal period. A uniform accounting system and adherence to that system along with the submitting of accurate financial reports will greatly assist the external auditors involved in the school's annual audit. However, common knowledge should exist that there is the possibility of impromptu audits taking place if the board and/or central office are of the opinion that such a direction is necessary.

B. THE BUDGETING PROCESS

Budgeting as it concerns the building level and the principal will vary from school district to school district and from state to state. Some principals are given considerable responsibility (by central office) in developing and administering a budget for their buildings. However, there are some situations in which the central office will dictate a total amount for the building's needs for a forthcoming fiscal period. The principal and the building staff (both instructional and logistical) are not allowed the opportunity to provide feedback to reinforce their cases for additional financial need.

The principal and his/her staff should be entitled to plan and organize their own budgetary needs for a future school district fiscal period. School buildings mainly operate on a fiscal period to fiscal period time frame. Building level administrative activity will find itself cutting across other time periods such as:

1. The state fiscal year
2. The federal fiscal year (if involved with federal programs)
3. The academic year (with its intermittent grading periods)
4. The calendar year

Time period involvement, as previously mentioned more or less places the individual school more in line with the short-term budgeting process rather than that of long-term budgeting. This is not to say that long term budgeting has no place in singular school budgeting practices. An introduction of a long-term educational program within a school building could lend itself to a long-term budgeting process. Long term budgeting procedures would be needed to ensure those extended programs proper fiscal control, quality control, and fiscal management procedures.

Budgeting provides the principal with the flagship of the building's financial management endeavors. The principal, the building administrative team, the instructional staff; the representative educational support team (library, guidance, personnel, media personnel, etc.); and the building logistical staff (clerical and custodial personnel) need to work as a unit in the construction of a budget.

A building administrator and his/her staff first need to determine the goals of the building's overall primary education program, plus the numerous goals concerning various secondary programs operating within the building (grade level instruction, subject and subject level instruction, educational support programs, logistical support programs, etc.). All of these items are part of the building's primary goal of educating the children of the populace. Each unit within the school needs to work with the building administrator in formulating the goal or goals that the individual unit desires to achieve during a future fiscal period. Once the principal and his/her various unit leaders have constructed and coordinated their future goals, projections are then formulated concerning program priorities and costs. This is the heart of budget construction in that total costs, program allocations, and priorities must generate an exchange of ideas and opinions between the principal and the individual unit leader. The results of the total input by building unit leaders will place the budget in the administrator budget evaluation phase. At this point the principal has the option to alter individual unit request (add to or reduce), or to allow approval for the projected fiscal unit cost of operation for the next period.

Once information has been collected, discussed, and revised, the principal will forward his/her budget to the school district's business or logistical manager for further discussion and possible alterations. After review by the central office logistical manager and the superintendent, there will usually be consideration and adoption by the local board. (Local government must approve of the budget if the school district is fiscally dependent. Fiscally independent school districts will require only local board approval of the school district budget.)

After school board (and possibly local governmental) approval of the budget has been received, it is then returned to central office for administration and appraisal. The office of the logistical manager in turn will revert the adopted building level budget to the principal who will in turn administer and evaluate the budget (along with various unit leaders in the building).

At the end of the fiscal period additional appraisal will be made by the building level administrator and his/her unit leaders. Central office evaluation will be made by the logistical manager and the superintendent, and further appraisal by the local board (and local government if fiscally dependent). Appraisal results by building, level, central office, local board, and possibly local governmental personnel will provide a springboard of knowledge in the preparation of the budget for a new fiscal period.

Building level budgeting provides for a dual thrust which offers to the school building administration and the school staff a means of financial control and quality control.

Roe and Drake are of the opinion that the principal and his/her staff may obtain benefits from working together in the building level budgeting process. These benefits are[3]:

1. Establishes a plan of action for given periods, long-term and short-term.

2. Requires an appraisal of past activities in relation to planned activities.

3. Necessitates the development of specific goals and objectives.

4. Necessitates the establishment of work plans to achieve goals and objectives.

5. Provides security for the administration by assuring the financing and approval of a year's course of action.

6. Necessitates foreseeing expenditures and estimating revenues.

7. Requires orderly planning and coordination throughout the organization.

8. Establishes a system of management controls.

9. Provides an orderly process of expansion in both personnel and facilities.

10. Should serve as a public information device.

In closing this particular chapter segment a closer look should be taken of the previously mentioned tenth item which touches upon public information. Principals are administrators of the community's schools and reside during the business day (and sometimes the evening hours) within the border of the community. Central office operates from within a fortress far from community's maddening crowd. The principal and his/her building plus the staff becomes a typical school district's only unit directly involved with the public. In these days and hours of public demand concerning accountability and the proper use of public funds, the budget of the building provides for an excellent and official public relations device. It (the budget) also serves as burden of proof concerning building operating expenses needed to conduct the educational program.

C. FISCAL REPORTS

Financial management procedures carried out within the school will call for a variety of financial reports. Some of these reports will serve as school records along with being forwarded to central office. Financial reports can further be classified as relating to the school building's general fund (for all students or the school as a whole), or for those restricted accounts which reflect fiscal action with certain individual school activities. These activities (or restricted activities) are of a benefit to only a segment of the school population.

In taking a more in-depth observation of the typical school fiscal report form and how the form is to be completed and handled, a series of questions should be answered:

1. What party (or parties) will complete the form?
2. Is the process of delegation allowed as to who authorizes and/or completes the form?
3. How is the report to be filled out?
   a. In ink or pencil?
   b. Any particular color of ink required?
   c. Is the report to be typewritten?
   d. Are typing space requirements needed?
   e. Are signatures required?
   f. Is there a requirement for a date-time stamp to be placed upon the report?
4. To what person and/or office unit is the report form to be sent (internal or external to the building)?
5. What are the copy, number requirements and distribution for the individual report?
6. Where are the copies to be stored (by computer or file cabinet)?
7. Is there a possibility for the original copies to be programmed and constructed by a word processor and yet stored within the computer device?
8. When are specific financial forms to be filled out and forwarded to their appropriate destinations?

School fiscal reports need to be evaluated on some periodic basis to determine their effectiveness in the building level fiscal management process. Appraisal actions will involve another series of questions to be asked:

1. Is the particular report form meeting all of its intended purpose?
   a. If partial success is only being achieved, then there is need for alteration or termination of the report format.
   b. If no success is being met by use of a particular fiscal report form then termination proceedings should be carried out.
   c. If a fiscal report form is terminated, then plans should be made to construct a more suitable form to meet the school's needs.
2. Does the form synchronize itself with other financial procedures and forms within the building's and central office's financial management operation?

3. Is the specific financial report form appropriate to the building financial management task?
4. Does the form reflect clarity of purpose?
5. Does the appraisal indicate that there is a minimum or no complexity by the user?
6. Does appraisal indicate that there is an economy of use concerning a particular financial report form.

The number and type of fiscal reports to be used in the school building environment will depend upon: (1) the building's needs, (2) the school district's needs, and (3) the requirements of the state. Some principals and their staffs will construct specific types of financial forms to meet the various fiscal requirements within their buildings. In order to meet the building's fiscal management goals, adequate specific financial report forms are in need for construction (with staff input during the planning stages for form construction).

Some typical building level financial report forms that may be used at building level will be presented in this chapter segment. Attention will be brought first to those financial reports that could be associated with elementary or secondary schools. Financial reports can vary from state to state and from school district to school district within a particular state. Many financial reports involving building level financial operations are tailor-made to fit a particular building and the building-central office needs. In numerous cases (excluding mandatory state reports if applicable) building level financial reports are conceived by the building administrator and his/her financial management unit, or the report forms may be developed under the directions of the central office financial management unit.

Accounting report forms (computerized or kept manually) that are used in the typical school could be:

1. Daily and monthly transaction reports of the school's journal.
2. Daily and posting reports to the various accounts in the ledger.
3. Monthly individual account reports for general and restricted accounts.
4. Budget worksheet.
5. The purchase requisition.
6. Payment authorization vouchers.
7. Activity ticket sales report.
8. The payroll report.
9. Ticket and concession sales reports.

10. School activity fund warrants.
11. Warehouse requisition.
12. Daily cash inflow report.

Financial reports allow the principal and his/her financial management team to have:

1. Evidence of financial transactions.
2. Greater accuracy for financial accounting.
3. Current knowledge regarding financial situations.
4. Auditing assistance.
5. Assistance to the central office financial management operation.

Figures 10–20 will provide illustrations of some of the typical financial reports which may be found at building level. Those items are:

WEEHAWKEN MIDDLE SCHOOL
WOONSOCKET SCHOOL DISTRICT
HIAWATHA, MINNESOTA 55515

CENTRAL OFFICE PAYMENT VOUCHER AUTHORIZATION

Check Issued To _____   Voucher No. _____
                    Name of Person or Firm

Amount of Check _____   School Check No. _____

TO THE CENTRAL OFFICE DIRECTOR OF ACCOUNTING

The goods and/or services indicated by the attached business forms have been received. Authorization is now given for payment from public school funds, and charges are to be placed against the following account: _____

Payment should be made only on the final approval of the school principal.

Date of Payment _____
                                              Activity Finance Office
Check No. _____   _____

                                              Faculty Sponsor
                                              _____

_____   Approved by: _____
Central Office Director   Principal
of Accounting   Weehawken Middle School

ATTACH ALL NECESSARY DOCUMENTS

Figure 10. Payment Voucher Authorization Form.

1. Payment Voucher Authorization—This form gives the principal the authority to direct central office accounting to issue a check for payment to an individual or business organization (see Figure 10).

2. Purchase Request-Order Form—An item of this type formally establishes the need for specific commodities or services by a building unit leader with the principal's signature acting as a symbol of approval. Once this form has signature approval of central office accounting and the purchasing agent, it (the form) automatically becomes a purchasing order ready to be forwarded to the vendor for commodities or services (see Figure 11).

PURCHASE REQUISITION-ORDER FORM

OHIO COUNTY PUBLIC SCHOOLS
RIVERVIEW, INDIANA 43764

School _____   Requisition No. _____

To: CENTRAL OFFICE PURCHASING AGENT

Upon approval of the Accounting Department your office is authorized to purchase the following items or services:

Quantity	Description of Desired Item or Service	Price Per Unit	Total
		$	$
	Grand Total	$	$

Catalog information _____   Date of Request _____

Account to be charged _____

Principal approval _____   School Department Leader Approval _____

Accounting department approval _____

Purchasing agent approval _____

Figure 11. Purchase Requisition Form.

3. Building Concessions Financial Report—Concessions activity at school events must be reported according to items purchased at wholesale price levels and the amounts received at retail sales prices. Such a

report of this nature will show profits or losses and the identification and date of the extra-curricular activity involved (see Figure 12).

```
                        CONCESSIONS REPORT
                      FREMONT ROSS HIGH SCHOOL
                 JACKSONVILLE JUNCTION PUBLIC SCHOOLS
                      JACKSONVILLE, OHIO  43807


Check One                                      Date _____

____ Football
____ Basketball
____ Other
     Specify _____


                                   Quantity
Items Purchased        Amount      of Items Sold        Amount

1.                  $ _____     1. _____      $ _____
2.                  $ _____     2. _____      $ _____
3.                  $ _____     3. _____      $ _____
4.                  $ _____     4. _____      $ _____
5.                  $ _____     5. _____      $ _____
6.                  $ _____     6. _____      $ _____
7.                  $ _____     7. _____      $ _____

         Total      $ _____            Total      $ _____

                                  Disbursement for
                                  Change            $ _____


Amount Sold           $ _____
Minus Purchasing Costs  _____
Minus Disbursements     _____
Balance               $ _____
(Positive or Negative
 Balance)
Please Circle


                            Event

        Fremont Ross vs. _____
```

Figure 12. Building Concessions Financial Report.

4. Monthly Financial Report for Restricted Accounts—A report form of this type will list the monthly account balances for the various restricted or special activity accounts within the school (see Figure 13).

5. Athletic Special Payroll Report—Athletic interscholastic contests will require the payment to game officials, security personnel, medical personnel, and ticket managers. Payroll information of this type will require that such transactions be recorded (see Figure 14).

6. Ticket Sales Report—The ticket sales report identifies the activity, student and adult ticket beginning and closing numbers, activity color code (to assist in identifying event and types of tickets), total adult ticket

BLUE PIKE ELEMENTARY SCHOOL
BISKATT PUBLIC SCHOOL DISTRICT #1
KUNCHREHAMM, GEORGIA   72143

MONTHLY FINANCIAL REPORT FOR BUILDING RESTRICTED ACCOUNTS

Total Current Balance $ _____   Date _____

Account No.	Account Title	Account Balance
Grand Total		$

Principal _____   School Clerk _____
Date _____   Date _____

Figure 13. Monthly Financial Report for Restricted Accounts.

sales, total student ticket sales, the grand total for ticket sales, and the total amount (grand total and specific totals) disbursed to ticket sellers for change making purposes (see Figure 15).

7. Monthly General Account Report Form—The building level organization must account for its general account by the recognition of the beginning balance, total deposits during the month, total expenditures for the month, the month ending balance, and the itemization of transactions involving the inflow and outflow of monies (see Figure 16).

8. Intra-School Activity Fund Warrant—This item represents an authorization by the faculty advisor and activity treasurer to inform the principal (and designated school building fiscal officer) to issue a check for payment to an individual or a firm (see Figure 17).

9. School Warehouse Requisition—A report of this nature represents the school's request (by the principal and a school unit leader) for commodities stored in the central office warehousing system (see Figure 18).

10. Daily Cash Inflow Report—A report of this type gives the school a

```
ATHLETIC DEPARTMENT SPECIAL PAYROLL REPORT
        COLUMBUS EAST HIGH SCHOOL
        CAPITAL CITY, IOWA  77777
```

COLUMBUS EAST v. _____   Date _____

Check One

____ Football   ____ Basketball   ____ Tennis   ____ Other

____ Track   ____ Baseball   ____ Golf   (Specify) _____

```
        GAME OFFICIALS, SECURITY, TICKET MANAGERS
                  AND MEDICAL PERSONNEL
```

Name	Position	Amount	Signature of Receipt

Figure 14. Athletic Special Payroll Report.

picture of all individual daily cash receipts according to time of day, receipt number, item of transaction, identification of the collector, account involved, and the amount received (see Figure 19).

11. Fiscal Year Ending Report—The end of the fiscal year and the financial status of the building at this point in time needs to be recorded. Total expenditures and receipts for the fiscal year along with the balance are recorded. All outstanding accounts payable balances are also identified in preparation for carry over into the next fiscal period (see Figure 20).

D. COMPUTER SERVICES

Computer services at building level are under the responsibility umbrella of the school principal. Due to the principal's involvement in a variety of instructional, community relations and other logistical tasks—

TICKET SALES REPORT
DONDERBAY HIGH SCHOOL
LORD BALTIMORE COUNTY SCHOOL DISTRICT
CRABNCLAMBAKE, MARYLAND 01122

Date _____   Opponent _____

Check One

____ Football   ____ Basketball   ____ Other (Specify) _____

Ticket Color Code Identifications _____

Ticket Number Sequence _____

Adult Tickets

Ending Number _____
Beginning Number _____
Total Tickets Sold _____ x @ $ _____ = Total $ _____

Student Tickets

Ending Number _____
Beginning Number _____
Total Tickets Sold _____ x @ $ _____ = Total $ _____

Total Disbursement for Change $ _____

Total Adult Tickets $ _____

Total Student Tickets   _____

Grand Total $ _____

Minus Change Disbursement   _____

Balance $ _____

Figure 15. Ticket Sales Report.

delegation of computer management procedures could well be in order. Such a delegation procedure may most likely involve the school office manager or an assistant principal.

Present day computer usage in the school will most likely include the administration of both the instructional and the logistical elements within the school's operation. The training of personnel in the operation, care, and troubleshooting of computer hardware and software will be identical to both instructional and logistical users of the system. This text will be concerned only with the logistical service use of the computer as it involves those tasks necessary for the building's daily program functions.

```
                    BLITZENBERG ELEMENTARY SCHOOL
                    KRUEZ COUNTY SCHOOL DISTRICT
                    PANZEREISEN, WISCONSIN 58602


        MONTHLY FINANCIAL REPORT FOR THE GENERAL ACCOUNT ITEM # _____

Account Title  _____


        Previous Balance      $ _____
        Total Amount Deposited  ================
        Total Amount Spent      ================
        Ending Balance        $ ================

Flow Itemization:

            Inflow              Date              Outflow              Date

1. $_____           ____      1. $_____          ____
2.  _____           ____      2.  _____          ____
3.  _____           ____      3.  _____          ____
4.  _____           ____      4.  _____          ____
5.  _____           ____      5.  _____          ____
6.  _____           ____      6.  _____          ____
7.  _____           ____      7.  _____          ____
Total $ _____         ____      Total $ _____        ____


Principal _____   Clerk _____

Date _____    Date _____
```

Figure 16. Monthly General Account Report Form.

Computer systems which can be used at building level could assist the principal and his/her staff in the following areas:

1. Building Level Financial Administration
   a. Electronic accounting procedures which would include:
      (1) General journal entries—which would record daily transactions (cash inflow and cash outflow) of the school
      (2) A general ledger which would contain not only accounts receivable and accounts payable accounts, but all those accounts involved in the school's daily transactions.
      (3) Construction of other accounting information and periodic account closings.
   b. Budgetary projections, construction, monitoring and appraising concerning time frames before, during, and immediately after the fiscal period of actual cash involvement with the building's functioning.
2. Storage Management
   a. Purchasing requests can be placed through a computerized system which in turn can verify financial ability (within accounts

```
                        BAKERMANN LOCAL SCHOOL DISTRICT
                        INTRASCHOOL ACTIVITY FUND WARRANT


School _____

Februarius, Florida  22204 _____/_____, 1997
                            Month   Date


          Issue a check in the amount of $ _____

to _____     for _____

   _____


Charge the activity account of _____

   _____


          _____     Faculty Advisor

          _____     Principal

          _____     Clerk

Paid _____          Amount of $ _____

Date _____          Time _____ a.m./p.m.

     _____          Activity Finance Officer
```

Figure 17. Intraschool Activity Fund Warrant.

involved) and whether or not there is a bona fide need (according to storage information). Purchasing requests through policy and computerized verification can become purchasing orders. Computers can also be programmed to order automatically when storage levels reach a selected low level.

b. The receiving of purchased items at the school can be inspected by the staff and recorded by computer. Distribution of the received item(s) to the school's storage area, or a particular unit or staff member within the school can also be recorded by the computer. The additional receipt of the invoice (along with a satisfactory inspection of the items received) can allow for the systems to construct a warrant for payment. This action can in turn allow for proper debiting and crediting of the accounts concerned in the transaction.

c. Supply and equipment inventory control can be better main-

WAREHOUSE REQUISITION FORM
BLOOMINGTON CITY SCHOOLS
BLOOMINGTON, COLORADO 87523

School _____   Date _____

School Department _____   Account # _____   Account Title _____

Catalog Number	Amount Requested	Unit Classification	Description	Unit Price	Number Shipped	Total Price
				$		$
		Grand Total		$		$

Principal _____

Clerk _____

Received on delivery by _____

Date _____

Time _____

Figure 18. School Warehouse Requisition.

tained through a computerized system at building level. The computer has the ability to categorize items as to supplies or equipment groupings. Further classification within these two major areas can also be made such as instructional, noninstructional, offices equipment, floor care supplies, etc.

Inventory situations of both supply and equipment items can be obtained at a moment's notice through input of the school's computer. Funds used to purchase these items can also

ISLE ROYALE PUBLIC SCHOOLS
MAUMEE-MENOMINEE, MINNESOTA 55555

DAILY CASH INFLOW REPORT

School _____

Time Period _____ a.m. to _____ p.m.

Date _____

Time of Day	Receipt No.	Description of Transaction	Collector's Initials	Account Involved	Amount Collected
					$
		Grand Total			$

Clerk _____

Principal _____

Figure 19. Daily Cash Inflow Report.

be identified and classified for accounting and auditing purchases. Distribution of supply and equipment items to the office staff, instructional staff, instructional media staff, the administrative team, and the building logistical staff can be monitored to detect rate of use or consumption along with possible indications toward waste, abuse or theft.

Equipment inventory allows for a more accurate upkeep of the school's property book by the principal. Equipment identification codes can assist the central office risk manager if insurance claims are needed due to loss situations.

KUCHENSTAUBLAPPEN TOWNSHIP SCHOOLS
PILLSBURY, MICHIGAN   48175

FISCAL YEAR ENDING REPORT TO THE CENTRAL OFFICE
ACCOUNTING DEPARTMENT

School _____   Date _____

Previous Fiscal Year Ending Balance $ _____
Cash Receipts for the Current Fiscal Year $ _____

Total Cash On Hand $ _____
Total Expenditures for the Current Fiscal Year $ _____

Balance Date _____ Check One _____ $ _____
                                  Positive   Negative
                                  Balance   Balance

Listing of All Accounts Payable Balances

Account Number	Account Title	Amount
1.		$
2.		
3.		
4.		
5.		
6.		
7.		
	Grand Total	$

Principal _____   Clerk _____

Figure 20. Fiscal Year Ending Report.

3. Personnel Management

Computer assisted personnel management can allow for better maintenance of employee records at the building level for both certificated and noncertificated personnel. Standard demographic data, payroll records, along with work evaluations can be maintained at the school without requesting information from the central office personnel unit.

Additional records concerning employee attendance, leaves, and tardiness could also be maintained by the school building's computer.

4. Student Personnel Management

a. Computerized student records can record the normal demographic information, parental information, medical and emergency information and contacts, educational program undertaking, testing results, past attendance records.

    b. Daily attendance and tardiness information for office and attendance officer use.

    c. Individual student, class, and room scheduling.

    d. Annual and/or semester registration.

    e. Grade recording and reporting.

5. School Library Management

    a. Computerized classification and inventory of all library books for better managerial purposes.

    b. Computerization of the library reference system for less complexity in student research.

    c. Computerization of the library circulation to allow library management to keep record of individual book use, individual loan periods, penalty records, loan records and procedures for circulation operations.

Computer use in the school's business and service tasks can reduce time and person power consumption. Readiness and convenience to computer stored information can free the principal and staff to attend to other pressing duties. However, the computer should not be viewed as some electronic superhuman device which will take over all of the school's managerial duties. Such thought may have building personnel looking forward to the allowing of staff members to take extended coffee breaks. Computers can be labeled as electronic managerial assistants to the school's business or instructional program. There will be a need for the proper programming of each computer task to fit the needs of the building. Programming needs should take into account any tie-ins with the central office computer system. Another aspect in need of consideration involves the training of administrators and building staff members assigned to computer usage tasks within the school's operational network. With the almost constant change of computer hardware and software, periodic or on call training will be necessary.

Computer use within the building will also call for building policy and security measures not only to protect hardware and software items, but also of stored computer information. Adequate locking and storage systems along with coding systems will be needed to offer a security blanket over the school's computer operation. Additional items such as electronic burglar systems within the building perimeter could reinforce an already established computer security network.

E. SUMMARY

Fiscal and electronic services logistically support the nerve center of the schools. This statement is even more essential in school systems that require the principal to be responsible for the construction and administration of the building's entire financial management system (the total budgetary requirements for the fiscal period). The accounting phase assists the principal and the school staff in maintaining control over daily transactions, cash inflow, cash outflow, and properly supervising the fiscal operations of intraschool activities. Accounting also allows for supervision of the building's external business transactions.

The auditing aspect of the school's fiscal services concerns an area of accounting which serves as a check upon daily accounting activities. This action is usually in accordance with accuracy and adherence to legal mandates concerning school financial procedures. Auditing tasks are initiated by bureaucratic bodies such as the local, state, and federal governments. Public schools and their principals are the custodians of public monies, therefore, auditing procedures must be taken by those levels of government representing the people and the tax monies of the people.

Another measure of fiscal control within the building setting is that of budget construction and administration of the approved budget (through the identified fiscal period). Budget construction at building level involves the direct leadership of the principal and the subordinate leaders within the school. For example, the building level administrative team, department chairpersons or grade level leaders, the head guidance counselor, the chief of clerical services, the custodial leader, the school librarian, the educational media coordinator, etc., are the subordinate leaders that will obtain financial data for the needs of their respective units. These actions should take place in order to prepare for a forthcoming fiscal period.

The principal must then determine each unit's actual needs (from a financial point of view) before he/she submits the total building budget to central office for approval. Further approval by the central office financial team (the logistical manager and the superintendent) will be made to the local board as part of the total school district package. Further approval will be required by a local governmental unit if fiscal dependence is practiced within the state.

Once approved the budget is then returned down the chain of command to the building level for proper budgetary administrative procedures. These procedures should be carried out by the principal and the building's subordinate leaders during the new fiscal period.

Fiscal reports may vary from school district to school district and from state to state. However, a typical report form should designate: (1) its intended use, (2) the party or parties involved with filling out of or signing the form, (3) whether delegation for filling out the form can take place, (4) identification of the forwarding unit, and (5) storage procedures concerning report copies.

Financial reports can assist in the school's accounting system and also support auditors in their periodic quests.

The central focus of the current electronic age is usage of the computer in education. Computers within the building environment fit into two primary categories. They are:

1. Instructional usage
2. Managerial usage

Emphasis of the school's business management endeavor within this book will allow for support to be placed on the logistical usage of the computer in managing the school. However, troubleshooting, maintenance, computer personnel training will involve both the instructional and managerial computer functions.

Administrator and staff input into the selection of hardware and software items to meet the building's need is imperative. This frame of thought is of prime importance if the building's goals are to be met.

Fiscal administration, personnel management, pupil personnel management, library administration, storage management, and purchasing are critical areas in which the computer can greatly assist the business management functions of the typical school building.

Proper fiscal management along with the electronic assistance of the school's computer system can support the principal's staff with greater accuracy and fewer demands for labor, therefore, freeing personnel for other essential duties.

REFERENCES

[1]Tennessee State Department of Education, *Tennessee Internal Financial Management Manual.* Nashville, Tennessee: State of Tennessee, 1977, p. 21.

[2]Ibid., p. 63.

[3]Roe, William H., and Drake, Thelbert L. *The Principalship, Second Edition.* New York: Macmillan Publishing Co., Inc., 1980, p. 353.

CHAPTER XII

FACILITY MANAGEMENT

A. COORDINATING CUSTODIAL OPERATIONS

Managing the custodial program is the responsibility of the principal. In some school systems the principal is given more control over the custodial operations than in other school organizations. There are some school districts where the major emphasis for custodial personnel administration, supervision, and general task assignment may come from facility managers quartered at central office. Within an organizational method of this type, the principal is not in a direct managerial line with the custodial staff. This situation more or less lends itself to a more advisory role concerning the building's custodial needs. If the custodial requirements of the building are not being met, the principal usually contacts the central office facilities management personnel in order that corrective measures be taken.

Regardless of whether custodial procedures are dominated by the principal, or central office facility supervisors, there is need for managerial coordination by the principal.

In order that there be a foundation from which to launch the building custodial program, there is need for central office and building level policies. Overall school district policy should provide for the establishment of general goals concerning district policy for custodial care and maintenance of school buildings setting. Building level policies would be more specific in meeting those maintenance and custodials goals that are concerned with the specific needs of the individual building. Building level construction of building level custodial and maintenance goals should be performed by the principal, head custodian, and the custodial staff. Additional input by the remainder of the school staff should be allowed and considered for possible input into the policies that are to be formulated.

Custodial operations and building maintenance are two distinct functions. Custodial operations involve those duties which are necessary to keep the school building operational to meet the daily educational program. These duties should involve:

1. General housekeeping
2. Sanitizing
3. Cleaning
4. Dusting
5. Floor care
6. Washing
7. Wall care
8. Deodorizing
9. Glass and hardware care
10. Lawn care
11. Ice and snow removal
12. Grounds policing and the sweeping of sidewalks, driveways and parking areas

Maintenance performance involves those tasks of:

1. Renovation
2. Unit replacement
3. Periodic and emergency servicing
4. Custodial personnel are mainly involved with user maintenance of noninstructional equipment operating within the school. Custodial personnel should also be aware of troubleshooting procedures (provided by the manufacturers of noninstructional equipment) that are involved with keeping the school operational. For example:

1. Heating units
2. Ventilating units
3. Cooling units
4. Various housekeeping equipment

Equipment breakdowns or malfunctions that are more serious in nature will involve the principal requesting central office for specialized maintenance personnel. Specialized maintenance personnel such as air conditioning and heating repair persons, plumbers, carpenters, etc., may be from within the school district or are contracted by the school board.

If the principal is charged with the personnel administration of the custodial staff, his/her duties will probably require:

1. Recruitment
2. Interviewing
3. Testing
4. Recommendation for hiring

5. Training
6. Supervision
7. Appraisal of work performance
8. Promotions
9. Leaves
10. Grievances

Custodial operations management of the school building will most likely involve:

1. Determining custodial and maintenance projections for the building. These projections should involve those planning periods that are concerned with:

    a. Daily needs constructed by the principal (or appointed designee) and the head custodian through a daily morning observation and inspection of the plant and grounds before the opening of school.

    b. Quarter to quarter or season to season plans as they effect the school operation. Items such as:
        (1) Rainy and muddy seasons
        (2) Winter season plus snow and ice removal
        (3) Heating, ventilating, and/or cooling requirements of the season
        (4) Leaf removal
        (5) Lawn cutting and watering
        (6) Lawn feeding
        (7) Floor wax removal
        (8) Floor wax application
        (9) Wall washing
        (10) General graffiti removal
        (11) Window washing
        (12) Dust storm periods
        (13) Filter exchanges
        (14) Football stadium cleaning and upkeep
        (15) Basketball arena cleaning and upkeep

    c. Yearly or yearly plus projections such as:
        (1) School plant budget construction
        (2) School plant budget administration and evaluation
        (3) Landscaping procedures
        (4) Supply ordering
        (5) Equipment ordering

(6) Building remodeling or additions

2. Organization of custodial and maintenance requirements and personnel.

3. Determining workload and the assigning of custodial and maintenance tasks.

4. Compliance with central office facility management concerning custodial and maintenance standards (as outlined in central office policies).

5. Adherence to housekeeping and equipment maintenance procedures as brought forth by central office policies and manufacturers recommendations and/or warranty procedures.

6. Use of supply economy, equipment economy, user maintenance, and economy of workforce task procedures.

In order to accomplish the satisfactory management of the school building's custodial and maintenance program, the principal must play an active role in coordinating all tasks required to keep the building in condition and operational.

B. MAINTAINING THE SCHOOL PLANT

Taking care of the school plant will involve prearranged tasks and the frequency in which these asks are carried out. In looking first toward task frequency periods, acquaintance with the following points would be of great assistance:

1. Emergency, daily, or as often as needed category. For example:
   a. Restrooms, including wash basins, toilets, urinals, bidets, restroom floors, mirrors, and trash receptacles.
   b. Foyers and entrances
   c. Shipping and dock areas
   d. Waste removal and the cleaning of waste containers (if plastic liners are not used).
   e. Drinking fountains
   f. Glass fixtures (excluding windows)
   g. Dust control (room floors, halls, woodwork and furnishings) through sweeping, dry mopping, and cloth application.
   h. Carpet vacuuming
   i. Campus policing
   j. Ice and snow removal

    k. Refilling of soap, paper, and sanitary napkin dispensers

    l. Gum and confections removal

    m. Locker rooms and showers

    n. Gymnasiums

2. Weekly Tasks

    a. Blackboard cleaning

    b. Hardware polishing

    c. Washing of floormats

    d. Thorough mop washing and sanitizing

    e. Cleaning rag washing and sanitizing

    f. Restroom stall cleaning and disinfecting

    g. Urinal trap cleaning

    h. Cleaning of doors and door windows

    i. Washing desk tops

    j. Washing table tops

    k. Adjusting clocks and bell ringing system plus fine tuning computer operated plant functions

    i. Take inventory of all cleaning and paper supplies. Reorder if necessary.

3. Fixed periodic tasks

    a. Floor scrubbing and mopping

    b. Floor stripping

    c. Floor waxing

    d. Floor polishing

    e. Carpet stain cleaning

    f. Carpet shampooing

    g. Window washing (interior and exterior)

    h. Lawn care

    i. Furniture care

    j. Shrub and tree care

    k. Heating, cooling, and ventilator filter exchanges

    l. Pest control procedures

    m. Periodic user maintenance and servicing of noninstructional equipment

    n. Budget projections for the next fiscal period

    o. Evaluation of building custodial operations and maintenance tasks

    p. Evaluation of safety, locking, and other security systems

Computerization and Energy Conservation

The managing of building operations and maintenance can be simplified through the school's computer system. The initial cost may be high, but one can witness a realization of savings over a period of time. This is possible if the proper computer system is selected (to meet the building's needs) and personnel are properly trained to operate the system. A computer can be programmed to monitor weather conditions and control the operation of the schools heating, cooling, and ventilation systems. Considerations for the operation of school activity hours, weekends, holidays, and vacations can be electronically controlled by the computer to allow for less consumption of electricity, fuels, and other utilities within the building. Building level control over the computer system should have the capability to allow for emergencies or other unexpected situations.

By controlling heating, cooling, and ventilating operations through the computer programmed within hours of building usage, both energy and financial savings can be gained by the building and the school system.

A building level computer system can also assist the principal and custodial personnel in providing for security through electronic locking devices and alarms to counter unauthorized entry. Security systems can so be arranged as to lock unauthorized personnel in particular areas of the building while informing local law enforcement agencies that the building's security has been breached.

Safety procedures can also be controlled by the computer in the area of fire control through actions such as: (1) sprinkler systems, (2) contacting local fire fighting agencies, (3) closing off building areas through the use of electronically controlled fire doors, (4) activating emergency lighting, (5) sounding alarms, and (6) reporting location of fire within the building.

Custodians can also use computer assistance in the printout of scheduled cleaning of the plant and maintenance of the school's equipment. Another area of custodial computer use is the printout of automatic reorders of janitorial supplies through computerized inventory procedures.

The school is the community's focal point. Popular prejudgment of the school's instructional program and its staff can be made concerning the physical appearance of the school. The school's condition is observed from three primary views. They are:

1. The exterior (of the building)

2. The interior, and

3. The condition of the surrounding campus

It is imperative that the principal, the custodial staff, the instructional staff, and the students cooperate to keep the building and its grounds attractive, free from litter, free from graffiti, and free from vandalism. Favorable public impressions of the individual building will also create favorable total impressions of the school district.

C. SPACE MANAGEMENT

Class scheduling in itself is an instructional effort, instructional support unit effort, a prime office management contribution with overall administrative guidance. Teachers, guidance counselors, the principal, the building level administrative team, and the office clerical management team usually take part in preparing students to meet their academic requirements. This action may be carried out at the beginning of each semester. The complexity of schedule construction increases as the educational program moves from the elementary to the middle school, and finally to the senior high school. Elementary staffs have less input to schedule construction than the middle or senior high schools. However, if the elementary school is departmentalized rather than self-contained student scheduling will involve more administrative and staff input. Use of the computer can greatly assist both school personnel and students in acceleration and accuracy while determining individual scheduling needs, and the total requirements of the master schedule. Computerization also lends itself to the adding and dropping of courses by students, therefore, allowing program elasticity. Additional elasticity is allowed by the computer in permitting student grouping (by sex, by grade point average range, by assignment to a particular school bus during the last period in order to avoid confusion, by educational program, etc.). Computer use can also identify class overloading, class conflicts, teacher conflicts, and room assignment conflicts.

Wood, Nicholson and Findley state that the following steps should be utilized in the construction of a school schedule with principal involvement[1]:

1. Registration of students.

2. Determining the number of students registering for each course.

3. Determining the size of classes—large group instruction, small group discussion.

4. Determining the length of the school day.
5. Determining the opening and closing times, intermission between classes, etc.
6. Preparation of a room availability chart, including the number of pupil stations in a room.
7. Preparation of the conflict sheet.
8. Preparation of teacher qualifications and preferences on subjects and activities.
9. Completion of the final schedule board, assignment of subjects, activities, etc., of other teachers.
10. Lunch period determination.

All of the above steps can be undertaken through computer usage. However, administrative, guidance and counseling personnel, teacher personnel, clerical personnel, and students need to monitor computer output to assure that all needs have been met.

Wood, Nicholson, and Findley are also of the opinion that in addition to the previously discussed steps to be utilized in schedule making there are certain factors to be considered in forming the master schedule. They are[2]:

1. Courses to be offered
2. Nature of subjects
3. Teacher qualifications
4. Student course requirements
5. Types of schedules available for use.
6. Room availability

In examining the factor of room availability movement is made from the instructional to the logistical element of administrative space management. Many school buildings are faced with the problem of space shortages for the overall building program (both instructional and logistical). However, there are in existence some principals with more space than what is required to operate the building's programs. If an overage of space does exit, there is need for central office to shift school attendance zones or close the building. Buildings operating far below their enrollment standards are producing cost overruns for the school district. Proper space management allows for economy of use of the building at lower per pupil costs.

The principal needs to look at his/her building from the point of view as to the use of each room (including closets, storage areas, attics, etc.) on how the space provided in each of these areas could assist the school according to instructional and logistical needs. Computers can be programmed to store the data concerning square footage provided by each room or specialized area. This data would include the main building and detached auxiliary building's on the school's campus.

In taking a critical view of each building area and the space that it provides, the principal needs to consider responses to the following questions:

1. What goal or goals are to be reached in a particular space?
2. What type or types of operations or tasks are to be carried out in a specific area?
3. What type(s) of personnel will occupy the area in question?
4. What are the equipment and supply needs of the area and how much space will these items consume?
5. Will the area require direct thermostatic controls? If so, what type(s) and why?
6. Are there special plumbing needs required for a specific area?
7. Are there special communications needs required for a specific area?
8. What are the safety and security needs for the area?
9. Are there specific illumination requirements needed?
10. Are exhaust and/or ventilation requirements needed in are area under consideration?
11. Can the room or space be converted to meet other goals, operations, personnel, supply, and equipment items, etc.?

Space management can be coupled with class scheduling, building storage, administration, office management, food preparation and service, custodial storage, custodial workshops, utility rooms, and any other specific needs required for building program operations. Great care should be taken in exercising the school's space management program. Administrators and office management personnel should have a thorough knowledge instructional and logistical space requirements of their building unit.

D. CAMPUS CONTROL

The condition of the school's campus as well as that of the building will prompt prejudgment of the school, its administration, and staff. A school site that is not kept clean and well-groomed provides a springboard for community negativism. A well-kept schoolground has the potential of teaching children to appreciate cleanliness, beauty, and school pride. The principal and the instructional staff can inform the student body of the importance of keeping the campus free from debris. The staff and student body also need to realize that it is everyone's duty to participate in trash prevention and the promotion of campus cleanliness.

In the process of keeping the school's grounds presentable, there is a need for both central office policy, central office education should outline: (1) general care, (2) supplies needed, (3) equipment needed, (4) procedures, and (5) evaluation. A more specific policy is also required at building level in order to: (1) carryout daily campus inspections, (2) carry out troubleshooting measures, (3) removal of campus problems and dangers, (4) repair and servicing of campus items, equipment and installations (such as fences, playground equipment, external buildings, etc., (5) campus grounds policing and pavement sweeping, (6) solid waste supervision through internal collection, waste storage plus storage unit management, and periodic waste removal, and (7) periodic care according to the seasons and climate conditions.

Campus care procedures can be divided into much broader areas than that of daily inspections and troubleshooting. We must go beyond sticking our fingers in the holes of the dike. Planning needs to be taken into account to determine those periods of intense storms and high tides which will place enormous and uncontrollable pressure upon the dike. A proper task of planning would better ensure us of reinforcing measures to allow the dike to strengthen its hold against the sea's fury. This frame of thought gives the principal and his/her custodial leader an opportunity to map out campus care according to seasonal and climatic conditions. By merging seasonal and climatic projections with those projections concerning the academic and fiscal projections, a campus management program is in order. Fiscal information is needed to determine personnel, supplies and equipment needed for care of the building's grounds.

Numerous school districts commence their fiscal year on July 1st and end it with June 30th of the following year. Budgets are usually constructed during the previous fiscal and academic periods. During the budget preparatory period all personnel, equipment, and supply items for campus care should budgeted and requisitioned for purchase to be paid for after the new fiscal year commences. July 1st places the care of the school campus into the early/summer season which usually requires:

1. Periodic lawn cutting (usually weekly and which depends upon rainfall and rate of growth. These factors may require additional cuttings

during the week). Lawns should not be cut lower than $1\frac{1}{2}$ inches in order to prevent solar root damage.

2. Periodic watering of the campus lawn (depending upon natural rainfall conditions).

3. The repair and repaving of sidewalks, driveways, and parking lots.

4. Clipping and care of shrubs and shrub areas.

5. The periodic feeding of lawns, trees, and shrubs.

6. Ordering of snow and ice removal equipment plus supplies.

With the starting of the academic year soon comes the fall season. This period of time can require:

1. Removal of fallen leaves

2. Lawn trimming until the first killing frost (in the more northern climates)

3. Continuation of periodic lawn and shrubs feeding until the first killing frost.

4. Prune trees during late autumn (after the leaves have fallen).

5. Service and repair of lawn maintenance equipment upon completion of the fall season

6. Prepare snow and ice removal equipment and supplies for next season's use

7. Removal of leaves from eavestroughs and drainage opening areas to prevent flooding and ice formation during late fall and early winter.

Winter will call for extensive use of snow removal equipment and ice thawing materials for sidewalks, driveways and parking areas. The principal, the head custodian and central office grounds and facilities managers should have an established weather watch program. During the winter season, the following steps should be taken:

1. Keep a periodic inventory of ice thawing supplies. Reorder before dangerous low levels exist.

2. Daily grounds policing should be maintained when snow melting has occurred.

3. Maintain a watch on solid waste storage areas. Periodic pickups may be delayed because of hazardous road conditions.

4. Order grass seed, shrubs, fertilizer, etc., during the late winter season.

5. Repair and service all snow removal equipment at the end of the winter season.

6. Project next year's winter supplies and equipment needs for the coming early summer ordering period.

Upon arrival of the spring season there is a need to survey winter's damages to the school campus. Duties which will probably be in need of undertaking are:

1. Removal of tree limbs, leaves, trash and other debris from the school grounds.

2. Replanting of grass in needed areas.

3. The feeding of existing lawn areas.

4. Pruning of shrubs.

5. Repair of damages to sidewalks, driveways, and parking lots.

6. Begin initial lawn trimming once the grass growth period commences.

7. Check for building eavestrough drainage areas (in anticipation of spring rains) for stoppages in order to prevent flooding of the grounds and possible water damage to the building.

Control of the campus area is a major task that needs the joint cooperation of both the building principal, the head custodian, and the custodial staff. Proper planning to meet fiscal, seasonal, academic and climatic periods is necessary if an adequate or a more-than-adequate attempt is made for proper care and beautification of the school grounds.

Seasonal and climatic differences throughout the United States and Canada will require various adjustments to meet the needs of presenting the community with a well groomed school campus. Regardless of climatic conditions the administrative-custodial alliance of the building organization is needed to provide a the quality product of an eye appealing campus.

E. SCHOOL SAFETY AND SECURITY

A building's safety and security program will require the need of an advocate and a manager. These two duties will rest among the various responsibilities of the principal. Building policy should be formulated to cover both safety and security measures which will be carried out by the administrative staff, the instructional staff, the logistical staff, and the student body. Safety and security of the building is the concern of all personnel assigned within the confines of its wall.

The Building Safety Program

The key to carrying out an adequate or more than adequate (safety knows no boundaries) safety program once policy has been established, is that of properly training both school personnel and students to be safety and security conscious in numerous areas. For example:

1. Fire safety, prevention, and evacuation procedures.
2. Highway and pedestrian safety.
3. The dangers of electricity.
4. The safe handling of flammable materials.
5. Safe storage procedures for flammable items.
6. Safety procedures that need to be taken on school grounds and within the building.
7. The reporting of contraband to school officials and teachers.
8. The posting of safety posters throughout the school and the issuing of safety literature to both students and staff personnel.
9. Coordination with food service personnel regarding safety of food preparation to storage areas. Plus the prevention of poisoning of foodstuffs.
10. Coordination with pest control personnel regarding pesticides and the potential of poisoning building occupants.
11. Remembering that safety cannot be overstressed.
12. Remembering to secure supplies, equipment, and sensitive areas.

Safety first begins in the protection of human life. Both staff and students should be aware of building evacuation procedures. These procedures must be taken in case of fire, explosion, gas leakage, or any other disasters that may strike. Disasters such as tornadoes, hurricanes, dust storms, or other violent reactions of the weather may place the school in position of becoming a shelter for its occupants and other community members. If a situation of this nature should arise plans should be made as to the protection of building occupants from falling debris and flying glass.

Fire protection equipment may consist of a manual or computerized alarm system, sprinkler system, high pressure hoses and release valves (in glass covered emergency points), or just plain old portable fire extinguishers. A number of school systems are working with computerized heat and smoke detector systems with sprinkler systems and automatic fire door closings to lock in and isolate burning areas (but not personnel). Some computerized fire control systems will electronically pinpoint fires plus notify local fire department units.

Regardless of the type of fire control system that are located in the school building, it must be serviced, tested, and monitored. A similar action must be taken by school occupants in carrying out state and local requirements concerning fire and disaster drills. In addition building administrators, instructional and logistical staff members along with the study body should be involved in observing and reporting fire hazards within and outside of the school. The principal (or designee) and the custodian can provide an additional hedge against possible fires through the neutralizing of hazards found during daily preschool inspections.

The Building Security Program

Security systems are designed to prevent unauthorized entry by unauthorized parties. No security system for the school building, the home, automobile, or even the local bank can be considered impregnable. Bypassing or neutralization of the locking system can be attained in time by experts. However, there is an item of consideration in this area—the fact that the more complex the construction of the locking system, the more time will be consumed to allow unauthorized entry.

Modern day schools are more or less business houses capable of handling up to thousands of dollars per day, along with the housing of thousands of more dollars of supplies and equipment which are necessary to carry out the daily educational program. One can simply look at the dollar worth of foodstuffs stored in the food preparation area alone and realize a typical building's dollar worth in contents. Security measures must be taken to protect (as much as possible) the building and its contents from theft and destruction. One may ask the question: How can the school be protected from unauthorized entry, theft, and vandalism? The response would need to take into account a number of variables, such as:

1. A building security policy.
2. An adequate locking system (manual or computerized).
3. Security measures concerning keys and computer entry codes.
4. Periodic alterations of key systems and computer entry codes (especially if there are personnel changes).
5. Use of a computerized security system that contains a variety of electronic countermeasures against intruders, such as:

   a. Electronic beams
   b. Pressure devices
   c. Audio monitors
   d. Television surveillance
   e. Audio and visual alarms
   f. Body heat sensors
   g. Automatic contact of local law enforcement agency
   h. Motion detectors

   6. Placing custodial shifts on a twenty four hour system (to keep the building occupied).

   7. Having custodial living quarters on the school site.

   8. Contracting security personnel services.

   9. Contracting security watchdog services.

   10. Telephone locking devices (to prevent unauthorized use after school hours).

   11. Locking devices for food storage units.

   12. Additional locking and surveillance systems for computer working areas.

   13. Nonuse of the office safe. Funds should be deposited daily through contract services of security organizations such as Brinks or Wells Fargo. If such services are not available in your community daily deposits (with police escort) should be made with a local bank. Funds collected at night or after banking hours from activities (such as sporting events, dances, parties, etc.) should be carried to a bank night deposit box (again with law enforcement escort).

   Funds should not be kept overnight in an office safe. An action of this type is an open invitation for unauthorized entry and theft.

   14. An accurate accounting system for monies, supplies, equipment, foodstuffs, computers, and other electronic equipment usage.

   The principal and the staff must cooperate in order that the building has a sound security system. Policy should be followed by all parties concerned in order that the building's defense perimeter can withstand criminal assaults from without and within.

F. SUMMARY

School buildings are the homes for the community's educational programs. They (school buildings) are dwellings that must be taken care of in order to preserve the structure and to be observed for its attractiveness along with the beauty of surrounding acreage.

The facility is maintained through management procedures by the principal, central office, and the custodial leader. Planned custodial and maintenance procedures should be carried out through policies formulated at the central office facility and grounds department, plus those policies of the school principal. Custodial duties keep the building operational in order to meet the daily demands of the educational program. Maintenance involves those items which are part of the building and its equipment. Maintenance procedures undertake the tasks of repair, replace, or servicing of building and equipment items.

Managing space within the building unit can become an obstacle for the principal. This situation is possible if car is not taken for the two-fold purpose of accurate class scheduling for instruction, and maintaining space within the building for noninstructional or logistical purposes. Computerization can greatly assist the principal in this area.

Maintaining a system of proper care for the school grounds will call for a well planned scheme to coincide with the fiscal, academic, and seasonal periods. Funds for personnel, supplies, and equipment along with school session periods and the changing seasons will determine the tasks to be performed. Lawn care, tree and shrub care, grounds policing; the cleaning of paved areas; along with ice and snow removal stand out as the prime factors of grounds care.

School safety and security involves the cooperation of the building's occupants. Safety can well be applied to all that dwell within the walls of the schoolhouse structure. Safety also requires the effort of all in order to be effective. The principal must provide leadership to the building safety program by serving as its manager. Fire prevention and emergency measures are considered by some to be prime features of the school's safety program.

Security of the school today may include electronic or manual locking systems. Security must also have the efforts and cooperation of all staff members. A school building and its contents must be protected from unauthorized entry, theft, and damages by criminal elements. Effective security measures will provide the school with a defense perimeter against unauthorized entry. The school administrator must realize that such a perimeter as previously mentioned is not impregnable. Good policy and coordination with local law enforcement agencies can help to prevent criminal assaults upon the school building.

REFERENCES

[1]Wood, C. L., et al. *The Secondary School Principal: Manager and Supervisor.* Boston: Allyn & Bacon, 1979, pp. 280–281.

[2]Ibid., pp. 281–282.

CHAPTER XIII

PURCHASING AND STORAGE MANAGEMENT

A. THE BUILDING LEVEL PURCHASING PROCESS

Purchasing involves a working system for the procuring of commodities and services to be used in an organization's operational scheme. Building principals serve the dual roles of instructional leader and building logistical manager. Purchasing is a logistical task that may be performed by the principal or his/her designee. The obtaining of certain supply and equipment items can sometimes be requested from the school district's warehousing system. These items are then forwarded to the requesting school as soon as possible. The final phase of this task will involve the monetary value of the requested items being charged against the building's account. However, there are situations when commodities or services are needed by the individual school which will involve the construction of a purchasing request for items not purchased in mass and stored by the school district for later distribution (on a "as needed" basis). Such items will require:

1. Proof of a bona fide need.
2. Determination of quality control procedures.
3. Construction of specifications.
4. Determination of commodity quantity, or the scope of service required.
5. Satisfaction and past evaluations of previous similar commodities and services.
6. Undertaking a building affordability check.
7. Forwarding a request to the central office purchasing agent.
8. Second affordability check by the accounting unit.
9. Bidding (if applicable by state law or local board policy).
10. Issuance of the purchase order by the purchasing office (copy sent to requesting school).
11. Receipt of goods and invoice to school district warehouse or directly to the requesting school.

12. Inspection of goods and comparison of requisition, purchasing order and invoice (by warehouse and/or requesting school).

If the commodities are received at the school district warehouse, they must be temporarily stored and later distributed to the requesting school according to established delivery schedules.

Services that are purchased from external organizations (for example: plumbing, building repair, electrical work, equipment installation, etc.) may require bidding (according to state law or board policy). Once the servicing unit is selected a time schedule is constructed for commencing and terminating points for service task action.

Once commodities are received and inspected, or services are completed and appraised, a warrant will be issued by the purchasing department and forwarded to accounting. Accounting will then issue payment to the vendor or servicing agent.

Prior to exercising the previously mentioned purchasing steps, the principal (or designee) will act as the building level purchasing agent. One of the tasks performed by this individual should include the evaluation of the various requests being forwarded by the building's staff. Considerations need to be made concerning:

1. **Time** — (a) To what fiscal period will the purchase be applied? (b) What is the current status of the account to be charged for the item of request? (c) What time period is projected for use or duration of the requested commodity or service? (d) What is the projected time consumption period between the original request and the receipt of goods (or the performance of services)? Time is an item that must be considered when the principal embarks upon the act of purchasing.

2. **Quality Control and Assurance** — Standards for quality concerning a needed commodity or service should be established by central office and/or building level. Administrative and user evaluation of the product or service should be kept on record. The reviewing of these records should provide adequate data to consider for future purchases.

3. **The Quantity Question** — The justified need and the time period to be covered by the product or service must all be coordinated if the proper determination of quantity for the purchasing request is to be made. Additional consideration would involve items like:
   a. The normal consumption rate.
   b. The normal fair wear and tear period.

     c. Cost and discount incentives.

     d. Internal damage and deterioration rate.

     e. Inventory control procedures.

     f. Market climate for products and services.

4. **Proper Inventory Accounting** — The avoidance of improper distribution of products by forwarding and using older products in storage. Actions of this nature can assist in avoiding waste through deteriorated or obsolete products. A building administrator needs also to take steps against hoarding by staff members. There is need for a system to be formulated (by computer if available) to keep an account of commodities issued to both the instructional and logistical staffs within the building.

5. **Observance of Commodity or Service Markets** — Information can be obtained from various business monitoring and service organizations concerning the marketing situations of manufacturers and service companies in regard to supply, demand, and pricing. The gaining of information in these areas will allow the principal to request a purchase at the right time in order to obtain the lowest price possible (in line with quality expectations).

6. **Source Identification** — Through the proper construction of specifications, the obtaining of quality standards along with low pricing is possible. Detailed specifications can automatically mark a certain product or service that a principal and/or his/her staff desires. Building administrators and the school's staff can better perform their assigned tasks plus meeting their goals through the use of satisfactory products or services.

7. **Vendor Credibility and Reliability** — Records should be kept at both central office and the building level to provide information regarding credibility and reliability of past vendors. Information also needs to be obtained concerning potential vendors that have engaged in business with the school system. Potential vendor information can be found through business monitoring organizations and other school systems, or organizations that have used the potential vendor's commodities or services. A listing of positive vendors and their products or services can assist in specification construction, and the seeking of lower price ranges.

Purchasing procedures carried out at building level by the principal and the building staff are accountable to the public. Items purchased by the school system for building use will involve the use of public monies, and the obtaining of products and services for public use. Therefore, a bona fide need has to be established along with proper use of the commodities once they are received. Services that are purchased must be for the good of the building, or to assist in the instructional or logistical tasks being performed at the building.

There is not only the concern for the credibility of the vendors, but also that of principals in their purchasing of products or services. Today's society offers an assortment of nefarious business organizations along with their representatives that are quick to offer shaded deals through incentives such as "kickbacks" and expensive, but illegal prize offers for the school's business. Once an administrator or staff member is involved with illegal action, he/she is "hooked," therefore, leaving the school and school district in a position for scandal. The principal must also remember the he/she is responsible for the deeds of his/her staff, whether positive or negative. Honesty in all of the school's business transactions should be impressed by the principal upon the school's staff.

B. PLANNING AND PURCHASING

The tasks of planning and purchasing should be well coordinated in order to provide a steady flow commodities and services needed for the conducting of the building's instructional and logistical programs. Most building level purchase planning will concern the preparation of providing goods and services for a fiscal year. The actual planning for the task of purchasing should also be coordinated with the approved budget. Funds for supplies, equipment and services need to be placed into the building's various accounts for the forthcoming fiscal period (during budget construction).

Administrative leadership in the planning phase of the purchasing task should involve the:

1. The Principal
2. The Building Administrative Team (assistant principals)
3. Department Chairpersons (middle or secondary schools) or
4. Grade Level Leaders (elementary schools)
5. Educational Support Leaders (guidance counselors, librarians, curriculum coordinators, student deans, educational media directors, etc.)
6. Logistical Support Leaders (chief secretary, head custodian, heating engineer, etc.)

Each building leaders represented in each of the above major groups needs to take into account, the needs of his/her unit in the areas of equipment, supplies, and services to accomplish those goals assigned for the forthcoming fiscal period (which will include the new academic year). A series of questions should be answered by each building unit leader before actually establishing quantity, quality, dollar amounts, and the time span to be covered by the purchased commodities and/or services. For example:

1. What type of program (or programs) will I be responsible for next fiscal period?
2. Will the program involve a series of steps or phases? If so, what commodities and/or services will be required at each series?
3. If the program I am responsible for does not involve a series of steps, what are its needs for the new fiscal period?
4. What is the current status of the inventory of various commodities used in my unit?
5. Will there be a need for commodities or services not used in the past?
6. What were the appraisal results concerning the synchronization of my unit distribution system (the issuing of commodities and service needs to the subordinates of my unit)?
7. What were the appraisal results concerning supply economy measures taken within my unit during current and past fiscal periods?
8. What has been the average rate of time consumption between purchase requisitions and actual delivery? Will this factor have an influence on my unit's needs and the accomplishment of its assigned objectives?
9. Is there any forecast concerning possible labor problems with manufacturers, wholesale jobbers, or transportation carriers which could possibly prevent the shipment of goods in time for the new fiscal period?
10. Are there any forecasts concerning labor problems in service organizations (such as janitorial service contractors, painting contractors, plumbing contractors, refuse removal services, etc.)?
11. Do incentives exists (by vendors) that would allow savings through the act of purchasing of commodities for use beyond the forthcoming fiscal period?
12. How does the building storage capability match with my unit's needs along with the storage needs of other building units.

13. What are the peak and low demand periods of my unit for specific commodity items during the fiscal year?
14. Are my unit's demands being currently met, and were they met during past fiscal periods?

Upon responding to each of the previous questions, the unit leader should be able to construct his/her unit's needs for the coming fiscal year. At this point, the principal and the building administrative team should coordinate the needs of the various staff leaders. Upon the completion of reviewing the various purchasing requests, the principal needs to decide approval or denial for each service or commodity desired. If a commodity or service item is denied, there is need to inform the subordinate leader as to the reason(s) for the denial. All approved purchase requests should be forwarded to the central office purchasing unit for further review and possible approval.

Supervision of the building's purchasing operation will require a significant amount of input by the chief building administrator. He/she (the principal) needs to make sure of:

1. Availability of supplies and equipment at the school district warehouse, or from wholesale jobbers, or direct procurement from manufacturers.
2. Will there be or are there trends indicating shortages of specific commodities? If so, will the central office business manager impose a rationing system upon the individual school buildings? Does the political climate in your school district foster favoritism for certain buildings to ignore the rationing system? From a more specific point does the district political climate involve the need for a principal to be combative in order that his/her building receive its share?
3. Has the principal taken into account the anticipated overall consumption rate of building supplies, equipment needs, and service needs for the future fiscal period?
4. Have all the supply, equipment, and service needs of each unit of the building been carefully constructed and reviewed?
5. Can the various units within the building anticipate a timely replenishment of needed supplies and/or equipment items.
6. How does the specific service or commodity need match with funds available within the account concerned?
7. How does the building's overall services and commodities needs coordinate with the budget for the new fiscal period?
8. Are special state or federal funds involved in specific programs

within the school? If so, have the special guidelines for purchasing been complied with?

9. Is the school district solvent? If so, what is the degree of solvency? Is there the possibility of the local board placing measures of austerity, because of financial conditions (during the projected fiscal period)?

Once fiscal and purchasing requests requirements have been met, orders have been received and inspected by the central office warehouse (if not already on hand in stores), those items will then be distributed to the school making the original request. The principal or his/her designee should take a second inspection and compare the invoice with the original purchase request. The received items should then be placed in the building's requesting unit. Items that are in critical demand should be immediately distributed to the requesting building unit.

Up to this point most of the attention of purchase planning has involved commodity type needs. Individual building may also have the need for various types of maintenance services to be performed in order that the various educational and logistical programs can be carried out.

By careful inspection of the building and grounds the principal and logistical staff can come close to the service needs of the building that must be carried out by specialists such as painters, refrigeration and air conditioning experts, carpenters, roofers, appliance service personnel, etc. These projected services along with estimated costs (within the proposed budget). The local board (and local government if the school district is fiscally dependent) will most likely proceed with the bidding process in order that both specifications and lower pricing are met. Once the contractor is selected, task performance by the contracting organization is assigned during the fiscal period. There are certain factors that may have to be considered before the contractor can perform the service to the building or grounds. For example:

1. The season
2. The weather
3. Demand for the service by others
4. Labor problems
5. Pupil presence
6. Staff presence

There are some service needs that are emergencies, such as wind damage; broken water lines, sewer line stoppages, gas line leaks, and electrical line breakage; riot damage; fires; floods; etc. These items cannot be planned for. However, central office should plan for a reserve account to supplement insurance claims for such matters.

Planning is an essential force in the principal's supervision of the purchasing needs of the building. Input by the building level administrative team (assistant principal(s)) and other instructional and logistical unit leaders is a must. This is necessary if the inflow of commodities and services are to be synchronized with the objectives achievement process of the building's instructional and logistical units.

C. MANAGING THE SCHOOL BUILDING'S STORAGE AREAS

Once commodities are received by the school district's central or regionalized warehousing system, they (commodities) will most likely be temporarily stored until distribution to the individual school building. There may be occasions when items will be shipped directly from the vendor to the school building. Whenever purchased items are delivered to the school procedures that were carried out at the central office warehousing unit should be duplicated. For example, the tasks of:

1. Receiving
2. Inspection
3. Comparison of the purchase request with the invoice
4. Unpacking
5. Processing and construction (if required)
6. Authorization to the central office accounting unit to pay the vendor.

need to be undertaken at building level by the principal or his/her designee.

When the commodities are accounted for by the building's representative, flow implementation is put into process to route the goods to the building's storage area(s) or requesting unit. Most school commodities will have a short time or temporary duration in storage due to demand and planning procedures which have identified unit needs to cover the school district fiscal period and specific program periods during the academic year.

The typical school building needs to have available space in its storage unit(s) to carry adequate:

1. Instructional supplies and equipment items for the academic and fiscal period.
2. Logistical supplies (such as clerical items and custodial commodities) for the fiscal period.

3. Disposable bulky items such as paper towels, toilet tissue, sanitary napkins, etc., should be able to support building needs on a monthly basis. This would permit valuable storage space to be used for other items and prevent possible storage damage (due to environmental factors such as humidity, pest destruction, spontaneous combustion, etc.).

Consideration needs to be taken in the operation of the school's storage facility as to the rate of outflow of specific commodities to determine their average duration of space occupancy. Due to the fact that various items do not necessarily arrive at a common time, requires the school's warehouse manager to determine (as accurately as possible) space vacancies, space requirements, and the rate of specific commodity outflow from the storage area(s). The rate of commodity outflow determines the rate of commodity inflow and space designation. Once goods are received, inspected and compared against the initial request, there is the need for sorting and space designation. If the space available is partially occupied by an item of similar specifications, the older items should be placed in front with those items most recently received placed in the back of the designated space (bin, shelf, rack, etc.). This action allows for the older items to be used first. There is a definite need for policy support, adherence, and enforcement in this area.

Goods placed in storage are in need of protection as specified by the manufacturer. This may involve:
1. Temperature control
2. Humidity control
3. Protection from sunlight
4. Protection from water
5. Protection from pests
6. Consumption or product activity within a certain time period.

The building warehouse manager must keep the above mentioned factors in mind. This will also assist in the inflow and outflow procedures to be taken by building personnel.

Various types of commodities will require a variety of warehouse equipment to assist in maintaining a proper storage system. This will also influence space availability within the building's storage areas. Some of the types of warehouse equipment and areas that may be in demand are:
1. Shelves
2. Bins

  3. Floor platforms
  4. Hangers
  5. Tables
  6. Racks
  7. Floor space
  8. Reels
  9. Cabinets
  10. Refrigeration
  11. Freezers
  12. Receiving area(s)
  13. Distribution area(s)
  14. Storage handling equipment area(s)

Storage managers at building level need to also consider safety requirements needed in the storing of various items for building use. Chemicals used in building care or in instructional programs should be stored in areas that coincide with safety and manufacturer's prescribed procedures. Dangerous items of this type need to be kept away from the items which may promote fires, explosions, or the production of toxic situations. Building policy is needed to establish the segregation of commodities according to need and safety.

Equipment Storage

Equipment items should also be stored (and kept in protective packaging after inspection) until the time of distribution. Space occupation and duration of occupation of equipment items is critical to overall space demands. Equipment items may also require storage in a particular type of environment in order to prevent damage and deterioration of the product. Electronic equipment is very sensitive and may require special care during the storage situation. Equipment items should be distributed to needed units within the building and placed into use as soon as possible. A process of this nature will provide less consumption of storage space, a reduction of special care procedures while in storage; and lessons the likelihood of damage or deterioration while in the storage facility.

Food Storage

Food storage procedures are usually under the direction of the cafeteria manager, however, the principal or his/her designee should supervise this activity since its operation is within the confines of the building. This fact places the responsibility factor upon the building principal. Food storage needs will require protection from spoilage, contamination, pests, damage to foodstuffs, and biological and chemical breakdowns within specific food items.

There is a requirement for food storage areas to have the following needs provided:
1. Refrigeration
2. Freezing
3. Dry Storage Areas
4. Temperature control
5. Pest control
6. Cleanliness
7. Identification (Specifications, date received and storage period)
8. Proper rotation
9. Timely distribution flow

Security of the Storage Area

Security measures should be taken in guarding the storage area from theft, vandalism, unauthorized entry and distribution, damage or spoilage, and fire. Along with proper inventory control procedures security is required to ensure adequate protection for the building level storage system. Key tasks which will help promote security of building storage areas are:
1. Allowing only authorized entry to the storage area(s).
2. Distribution of keys or electronic locking systems to personnel only involved in storage matters.
3. Maintaining a building policy on storage security.
4. Inspection and removal of storage room hazards.
5. The securing of all storage areas when not in use.
6. Coordination between storage room security and inventory control.

Security policies for the building's storage facilities must be formulated, adhered to, and enforced by administrative personnel if a satisfactory security system is to be achieved. Cooperation by the entire building staff is essential in order to create a positive climate of keeping the building's storage areas secure.

Computers and Building Level Storage Centers

Computers can facilitate building level storage management through electronic memory, rapid computation, swift and broad monitoring, budget and fiscal input, and electronic surveillance of the overall storage operation. Human input toward the storage task can be reduced by the computer through a variety of electronic task performances such as:

1. Record keeping of all storage inflow and outflow.
2. Coordination procedures between central office warehousing and building storage efforts.
3. Inventory monitoring and control.
4. Commodity distribution information.
5. Specific unit consumption data.
6. Automatic reorder systems.
7. Storage area security and fire control systems.

Computer procedures concerned with the building setting should be outlined by building level procedures as outlined in the building policy book. In order that the computerized storage system functions in a more positive environment, there will be a need for employee cooperation. Another area of concern involving computer usage is that all individuals involved with storage procedures (administrative, instructional, and logistical personnel) be adequately trained. Training programs can be administered by central office computer personnel, or by computer manufacturing company training staffs.

D. AN EQUITABLE SYSTEM OF DISTRIBUTION

The length of storage item for commodities within the building's warehouse area(s) will depend upon the distribution factor. Items should be distributed to requesting units within the building as soon as possible. This action will allow for space gains which will free storage space for the future inflow of commodities. Distribution at times may involve a unit (within the building) requesting supply or equipment items on a "as needed basis." Regardless of the distribution or outflow procedures from the building storage area(s), there must be an accounting as to the:

1. Building unit identification.

2. Date and time of distribution.
3. The quantity to be taken.
4. Reason for item(s) requested.

Past records and prior planning procedures should enable building storage personnel to be able to predict approximate building unit consumption rates of specific items during a typical fiscal period.

Distribution procedures may be preplanned by the principal in order to prevent hoarding and waste by school personnel. Procedures of this type are largely determined by the overall general characteristic of the school staff. Selecting a particular philosophy concerning commodity control will enable the principal, or his/her designated storage manager the proper leadership needed in distributing commodities to the diverse building units. Such a procedure will also lessen the complexity of commodity accounting and inventory control. Accounting for distribution within the building can benefit the principal in the area of inventory control of commodities. Rates of unit consumption (as mentioned previously) of assorted commodities can be determined through inventory control measures. This action can prove valuable in purchasing for future fiscal periods. Inventory data will also assist the principal in budget construction (which places the dollar figure upon needed supplies and equipment). Computerization in this area would provide a boon to building administration procedures.

The Building Unit and Equitable Distribution

Earlier chapters mentioned that the typical school building is divided into a number of units which can be identified according to task. The three primary categories according to task are:
1. Administration
2. Instruction
3. Logistics

The administrative unit of the typical school building will involve:
1. The Principal
2. The Administrative Team (which can consist of one or more assistant principals with responsibility for various managerial tasks performed within the school setting).

In smaller schools there may be only the principal or a principal-teacher (a building administrator that is assigned part time teaching duties). Single principals or principal-teachers are not allowed a great deal of latitude in the practice of delegation. "The buck stops" at the principal's desk and he/she is forced to wear a number of hats (perform a number of tasks) in carrying out those duties needed to operate the school building.

Larger schools offer the principal the opportunity to have an administrative team (assistant principals) for the delegation of various building administrative tasks.

Instruction tasks performed within the building involves a number of operational units. For example:

1. The teaching faculty.
2. Instructional units (with unit leaders) according to subject area (departments in middle and secondary schools), or grade level units (in kindergarten, primary, and intermediate settings)

Instructional support units, such as curriculum coordinators, guidance counselors, librarians and the library staff, instructional aids, educational media, etc. Each of these units are usually assigned a leader.

Logistical support for the building can involve a number of personnel, their units and their unit leaders. For example, clerical support, food services, custodial and maintenance support, and pupil transportation coordination and control.

All of the leaders of the previously mentioned building segments are responsible for their units obtaining of an equitable share of commodities which are distributed through the building's storage system. Each leader needs to take a critical review of goals of their respective units and the design(s) used to accomplish those goals. Past accomplishments of unit goals have required time, funds, personnel, various service supports, and those *SUPPLY AND EQUIPMENT ITEMS* needed to allow the units to be successful (in undertaking assigned tasks). Another guide which will be of assistance to the leader and his/her unit is that of established standards which are avenues of approach to goal accomplishments. Subordinates within an individual building unit should be made aware of the standards of operation required and the units' primary and secondary goals. Secondary goals within the unit are segments of subordinate responsibilities. If these responsibilities are carried out properly, dividends will be reaped in true accomplishment. The accomplishment secondary goals by subordinate personnel are systematic parts of an overall or primary goals accomplishments system of the unit. Approval by the unit leader will provide information to numerous items related to subordinate and secondary goal accomplishment. Data collected and evaluated at this point will measure overall objective achievement. If the unit and its personnel were not successful in undertaking their objectives, appraisal data should indicate why. It is a known fact that various commodities are needed by a specific unit in order that it can function and achieve its prescribed goals. Therefore, the unit leader and his/her subordinates should be aware of the number, quality, and type of commodities that are needed to function in normally over the fiscal period.

Both leader and subordinate input are required to determine projected commodity needs, and thereby assure themselves of an equitable distribution from individual school stores.

Principal-building unit leader, planning, coordination and cooperation are required in order to lay the groundwork for an equitable distribution of various supply and equipment items. The principal (or his/her designee) must plan, coordinate, and cooperate with all unit leaders within the building. This type of combined effort can allow for proper budget building, adequate purchasing, and an equitable program for the distribution of commodities within the building. Through these actions the building administration can also become aware of various service needs which will meet through external service agencies (through the central office business management organization).

Distribution Techniques

Methods of distribution can also influence the equity situation among units within the building. There are two prime types of distribution methods. They are:

1. General Building Distribution—This pattern of apportionment will concern those commodity items received from central office warehousing and are sent to the school and then forwarded to the building unit which made the original request.

2. Intraschool Distribution—A system of this nature will involve units within the building making requests to the individual school storage manager (principal or designee) for those commodities that have been stored and are available in the school storage area.

Equity distribution in the above stated categories will require different efforts to ensure equity of distribution. Units making specific requests for particular items should be supervised by the school's administration. This type of action is necessary in order to establish that the requesting unit in need is in good faith and not at the expense of other units within the building. Intraschool distribution will involve a heavy concentration of supervision by the stores manager to guarantee that unit infighting and hoarding does not take place. Computerized inventory accounting and proper unit rationing procedures would greatly assist the school's administration of this area.

Distribution procedures within the limits of the school setting will involve a series of actions for which the principal (or designee) as storage manager will be responsible for. They may include the following:

1. Commodity identification and description.
2. Quantity and quality desired.
3. Determination of a bona fide need.
4. Does the item assist the unit in meeting its standards and the accomplishing its goals?
5. Inventory survey as to:
   a. Requesting unit's previous requisitions and consumption or usage rate.
   b. Availability of desired commodity.
   c. Current status of item inventory and rate of demand within the school.
6. An open communications system (two-way) between the principal, storage manager, and individual unit requester.
7. Intrabuilding transportation system between the storage area and the unit confines.

By having a strong program of equity distribution of commodities within the school, certain dividends can be earned. Assets such as high morale, esprit de corps, and proof of administrative fairness will promote a positive atmosphere within the building's instructional and logistical staffs. Positive relations between the principal and his/her staff can provide for higher productivity and positive goal achievement.

E. SUMMARY

Building level logistical management will most likely require the task of purchasing of supplies and equipment to sustain instructional and logistical operations. For the most part purchasing requests are usually constructed at unit level (which is within the building's organizational format). Unit leaders (such as department chairpersons, grade level leaders, the chief secretary, the head custodian, etc.) with the assistance of their subordinates will determine the need for various types of service and commodities. The service or commodity item(s) in need will become a purchasing request which is filled out to determine: (1) Identification, (2) Specifications, (3) Quality input, (4) Quantity, (5) Cost, and (6) Urgency status.

Purchasing requests are usually monitored by the principal or his/her designee to determine if the commodity need is bona fide and affordable. Principals need to plan purchasing needs with their unit leaders in advance of the fiscal and academic year. There is also a requirement to coordinate purchasing planning with budget construction in order to satisfy both need and affordability. Approved purchasing requests are then forwarded to the central office purchasing department. At central office the purchasing agent or his/her designee will usually determine (for the second time) if the building's need is genuine. Central office accounting unit checks are needed to determine if the school's financial situation (through the school's account) is adequate to pay for the items or services requested. Once these two situations are cleared, the purchasing office will issue a purchasing order to the vendor or service agent (organizational representative for a service firm such as plumbing, roofing, electrical, etc. contractor). However, if the item(s) being requested has a value over an established limit (according to state law) the bidding process must take place. In states where school districts are fiscally dependent, local governmental bodies (cities, counties or metropolitan areas) will exercise control over the bidding process. Fiscally independent school districts will oversee their own bidding procedures.

Serious thought is required when selecting a vendor or service agent for commodities that are straight purchases, or in instances where bidding has taken place. Both building level and central office purchasing personnel are in need of a vendor's and service agent's catalog (with ratings) which will enable a better means of selecting premium business organizations. In numerous situations, the lowest bid does not have to be accepted, however, the reason for doing so must be established. Specifications can be constructed in such a manner as to almost guarantee certainty of particular items or service company to be selected.

Storage areas within the school building should be established according to commodity requirements (involving both inflow and outflow of goods plus space availability). Other needs required in building space management will be in the areas of: (1) Inventory control, (2) Security of the area and its contents, and (3) the establishment and maintenance of an equitable system of distribution to building personnel.

CHAPTER XIV

FOOD, TRANSPORTATION, HEALTH AND SOCIAL SERVICES

A. THE BUILDING FOOD SERVICE OPERATION

Direct administration of the school building's food service program will normally rest with the central office director of food service. In the school building the cafeteria manager will exercise specific control over food service operations. Food preparation, recipe selection, menu planning, storage equipment, accounting and cash management, personnel management of food service employees, sanitizing and housekeeping of the food preparation center, ordering procedures for foodstuffs, plus ordering and inventory procedures for food service supplies and equipment will be administered by the building cafeteria manager and the central office director of food services. Liaison with the governmental organizations such as local, state and federal health units, the United States Department of Agriculture, state departments of school food services, and food brokers will also be under the direct administration of central office and building level food service personnel.

A factor which should be kept in mind regarding building level feeding programs is that this particular operation (food service) is being carried out within the confines of the school building. Therefore, food service automatically becomes a part of the principal's overall responsibility. The responsibility factor requires an administrative need for coordination between the principal, the cafeteria manager, and the central office director of food services. Such coordination could be in the areas concerning:

1. Menu planning, recipe construction and meal rotation. Tasks of this type can require building administrative input in the areas of:
   a. Menu acceptance by the student body.
   b. Ethnic make up of the student body.
   c. Religious make up of the student body.

    d. Monthly notification to students and parents regarding daily menus for the forthcoming months.

    e. Student input regarding recipes and menus.

    f. Average daily student and staff participation in breakfast and/or lunch offerings.

2. Food service sanitary and safety precautions.

    a. Cafeteria manager—principal coordination regarding standards of cleanliness of food preparation, serving, and eating areas.

    b. Sanitization procedures of the food service area.

    c. Organic and nonorganic waste removal and refuse storage procedures of the food service area.

    d. Fire safety procedures for the food preparation and serving areas.

    e. Pest control procedures for the food service area.

    f. Poison and chemical (cleaning agents, etc.) plus storage and security within the food service area.

    g. Proof by cafeteria manager that governmental health requirements are being met.

3. Coordination with the building food service manager that accounting and cash management procedures are correct and financially sound.

4. That all free meal recipients have been properly identified and accounted for.

5. Personnel management of food service personnel will primarily be the responsibility of the cafeteria manager. However, all cafeteria personnel should obey building staff policies.

Satellite, Regionalized and Centralized Food Preparation

There are some school districts that have organized their food service offerings through channels which differ from the school building's in house cafeteria operations. Methods such as the satellite, regionalized, and centralized food preparation centers have moved the process from direct building level operation.

Satellite food preparation involves the preparation of breakfast and lunch offerings at one school (for example, a nearby high school), with the prepared meal then being transported to elementary schools and possibly middle schools within the vicinity.

Regionalized food preparation operates in a similar fashion, however, these centers are not located in schools. The primary purpose of the regionalized food center is to provide those essential food services to all schools within a certain specified region of the school district. Prepared foods are then shipped to those schools within the region.

Centralized food preparation can provide breakfast and luncheon offerings to all schools within the district. The service provided by a central kitchen does not focus on a segment of the school district as found in the regionalized plan. Transportation requirements of this plan of organization will require shipment to all schools within the district. Foods prepared by satellite, regionalized or centralized kitchens may be of two general varieties which are either: (1) box lunches or (2) complete hot meals.

Requirements placed on the principal in complying with the satellite, regionalized or centralized food preparation schemes will involve interaction with the central office food service administration concerning use of part-time food service workers and possibly parent aides. Such personnel will assist in establishing serving arrangements, serving procedures, dining room arrangements, accounting and cash management, plus health and sanitation measures. Here again overall building responsibility of the principal will require his/her knowledge of the operation, keeping abreast of daily food service tasks within the building, seeking plus maintaining communication, and administrative liaison with the building food service leader plus central office director.

Other Principal-Cafeteria Manager Coordinating Procedures

In buildings which contain an internal food preparation center the principal and the building food service manager need to establish building access procedures for food service employees. If a building does not operate its custodians on a 24-hour shift (around the clock coverage through three eight hour shifts) arrangements are needed to allow food service personnel entry to the building. Some building food service staffs will provide for their bakers to work a 10:00 p.m. to 6:30 a.m. shift to prepare the cafeteria's baked goods. The master baker is usually in charge of the night operation and has responsibility for gaining access to the building. He/she (the master baker) will also provide for security measure during the night shift. The cafeteria manager, day cooks, and other personnel will usually operate from 6:00 a.m. until 2:30 p.m. If the school has a breakfast program this may necessitate an earlier start by the day food preparation people. Flexibility is needed in allowing for the scheduling of food service personnel. The principal needs to arrange for their authorized entry and construct a policy to limit food service personnel to the food service and rest room areas only.

Social indicators are pointing to the plight of America's "Latch Key Child." Future governmental involvement in this issue may require the public schools to provide programs to temporarily house, provide activities, and feed children in this category. An action of this nature could possibly involve the schools in providing three meals a day (breakfast, lunch, and supper) to a segment of its student body. If such an action is implemented, there will be a requirement for additional building administrative responsibility. There will also be an expansion of the duties of both building level cafeteria management along with the central office administrative input.

Principals and cafeteria managers need to project the numbers of children to be fed each day of the week along with that of staff members. Additional items needed to be taken into account can include the student absence rate (excused and unexcused), free lunch recipients (along with a coding system for these individuals), noncafeteria participants, and moderate noncafeteria participants (students that may purchase only limited products such as milk, desserts, etc.). These same features will also apply to building staff members that partake of cafeteria services. Information of this type will assist the cafeteria services. Information of this type will also assist the cafeteria manager in determining the daily serving output.

Cafeteria managers, along with building principals, need to plan for total cafeteria seating capacity both for students and staff. This information can support the building administrative team in determining the total number of lunch periods per school day, and the total length of time for adequate meal consumption. This information will help the school administrator to determine the length and total number of serving periods per day.

The establishment of a system for student control, student responsibility for cleanliness, and trash removal procedures should have the input of the cafeteria manager and his/her staff. These actions would also blend with student traffic patterns within the cafeteria involving:

1. Entry.
2. Serving line flow.
3. Seating.

4. Trash removal.
5. Used tray depositing.
6. Exiting the dining area.

Cafeteria manager-principal input is needed to coordinate custodial removal of waste materials (in plastic bags during and after the feeding periods) to external waste storage containers to await scheduled removal. Waste removal storage areas are usually in constant need of pest control operations (as both a prevention and eradication action). The placing of at least 3 cups of liquid ammonia into each 30 gallon plastic trash bag (filled with organic waste material) can minimize scavenging by dogs, cats, and other animals.

The building level administrator needs to plan for the school food center's receiving point (for delivery trucks containing various foodstuffs, supplies, and equipment for the cafeteria). There will also be a need for internal receiving space in or near the food preparation center for the inspecting and sorting food service supplies, equipment, and food items. Convenience needs to be taken into account in order to quickly transport the received commodities to specific storage areas within the building's cafeteria system.

An observance of the building's food service receiving area should provide for an ease of access for delivery trucks (through the campus driveways plus ease of exiting from the school ground. If the school's parking area is congested, food service and other receiving areas should be cleared of all parking, therefore, permitting delivery at any designated time of the day.

The principal needs to incorporate the security of the food service area's stores, vending machines, and daily revenue within the building's overall security networks. It is necessary to confer with the building cafeteria manager and possibly central office food service administrators in the area of security. Present day building break ins and thefts not only include normal supplies and equipment, but also foodstuffs.

Criminal action of this nature also creates a situation for possible intended food contamination for nefarious reasons.

Principals need to consider the building cafeteria manager and the food service staff as part of the school's logistical team—and a team which is necessary not only for the school's daily operation, but also its well-being.

B. COORDINATING THE CENTRAL OFFICE
TRANSPORTATION PROGRAM

Transportation like food services is primarily a function of the central office logistical system. Depending upon the school district's organizational scheme the transportation operation is usually a task of the school district logistical manager (or business manager). Middle to large sized school districts may delegate the transportation task to a director or supervisor of transportation.

Building level administrative responsibility for pupil transportation will be in the areas concerning:

1. Bus thoroughfares on the school's campus.
2. Pupil mounting and dismounting areas.
3. Pupil holding areas (within the building or external to the building).
4. Pupil transfer point operation (when pupils from other schools within the district are transferred from one bus to another, but will use part of the school's campus only as a holding or waiting area).
5. Pupil conduct and control from the bus stop area to the school building.
6. Coordination between the principal, bus drivers, and central office transportation administrator regarding pupil conduct, control, and riding privileges.
7. Coordination between the principal and central office transportation administrators regarding schedules, pickup points, transfer point operations, and the establishment of minimum "in transit" time.

Building Level and Pupil Personnel Procedures
for School Transportation Operations

The building administrator and his/her administrative team (in conjunction with the central office transportation unit) should plan a bus safety program for students at the elementary, middle school, and high school levels. Pupils should be given orientation regarding:

1. Proper overall conduct while riding and at bus stops.
2. Seating rules.
3. Emergency evacuation procedures.
4. Road crossing procedures.
5. Proper mounting and dismounting protocol.

6. Conduct in holding areas.
7. Noise control.
8. Respect for the driver.
9. The nonlittering of bus units.

A principal should make use of his/her administrative team and building staff (teachers and teacher aides) in assisting with supervision of pupil holding, mounting, and dismounting areas. There is also need for a system for reporting pupil infractions at (1) pickup and release points, (2) during transit between hone and school, and (3) in campus or building holding areas. Another reporting system that is in need of development by the principal is that of a report for pupil injuries while in transit. Bus drivers should be required to have primary input in reporting systems involving conduct (in transit and bus stops) and injuries (while in transit). Bus drivers should also be authorized by central office to provide written reports to the school principal concerning misconduct by pupils. Serious and chronic situations regarding pupil behavior should be part of a building level disciplinary system which allows for:

1. Possible immediate suspension of riding privileges or warnings of this action.
2. The establishment of meetings between the principal (or his/her designee), the bus driver, the parents, and the student offender.
3. The distribution of a notice of violations should be given to the school office, the driver, the parents, and the central office transportation office.
4. Upon completion of the meeting the decision regarding judgement of the rule infractions should be given to the parents the child, the driver, and the central office transportation unit. This may involve:
    1. Temporary suspension of riding privileges.
    2. Permanent exclusion of riding privileges.
    3. A warning.

Problems arising from bus stop situations may or may not include input from the driver. In cases of this nature there is need for a meeting between the principal (or his/her designee), the parents and the student(s) in order to resolve the issue at hand. A periodic drive through and careful observation of various bus routes by the principal or a member of his/her administrative team may help to minimize problems at bus stops.

Developing the School Campus for
Proper Transportation Administration

The school campus should be designed in such a manner as to keep the pupil transportation operation separate from:

1. Staff Parking.
2. Student Parking.
3. Delivery Parking.
4. All thoroughfares for the above.

Bus entrance and exit thoroughfares need to be separate in order to promote a more positive campus safety program. Pupil loading and unloading areas should provide for direct pupil access to the buses without crossing school bus thoroughfares on the campus (by the use of one-way thoroughfares). Staff, student, and delivery traffic should be forbidden to use campus bus routes.

Special Transportation Operations

Field trips, athletic contests, and other events will require the building principal to request the school district transportation office for special transportation support. Central office guidelines regarding such requests should include:

1. Advance notice limits.
2. Trip dates.
3. Passenger numbers.
4. Chaperone identification and numbers.
5. Sponsoring party identification (athletic director, speech club sponsor, etc.).
6. Number of buses needed.
7. Destination and projected time in transit.
8. Projections of waiting period by driver personnel.
9. Accommodations for driver personnel (if overnight stay is involved).
10. Method of payment for special bus use.

A building principal is in need of formulating a request system for special bus use by the instructional staff. The previously mentioned ten points (which should be a part of the central office transportation scheme) will suffice, however, a principal needs to determine whether the staff members request is bona fide. A "go" or "no go" decision should be made by the principal after careful study of each request.

Principal-Staff Cooperation

The principal and the building staff need to cooperate in assisting the pupil transportation program as it concerns the school. Teacher and administrative effort is needed to supervise and control:

1. Dismounting and mounting areas.
2. Pupil holding areas.
3. Transfer point areas.
4. Special trip planning and supervision.

Both the principal's administrative team and the instructional staff should participate in appraising the building's responsibility of participating with the central office transportation program. Conflicts and other problems which are determined by periodic evaluations should be discussed and resolved by the principal, the building administrative team, the instructional staff, and the central office transportation office.

C. SCHOOL HEALTH SERVICES

Health services at the school level mainly involves the building administrative and instructional units acting as a major referral system. Pupils are usually identified as having a need for: (1) medical, (2) dental, and (3) psychological services are directed to the attention of representatives of these three areas. The principal is responsible for the health of the student body (as it concerns the school setting), and for the training of the administrative team plus the instructional staff to recognize actual and possible health problems within the student body. Additional positive features to the building level health service program is to enlist the input of parental and community persons and organizations. Assistance by the community and its organization can be beneficial to normal student health operations and any health emergency situations that may arise.

Major emphasis for the school health program should be at the central office level. Depending upon the district size and enrollment of the school district, health services maybe directed by physicians, nurses, or public health specialists. A principal and his/her building organization needs to tie-in with the central office health operation through:

1. Compliance with central office and governmental health department directives.
2. Coordinating with the central office health unit for the establishment of training programs for the building staff.

3. Coordinating building level health measures and countermeasures with those of central office.

A building level school health committee should be established to recommend policy and direction for the school staff. A committee of this type should have built within its guidelines, a periodic change of membership and office positions. This group *will not* dictate action for the principal or the school. It (the health committee) should have as its main tasks—recommendations for health practices and procedures to be taken within the school. The principal should and always make the final decisions after careful study of the health committee's recommendations.

Individuals that could be a part of the health committee (ten to fifteen members would allow a variety of input) are:

1. A physician (general practitioner),
2. A dentist.
3. A public health nurse.
4. A psychologist.
5. A representative of the building administrative team.
6. A guidance counselor.
7. Faculty representation.
8. Parental representation.
9. Community organizational representation (for example, various civic groups).

A monthly review of the school and the community health status should take place with the group making recommendations to the school principal.

After careful consideration of the committee's input (toward the school's health program), the principal should decide the actions that the school will take, plus make arrangements for assistance by: (1) the central office health operation, (2) the local health department, and (3) the extent of assistance by the school staff.

There are major health problems in society that have a direct influence upon the individual school and its health environment. Building staff members are in need of in-service training by health officials to recognize health problems within the pupil population. Such training should be well planned and evaluated by the building administration.

Teachers are in almost constant contact with students during the school day, and they (the teachers) should be adequately trained to recognize actual and possible health problems of individual students. Guidance counselors through referral or by normal assignment should also be trained to observe for any health irregularities among the student body. The principal and his/her administrative team are in need of the same training.

Identification of health problems such as the normal childhood diseases (for example, measles, chicken pox, mumps, etc.) are considered fairly standard health problems. Ringworm, lice, plus other fungal and parasitic diseases should be considered serious and having the potential to infect the entire student body and staff. However, for more serious situations lurk in our school corridors. Society has introduced to those micro-social organizations that are termed schools, a variety of scourges which have had a negative effect upon humanity. Some of these problems are found in:

1. Acquired immune deficiency syndrome (AIDS) epidemic, and other venereal diseases which are difficult to detect and cure.
2. Drug addiction.
3. Alcohol addiction.
4. Childhood suicide.
5. Physical and mental injuries as a result of child abuse.
6. Mental illness (including mental illness that has been induced by drugs and alcohol).

The American judicial system has the authority to override the decisions of school officials to bar enrollment of children suffering from diseases such as AIDS[1]. Courts may also give decisions as to how the schools will function with other internal health problems. Court decisions can determine alterations to local board of education policies and the policies at building level. Principals need to be able to adjust their health and educational programs to adhere to court decisions and board policies. Individual schools should have health systems developed (with the assistance of central office and the building level health committee) to handle children attending classes with AIDS. This may involve separate restroom facilities, eating areas, etc. Additional health program systems are needed to work with other problems such as drug and alcohol abuse, suicide prevention, the termination of child abuse, recommendations for treatment, and the education of those children that are mentally ill. If the mental illness of a child is beyond the school's ability to serve his/her needs, then the school should be able to refer the parents and the child to an organization which can provide those needs.

A principal's administration of the school health program needs the assistance of the central office school health unit/ the building school health committee, and an ongoing school health training program for the building staff. The key to a successful school health program is having an adequately trained staff to recognize negative and possible negative health situations within the student body.

D. SOCIAL SERVICES COORDINATION

A typical American public school has the primary objective of educating the community's children. One must also realize that the school owes an overall duty of care to its student body—including their social welfare. In taking a closer observation of the social welfare of the school's children, the principal and his/her school staff need to rely upon the services of the school social worker. Many school social workers operate from two major patterns of organization which are as follows:

1. Some public school districts will have a social welfare agency unit built into its central office organizational pattern. Social workers within this unit will usually be assigned to regions (and their schools) constructed within the school district.

2. There are some public school systems that do not have a social welare agency unit that is organic to the district. Therefore, in situations of this nature, social workers are provided to the schools by local governmental bodies (city, county or metropolitan governments).

The School Social Workers and the Building Staff

School social workers and the building staff (especially the principal and his/her administrative team) are in need of a combined effort concerning the factors of:

1. Cooperation
2. Coordination
3. The providing of factual data
4. Making a solid and sincere effort to resolve each individual student problem
5. The establishment of a sound system for referral, and the use of proper space management to provide the social worker with more-than-adequate quarters from which to perform the social work task.

Hancock places a great deal of emphasis on the first contact between the principal and the school social worker. She (Hancock) looks upon the initial meeting as establishing good relations, a blending of the two professional tasks (education and social work), the establishment plus maintenance of a proper building level referral system, and use of the principal's expertise in the area of space management in order to obtain sufficient quarters for school social work procedures[2].

"The principal's perception of good social work practice may be very different from the school social worker's perception. Whatever the circumstances, this initial interview is a time for new beginnings and a fresh start. If the school social worker keeps in mind that the principal is interested in how the school social worker can be of greatest benefit to the school, social work services can be interpreted in this light. This does not mean that the school social worker thinks only in these terms. The school social worker must think in terms of helping the school to meet the needs of the client most beneficially and social work services must be presented in this light as well.

Every aspect of the principal-social worker relationship cannot be resolved or even approached during the initial interview, but there are two areas that should be decided on before the social worker actually begins working in the school: the manner of referral and space."

In the establishment of a referral system which will combine the school social worker with the pupil and the parents. The instructional and counseling staffs should be orientated (through in-service training) in the methods of observation and inquiry to determine pupil problems (actual and suspected). The referral system needs to allow for formal written statements by individual teachers and counselors in their construction to establish special assistance for the child concerned. Recognition of various student problems by a properly trained staff member could include:

1. Drug use
2. Drug trafficking
3. Physical abuse
4. Sexual abuse
5. Hunger and malnutrition
6. Mental problems
7. Physical problems
8. Medical problems
9. Dental problems
10. Suicidal tendencies
11. Possession of contraband
12. Pregnancies

13. Handicaps
14. Poor study habits
15. Unusual stress

The referral system should allow for the principal to have initial contact with the formal notice and a conference with the instructional staff member(s) involved. Upon obtaining a more detailed picture of the student problem (through the principal-teacher conference), the referral should be forwarded to the building level Special Services Unit. This unit should consist of the principal or his/her administrative designee), the school social worker, the school guidance counselor, a school psychologist, a school health representative, a speech and hearing specialist, and faculty representatives. Upon hearing input concerning the case of the student referred, the committee could direct the child and/or the parents to the governmental or community services available to counter and assist in solving the problem(s) of the child concerned. The school social worker's position on the Special Services Unit is of vital importance in the identification and contact with governmental and community social agencies. This action would also include the input and orientation of the concerned child's family.

As brought forth in the presentation of the building's social services referral system, one notices that the school social worker and the social services format encompasses nine main segments. They are:

1. The Principal
2. The Building Administrative Team (assistant principals and the guidance and counseling staff)
3. The Instructional Staff
4. The Building Special Services Unit
5. The School Social Worker
6. The Student Body
7. Parents
8. Governmental Agencies
9. Community Agencies

In spite of the fact that once a problem of social welfare concern is identified and processed through the building's referral system, the Special Services Unit, and referred to external agencies, the principal and the school still bear responsibility and there is a need to follow-up each case. Responsibility places upon the principal a need for proper administrative control over the social services operation. This measure will also call for an appraisal of the building's Special Services Unit (including both internal and external specialists') and the procedures for recommendations concerning pupil and family problem treatment. The administrative evaluation procedures should also call for the outcome of external agency ability to successfully handle individual student and/or family problems.

E. SUMMARY

Food services, pupil transportation, school health services, and school social services are under primarily central administrative control which is external to the building. However, the principal bears the responsibility for these services since they are operating within or in conjunction with the school building. Problems which could arise in the previously mentioned services areas can well cast a shadow upon building administrative responsibility. Externally controlled services are in need of supervision by the principal and his/her administrative team in order to provide:

1. More efficient services.
2. Proper coordination.
3. Cooperation.
4. Synchronized daily building level operations (including education and support services).

Food service operation within the building will require the coordination between the principal and the food service manager regarding: (1) Servicing schedules, (2) Dining room capacity, (3) Traffic flow within the lunchroom facility, (4) Periodic refuse removal (during the serving periods), (5) Pupil control in the dining area, (6) Free lunch management and procedures for students, (7) Menu notification, (8) Foodstuffs, supplies and equipment ordering plus delivery to the school plant, and (9) Building access for food service personnel beyond standard instructional hours.

Satellite, regionalized, or centralized food preparation will require varied administrative actions by the building administrator. Building coordination with external food service management will cover delivery schedules to the individual building and menu notification. The principal will have to arrange for part-time building food service personnel or school aides to arrange dining areas for serving and meal consumption. Serving schedules will have to be constructed by the principal with the input of part-time food service personnel and school aides.

Central office pupil transportation administrators and the building principal will require a major emphasis concerning scheduled arrivals and departures, holding and transfer point area supervision, and student control at bus stops and while in transit.

Driver-principal-child-parent coordination is needed to systematically neutralize behavior problems associated with bus transportation. A number of local boards allow the principal discretion in withholding a student's privilege to partake of the district's transportation service. Misconduct that is associated with school transportation can create unsafe environment for bus operation.

School health services are to provide the school administration and instructional staff with assistance concerning the health climate of the school, student body, and the community. The school staff should be trained (through in-service procedures) to recognize actual and possible health problems and conditions within the school environment. A referral system should be established to identify student needs in the following areas: (1) Medical, (2) Dental, and (3) Psychological services. Coordination between building and health personnel is a must if the health service program is to be successful.

Social services will also require an adequate referral system by properly trained building personnel to identify acutal and potential social deficiencies among school children. The school social worker and other professionals (such as school or public health personnel, guidance counselors, building administrators, instructional staff members) should be part of the building Social Services Unit. This unit would determine the disposition of individual referrals along with both student and parental counseling.

REFERENCES

[1]Black, J. "AIDS: Preschool and School Issues." *Journal of School Health,* Vol. 56. No. 3, 1986, pp. 93–95.

[2]Hancock, Betsy L. *School Social Work.* Englewood Cliffs, New Jersey: Prentice-Hall, Inc., 1982, p. 50.

CHAPTER XV

MANAGING THE PUPIL PERSONNEL TASK

A. THE STUDENT BODY POLICY BOOK

The school's student body needs to be under some element of control. The type of control needed should be one which is beyond that of teachers and administrators. The device needed in such situations would be that of a reference point which would outline an overall plan for governance and operations procedures that would apply only to student personnel. Such a device would be that of the student body policy book or student handbook. Rules that are contained within the handbook would be constructed by the input of the building's administration, guidance staff, teachers, clerical staff, custodial staff, food service staff, and the students (depending upon grade level). The bulk of the input for student policy book construction would be that of the building's administrative team, however, the input of the other above mentioned groups is necessary in order to cover all operational aspects of the building. Periodic review and appraisal of the student policy handbook should be undertaken by the school's staff along with the administrative team. The principal should make the final approval to any alterations or termination of policy (or policies) within the student handbook.

The school's guidance unit should be delegated the authority to provide student orientation programs to the entire student body at the commencing of the academic year. Special orientation sessions should also be held for new students, transfer students, and parents. A typical orientation program should provide an explanation of the school's: (1) educational programs, (2) extracurricular programs, (3) the school plant interior and grounds, and (4) the method of governance of the student body. Presentation and explanation of the student policy book should be made during the orientation. Conclusion of the orientation program should be with the presentation to the policy book to students and/or parents in attendance. Proper orientation with the student handbook as a guide has the possibility of providing dividends and goodwill to the school, its students, and the community.

Student Policy Book Coverage

Prime areas which should be covered in the student policy book are:

1. Student Expectations—This area should provide coverage in the student's sphere of developing a high level of self-esteem and self respect. Another point of significance would be the fact of treating others as the individual student would desire to be treated in return. The nerve center of the desire for high expectations will be aimed primarily toward student success in academics and human relations. Secondary achievement is also desired in extracurricular affairs.

2. Standard School Rules and Regulations regarding:
   a. Attendance and absences
   b. Tardiness
   c. Telephone usage
   d. Early individual dismissal procedures
   e. School transportation procedures
   f. Lunch period procedures
   g. Fire and emergency evacuation procedures
   h. Class periods and bell schedule
   i. Arrival and dismissal flow
   j. Student off limits areas
   k. Hall passes
   l. Personal locker management (gym and hall lockers)
   m. Intramural sports and attendance
   n. Interscholastic athletic programs and attendance
   o. Student fees
   p. Library procedures

3. The code of Discipline—There should be a requirement to demand proper student behavior in order to attain: (1) an ideal environment which would allow the process of learning, and (2) daily general school operations to take place. Whenever there is disruption in these two areas, the perpetrators must be dealt with quickly and appropriately. Punitive actions (according to state law and local board policy) are normally in the areas of:
   a. Long and short-term suspensions

    b. Expulsion

    c. Corporal punishment

    d. A penalty system

    e. Detention

    f. Legal charges filed through the judicial system.

  The above mentioned actions will cover a variety of student offenses in which some may be:

    a. Insubordination

    b. Possession of drugs, alcohol, or tobacco products

    c. Violation of the dress code

    d. Truancy

    e. Harassment and assault of students and school personnel

    f. School bus conduct

    g. Profanity

    h. Excessive displays of affection between male and female students

    i. Immoral acts

    j. Destroying the operation of the school

    k. Damaging of school property

    l. Disregard for campus motor vehicle operation and parking

    m. Motor vehicle operation

    n. Violation of school rules and regulations on school property, or at school sponsored events away from the campus

    o. Bringing contraband to the school site

    p. Attendance procedures and standards for student assemblies

    q. Prohibiting of electronic equipment such as radios, tape players, etc. on school property.

    r. Adherence to the school's visitor procedure system

    s. Prohibiting of excessive noise

4. The Individual Class Schedule (self-contained or departmentalized classroom system)—An individual schedule can possibly provide an opportunity for the student to construct and keep a record of his/her homeroom plus instructional areas for each school day. Each student should also have the school's master schedule (if departmentalized) to use for reference.

5. Procedures Concerning the Development of Positive Study Habits—Handbook explanation in this area should cover:

    a. Time management

    b. Planning for each day's assignment

    c. Use of the dictionary and thesaurus

    d. Use of the school library

    e. Develop a mind set for "business before pleasure"

    f. Review the previous lesson before advancing to the next

    g. Completion of each assigned lesson

    h. Selection of a quiet area for home study

5. The Academic Calendar—A copy of the school's academic calendar should be included in the study policy book in order to give notice to:

    a. Grade report dates

    b. Semester and quarterly examination periods

    c. School events

    d. Testing periods

    e. School event calendar

    f. School and/or class trips

    g. School holidays

    h. Registration

A school's student policy book serves as a point of reference for students, teachers, counselors, and administrators. It gives the student a printed guide which creates a highway to the student's positive contribution to the school's program, other students, and staff personnel. The handbook also serves notice to those who wish to violate the school's established limits in the area of student conduct.

B. PUPIL SERVICES

Chapter fourteen has already presented student services in the areas of health, social work, bus transportation, and daily feeding operations. This chapter segment will cover the areas of guidance, psychological, speech, and hearing services.

Guidance and Counseling Services

The school's guidance and counseling department should be considered as a specialized unit established not only for assisting students, but for helping and coordinating with both administrative and instructional personnel.

Schools having large enrollments and with more than two guidance counselors are in need of a building level supervisor or assistant principal over the building's guidance program. A maximum guidance counselor-student ration of 1:300 would most likely provide an adequate base for guidance operations within the typical elementary or secondary school. However, a number of schools may find themselves operating at a much higher counselor-student ratio.

A typical guidance counselor should coordinate with both administrative, instructional, and other special services (health, social work, etc.) personnel concerning individual student problems. Concentration by guidance personnel servicing the student will cover those areas involving:

1. Assisting students in developing personal attitudes and values which are positive to and accepted by society.
2. Career development and planning.
3. Promoting student participation in academic and extracurricular programs.
4. Assisting the student in time management procedures.
5. Assisting the student in developing a high level of self esteem and the ability to participate in society.
6. Informing the student of personal health needs.
7. Synchronization of the student with the school's program.
8. Assisting the student in the development of academic success and goal achievement.
9. Giving the student direction to needed resources (internal or external to the school).
10. Informing the student that counseling information is classified (and open only to those within an official "need to know" category).

Psychological Services

Administrative, instructional and/or guidance personnel may refer (depending upon school district policies) students to the school psychologist. The school psychologist needs to assist the school program through interaction with guidance and teaching personnel concerning:

1. The screening process systems used to diagnose emotional or personality problems.
2. Identification of gifted children.
3. Referring or placing diagnosed children in appropriate educational settings.
4. Providing group or individual psychotherapy with school children.
5. Coordinating with parents.
6. Coordinating with the school staff.

7. Appraisal of psychological performances with referred students, parents, and the school staff.

The psychologist should maintain contact (through conference sessions) with principals, counselors, teachers, and parents regarding student progress. A psychologist may refer some cases to agencies outside of the school setting in order to provide the best possible treatment for a student. A school psychologist needs to be considered as an integral member of the school team.

Speech and Hearing Services

Hearing examinations should be undertaken on annual basis at the elementary, middle and high school years. However, if any teacher, counselor, or administrator is suspicious of or detects a hearing problem, the student should be referred to the hearing specialist.

Planned or unscheduled hearing examinations would determine the extent of hearing loss. The hearing therapist would then refer the student to the proper medical personnel for additional testing and treatment.

Teachers need to observe their classes in order to identify children with speech defects. Upon identification the teacher needs to coordinate with the school's administration and/or guidance (depending upon local board policy) and construct a notice of referral to the speech therapist.

The speech and/or hearing therapist normally approaches those children with deficiencies through:

1. Testing the student's abilities in speaking and listening.
2. Determining whether the student has other physical or mental deficiencies along with the student's speaking or hearing problem.
3. Taking a review of the student's academic record.
4. Takes a check of the student's health and psychological records.
5. Makes referrals to medical personnel regarding the student's conditions.
6. Confers with teachers regarding special individual programs which can provide assistance to the student.
7. Confers with administrative and guidance personnel concerning the child's condition.
8. Confers with the child's parents.

The speech and/or hearing specialist plays an important role (as part of the student services team) in assisting the school to meet the needs of its children. Coordination of both the speech and hearing therapists may be made with the school social worker in order to refer poverty stricken children and parents to social agencies. These agencies can also assist in providing needed services to the members in the more upward socioeconomic groups.

C. CONTROL OF THE STUDENT BODY

The main reference volume for student control is the student policy book. However, there is a point in time when policy is violated, and when administrative and instructional units (within the building) must counter acts of perpetration. Whenever a violation is committed by a member of the student body, the school staff needs to take into account:

1. An immediate close review of the rule (or rules) violated.
2. Is there actual proof that the alleged student violator broke the rule(s)?
3. How severe is the violation?
4. What punitive actions within the school's and school district's policies for this particular classification of offense?
5. Is the recommended punishment in line according to severity of the infraction.
6. Has the matter been completely reviewed (also including: (1) actual and possible legal issues, and (2) the physical and emotional condition of the child involved before the administering of punitive action.

An aware administrator needs to study the school's system of pupil control for:

1. Obsolescence
2. Legal violations
3. Severity
4. Deterrent effect
5. Community acceptance

Community input is necessary in the principal's construction of the school's system for pupil control. Each school within the school district serves a unique community with a unique attitude toward the school's measures in controlling the actions of their children. A standing school *Student Control Committee* consisting of a member from the administrative team, a guidance and counseling representative, representatives of the instructional staff, and selected citizens of the community should assist the principal and the school concerning pupil control. There is a need for periodic personnel changes of the committee and its officers in order to provide new ideas and input to meet a constantly changing school setting. A principal will also need, in addition to the input of the *Student Control Committee,* the school staff and the students to periodically appraise the building's student control program. Middle and senior high school students should be represented on the school's *Student Control Committee* in order to more directly grasp student body attitude toward control measures being carried out in the school.

Student representatives to the *Student Control Committee* can more vividly express the needs of the student body. Some of the possible prime needs of students in their relationship with the school's control mechanism could be in areas of:

1. Having input (by representatives or popular vote) concerning how they (the students) should be governed by school personnel.
2. Having constitutional rights as an American citizen.
3. Allowing for individuality within the realm of social acceptance.
4. Fair treatment to all members of the student body.

The school's student control mechanism is only as powerful as those who enforce it. Guidance, instructional and other personnel should be trained through in-service on how to interpret and fairly carry out school policy. A building's entire staff should work as a team to assure that all facets of pupil policy and control are carried out according to plan. The building team approach has the possibility to determine a building's reputation within its own community and that of the overall school district.

D. STUDENT GROUPING

Student grouping since the 1960's has caused considerable problems within American society. These problems have placed public school districts in courts of law for judges to determine if racial, sexual, handicapped, or socioeconomic discrimination had taken place. Representatives of four previously mentioned groups have accused the schools of malice or other assorted underhanded tactics in preventing children of certain classifications from a fair share of America's opportunity.

Student organization for instruction can be classified into two main thrusts which are: (1) Heterogeneous grouping, and (2) Homogeneous grouping. The act of placing students in these two prime areas usually comes as a result of individual student achievement as brought forth through academic grade records and achievement testing. Additional information which may be fed into the classification machinery is that of projected ability of the student. This aspect (ability) needs also to be considered in the act of organizing students for academic grouping.

Heterogeneous grouping lends itself to a more ideal situation which is representative of America's society. Unless we as citizens place ourselves in totally sheltered environments, we will find that there is an almost daily contact (direct or indirect) with various societal levels.

One can find contact with various social elements on a frequent basis which may include the work place, church groups, a variety of social organizations, contacts with various levels and organizations of government, and acts of carrying out the business of the daily requirements of living. Heterogeneous grouping with the student structure allows for students to intermingle with individuals of various backgrounds of social status achievement and ability. Such a practice allows for a student mix of achievement and ability. This action makes for a more synchronized blend with individual teacher or teacher team assignments. Heterogeneous grouping also allows for the individual teacher or the teacher team to recognize individual differences and the aptitude to plan plus carry out instruction to meet the needs of all children (regardless of achievement and ability). Another facet within the realm of heterogeneous grouping is that of the teacher having the opportunity to bolster plus push forth the underachiever. The teacher is also allowed to increase the achievement of those students who may not be working at their top performance levels.

Homogeneous grouping should not be cast aside for the more popular heterogeneous mix of students. It (homogeneous organization) can be more beneficial to the students, the teachers, or teacher teams when two major situations exist. They are:

1. Students that are ultrahigh achievers and are not challenged in the standard heterogeneous classroom mix. Here one can see that the need is competition by other students that are also ultrahigh achievers. The homogeneous arrangement would be beneficial to such students.

2. The second situation looks at the other extreme polar region which involves those pupils that are extremely low achievers (due to environmental or other reasons). Pupils within this classification may require extra effort by the individual teacher or teacher team to acquire established levels of performance. Pupils within this

category will most likely operate at a pace lower than that of students in the standard learning environment.

Homogeneous grouping can easily lend itself to fit those that are within the zones of below average, average, or above average. Emphasis is usually placed on those individuals that fall in the superior and failure areas of instructional operations.

E. SCHEDULING

The degree to which an individual school schedules its classes depends upon the overall educational program offered and the system of classroom management.

Elementary Schools

Some elementary schools tend to have a self-contained classroom organizational and management scheme which usually lends itself to a minimum of scheduling. Such scheduling would involve synchronization with the building's overall program. Scheduling at the elementary level would probably involve those areas other than the basic grade level subject offerings. Such areas could be:

1. Music
2. Physical education
3. Specialized reading assistance
4. Specialized mathematics assistance
5. Extracurricular events
6. Science laboratory presentations
7. Library research periods
8. Art

Elementary schools usually do not require a heavy administrative and instructional staff input in construction of the master schedule.

Middle and Secondary Schools

At the middle and high school levels with their program offerings and the departmentalized classroom operation, the construction of the building master schedule becomes a major effort by the school's administrative team. Consideration in this area (schedule construction) is given to the subject department chairperson's and their staffs for input. Guidance counselors should aid in registering students for fall and winter semesters on a preliminary basis. This can assist the school administrative team (including subject department chairpersons) in placing:

1. Teachers
2. Students
3. Classrooms
4. Class sections
5. Class periods

in prearranged cells.

Other considerations in the construction of the school's master schedule is that of:

1. Location, assignment and number of homerooms.
2. Number of lunch periods.
3. Length of lunch periods.
4. Number of students per lunch period.
5. Length of the individual academic period.
6. Total number of academic periods during the day.
7. A flexible arrangement for school activity periods.
8. Classroom and time availability for specialized instructional activity.
9. An adequate system of space management and availability synchronized with the element of time.

Whether the construction of the school's schedule is determined by computer or manual input, there is a need for teamwork on the part of a number of members of the school's staff. This would include the:

1. Guidance and counseling staff.
2. Subject area department chairpersons.
3. The instructional staff (according to departmental subject areas).
4. The clerical staff and its computer team.

These four elements along with the administrative task mastership of the principal and his/her administrative team are the key subjects in determining the proper direction for master schedule construction. Goals that the building's administrative team should strive for in schedule construction are:

1. Providing the proper mix of instructional staff and student personnel to assure that adequate and timely instruction in the various subject areas taken place.
2. To provide the school with a suitable blending of academics and school sponsored extracurricular offerings.

3. To merge the offerings of the school plant with the educational curricular program.
4. Use of the building's master schedule as a reference point and as a medium of control over the academic and activity programs.

F. STUDENT EVALUATION, REPORTING, AND RECORD KEEPING

Student Evaluation

Teacher evaluation of student progress is a must if proper instructional procedures and the attaining of student goals are to be achieved. Student achievement in the classroom also reflects upon satisfactory instructional achievement by the instructional staff. Teachers are placed in a position to determine the level of individual student progress. Whether a student passes or fails, the school district should have established a system of evaluation (for the student, his/her parents or guardians, and for the permanent school record). There is also a requirement to the school to assist (through instruction, guidance and counseling, and administrative leadership) the passing or failing student toward his/her ultimate level of achievement by way of the student's innate ability.

Reporting and Record Keeping

Another point of administrative input concerning student evaluation is the supervision of the school's grade reporting system. Again direction is given to other members of the school's team such as:
1. The instructional staff.
2. Department or grade level leaders.
3. Guidance and counseling personnel
4. Clerical personnel (and the building computer team if applicable).
The system should allow for scheduling:
1. Teacher determination and submittal of student grades.
2. The transferring of grades to report cards and permanent records (manually or by computer).
3. The distribution of grade reporting cards directly to students or by mail to parents.

4. The allowing for parent-student-counselor-teacher conferences concerning grade reports.

Student permanent grade records may be placed on recording file cards or as part of a computer storage bank. Regardless of the method used, there needs to exist both school district and building policies regarding security and excess to student records. Excess to these items should be placed to only a official "need to know" basis.

Evaluation procedures by the school needs the input of a variety of individuals—from central office to building level and to that of the School's community. For example:

1. The central office needs to construct the overall procedure for a uniform grade marking system concerning:
   a. Elementary schools
   b. Middle schools
   c. High schools
2. Central office instructional directors and supervisors (subject area and grade level) should develop student and teacher goals in each subject offered.
3. Central office personnel should also develop a system for teacher determination of individual achievement levels and grade awarding. This system also needs to allow for some degree of elasticity in order to better meet individual needs and situations.
4. Building administration, subject department chairpersons, and grade level leaders need to supervise the teaching staff to ensure that central office student evaluation directives are being carried out.
5. Community members should be allowed to place input at central office and building level (through use of committees) concerning student evaluation systems.

Student evaluation procedures are critical to the school's educational program. Individual student grades serve as determinators to success or failure in: (1) Upward mobility in academics, (2) employability once one leaves school, and (3) Level of socioeconomic success as an adult.

G. THE EXTRACURRICULAR PROGRAM

Extracurricular activities are offered with the educational programs at the elementary, middle and high school levels. In moving from the elementary school to the secondary school these activities increase with the grade levels.

Classification of the building extracurricular (or cocurricular) program could be as follows:

1. Democratic student governmental organizations.
2. Academic clubs.
3. Leisure time and relaxation activities.
4. Sports clubs.
5. Intramural athletics.
6. Interscholastic athletics.
7. Homeroom organizations an activities.
8. Student honor groups.
9. Cheerleader groups.
10. Junior R.O.T.C. drill teams and military associations.
11. Student publications.
12. Class level offices and organizations.
13. Student assembly programs.
14. School-community organizations.
15. Band and music organizations.
16. Social assistance organizations.

Regardless of the school level (elementary through high school) the principal is charged with overall responsibility for the building's extracurricular program. In order that the school's chief executive can have input and supervision in numerous school activities (that are operating during the typical school day), the process of delegation should be used. Principals usually delegate authority for managing the co-curricular program with: (1) Members of the building's administrative team, and (2) Members of the instructional staff. The process of delegation will vary from school to school with the key factors being: (1) Size of the building administrative team, (2) Size of the instructional staff, (3) Student body number, and (4) The extent of the extracurricular program.

Another variable which must be considered in the delegating of cocurricular supervisory authority to members of the teaching staff—is that of the contract negotiated between the school district and teacher organizations. Some teachers may desire extra pay, reduced workloads, or nonparticipation of teacher personnel with student activities. Nonparticipatory practices may open the doors to the use of paraprofessionals as sponsors for some activities. If this method is used the principal must still delegate and carry the load of overall responsibility for extracurricular activities.

There are a number of tasks which need to be made by the principal and those delegatees involved with the school's extracurricular program. These tasks may concern:

1. Precise activity planning.
2. Proper delegatee recruitment.
3. Delegatee in-service training.
4. Student recruitment.
5. School activity policy and control enforcement by the building staff.
6. Synchronizing the co-curricular program with the educational program.
7. Allowing for community input toward the extracurricular program through committees or school-community organizations.
8. Establishing new activities to meet the various needs of the student body.
9. Maintaining proper fiscal planning and management.
10. The establishment and maintenance of a periodical appraisal system for the school cocurricular program.

Extracurricular activities within the school should not be taken lightly by the building administrator. Bearing the brunt of the overall responsibility factor places upon the principal an all-out effort to properly manage the cocurricular program. Dependable and competent administrative assistance (by assistant principals, guidance personnel and athletic directors) and teacher personnel should be obtained in order to provide a broad coverage of the building's activity program.

H. SUMMARY

The student body policy book is the key to a proper school environment through student self control and control enforcement by the school staff. Policy books serve as reference points, therefore, creating a proper guidance system for the student. It (the policy book) also creates a penalty system for those that desire to transgress and/or destroy the building policy system.

A school not only educates its pupils, but provides for their needs in a number of ways. Socioeconomic status, health (physical and mental) and other circumstances may place a hardship upon students and their parents. Schools can provide assistance along the lines of:

1. Medical and dental needs
2. Psychological and psychiatric needs.
3. Social needs.
4. Guidance and counseling services.

Control of the student body goes beyond the rules and regulations brought forth by central office and building level policies. Building staff members must also be aware of such policies, and be properly trained and prepared to enforce those measures. Policy established for student control must be clear and concise, therefore, eliminating problems of interpretation by the students and the school staff.

Student grouping should be heterogeneous in order to provide each student with the opportunity to work and have social contact with individuals of all levels. This approach provides the individual student with a microcosmic plus panoramic view of the society he/she will most likely encounter as an adult. Homogeneous grouping can become positive in situations where extremely high achievers and extremely low achievers can benefit from specialized instruction which will enable these individuals to fulfill their needs for academic success.

Scheduling construction efforts by the principal and his/her staff are completed either manually or by computer assistance. Breadth and depth of the schedule construction effort depends upon: (1) The school level (elementary, middle or secondary), (2) Overall student body size, (3) Departmental or grade level offerings, (4) Classroom management system (self-contained or departmentalized), (5) Teacher numbers according to grade level or specialty offering(s), (6) Space availability, (7) Lunch period offerings, (8) Activity period offerings, (9) Time periods, (10) Overall school hours, (11) Course offerings, (12) Course requirements, (13) Student needs, and (14) The offering of a degree of flexibility.

The student evaluation, grade reporting and record keeping system needs to meet the needs of the school environment according:

1. Administrative supervision.
2. Guidance input and coordination.
3. Grade level leader or department chairperson supervision.
4. Teacher task performance.
5. Clerical staff input and coordination.
6. Community input (through committee participation at building or central office levels).

There is also a need for the establishment of rules and goals regarding the earning of various grades by students. This undertaking needs to be accomplished by both central office and building level administrations.

A building's extracurricular program needs to be managed by the building principal who has been assigned overall responsibility in this area. In order to provide a 360° coverage of the building cocurricular program, there is a need for the principal to delegate authority in this area to his/her:

1. Administrative Team and
2. Teacher Staff.

Building personnel selected to assist in extracurricular activities should pass the scrutiny of the principal. Activity sponsoring personnel need to be able to work with variety of student personalities, plus have an interest and knowledge of the assigned activity.

CHAPTER XVI

OFFICE MANAGEMENT

A. SCHOOL OFFICE—THE BUILDING NERVE CENTER

The school office is the hub of the school's managerial and clerical activity. A building's clerical unit provides for an adequate flow of the school's educational program. It (the clerical unit) also synchronizes the instructional and the logistical tasks in the areas of planning projections, organization, guidance, and supervisory control. Building enrollment, teaching staff, and program function will most likely determine the size of the clerical unit. Some smaller schools will operate with only one secretarial person, while larger schools will function with a chief secretary (or clerical manager) and a secretarial staff. The size of the secretarial staff will also depend upon the building's clerical needs to support the daily operational program.

The building clerical manager is responsible for the school's overall clerical effort, and for subordinate secretarial personnel assigned to the clerical unit. This responsibility may involve:

1. Computer operations.
2. Typing and/or word processing.
3. Electronic dictation procedures.
4. Reproduction copy services.
5. Record keeping (manual and/or computerized).
6. Filing (manual and/or computerized).
7. Supervision of subordinates.
8. Workload allocation and schedules.
9. Providing for the building's communications service system.
10. Purchasing, receiving, plus stores and inventory management.
11. Standard and emergency telephone management.
12. Building staff personnel management.
13. Student personnel management.
14. Supervision of clerical personnel orientation and inservice training.

15. Management of the building's policy, catalog, and other assorted reference systems.
16. A center for requests concerning maintenance and other building needs.
17. Financial and accounting services.
18. Construction of projections for the clerical unit.
19. Appraisal of subordinate secretarial personnel and the clerical unit.
20. Coordination with the school principal.
21. Use of the clerical unit as a public relations tool in parental and other community contacts.

The typical school office, if used effectively, can assist the leadership task format of the principal and the administrative team. Clerical coordination and support can provide the building with a greater umbrella coverage to meet both instruction and other logistical demands. Another point which should be brought forth at this time is that of using the school office and clerical staff as a means for promoting school public relations. Parents and community persons are usually directed to the school's office upon arrival to the building setting. This action provides the clerical unit to create a positive environment before the discussion of business with the school administration and staff.

In order that the secretarial unit function at its maximum potential, there is a need to centralize the building's clerical needs and place them under the supervision of one clerical person. A procedure of centralization has possibility in allowing for an adequate coverage of the building's clerical needs.

B. CLERICAL SUPERVISION

Being the school's secretary, chief secretary, or office manager (with subordinate secretarial personnel) indicates a need for responsibility in supervising the building's clerical operation. Primary points for such supervision can involve: (1) the subordinate staff, (2) orientation and inservice, (3) task streamlining, (4) management functions, (5) task performance, and (6) service provisions. A closer observation of the previous six points will bring forth the following:

1. The subordinate secretarial staff needs supervision along the lines of:
   a. Work assignment and completion.

    b. Appraisal.

    c. Promotion, demotion, and termination.

    d. Employee-manager relations.

    e. Employee selection.

    f. Employee development.

2. Responsibility in the areas of orientation and inservice can cover:

    a. Planning and coordinating the clerical staff with external, central office and building-level training programs.

    b. Obtaining subordinate feedback regarding training programs.

    c. Measuring possible subordinate improvement due to training opportunities.

    d. Developing pride, quality and team participation within the clerical unit.

3. Using task streamlining to:

    a. Reduce the overall clerical workload.

    b. Supply and cost economy.

    c. Terminate obsolete and costly work schemes.

    d. Obtain a high productive rate and quality of service at minimum cost.

4. Management functions involved in the clerical supervisory scheme could include:

    a. Policy construction, enforcement, appraisal, alteration, and termination.

    b. Projection construction.

    c. The clerical unit organizational scheme.

    d. Task construction.

    e. Unit direction.

    f. Operation and maintaining of a two-way communication system.

    g. Development and carrying out of a proper public relations program.

5. Task performance within the school clerical unit can touch upon:

    a. Quality control and quality assurance.

    b. Knowledge of unit production capacity.

    c. Synchronization of the building's overall clerical effort.

    d. Providing subordinates with a suitable work environment.

    e. Placing the teamwork ethic upon subordinate personnel.

6. Providing needed services to the clerical team through:

    a. Adequate space management.

    b. Adequate supplies.

    c. Adequate equipment.

    d. Providing services such as:

        (1) Training for new procedures and equipment.

        (2) Troubleshooting equipment malfunctions and requesting repairing and servicing of equipment.

        (3) Providing adequate heating, cooling, ventilating, illumination, and power systems for clerical space requirements, personnel, and equipment.

        (4) A clerical staff area for relaxation and recreation.

Supervision of the building's clerical effort should be taken seriously. Not only should quality clerical personnel be hired, but they (clerical personnel) should receive quality treatment through services, supplies, equipment, and working conditions. It is the duty of the principal and chief clerk or office manager to provide the quality measures needed in order to obtain premium production output.

C. SCHOOL COMMUNICATIONS MANAGEMENT

Building level communications network centers are located within the school office. External communication from central office and the community are received at the school office scene. Upon the receiving of information the principal and/or the building's chief secretary will disseminate information to identified personnel within the building's staff or students.

The communications vehicle is also used internally regarding the school's intrabusiness operations. The school office also provides the vehicle and dissimination procedures to both students and staff members.

Communications received by the school from external sources could involve:

1. Computerized messages.
2. U.S. mail.
3. School district mail.
4. Radio transmissions.
5. Television transmission.
6. Standard telephone reception and transmission.
7. School district telephone emergency reception and transmission.

Items of communications involving the school office in the area of internal communications may involve:

1. Typewritten or handwritten messages.

2. The building intercom system.
3. The building internal telephone system.
4. The building's bell, alarm, and other audio systems.
5. The pure spoken word.
6. Programmed and designated signal lights.

All of the previously mentioned internal and external means of communication should be viewed as being two-way. If a communications network is to assist in objective achievement, it is necessary that it be two-way in order to assure clarity and direction.

The school office operates as the building communications center. A building clerical unit is the prime receiver of all communications thrusts to the building scene. It is the duty of the clerical unit to disseminate to the designated building unit for further dissemination and/or processing with the possibility for return transmission.

D. THE SCHOOL OFFICE, THE PRINCIPAL, AND TIME MANAGEMENT

The controlling of chronographic dimensions will most likely require that the chief building administrator set the pace, and require his/her subordinates to stick to task in order to be timely in meeting building level objectives. Subordinate leaders (the building administrative team, guidance director, grade level leaders, subject department heads, etc.) must also have a degree of latitude and autonomy in determining the management of time.

Time is not stationary, but constantly being consumed, taking personnel, programs, finances, supplies, equipment, and other services from the current to elapsed dimensions. The golden keys to success in managing time is careful planning, determining priorities, and the allowing of predetermined elasticity to absorb those situations which are impromptu, spontaneous, or unforeseen.

1. Commencement of the building's time management program will most likely require the principal's overall format (for the building's instructional and logistical programs) along with those subsidiary time management programs of subordinate leaders operating within the building's organizational format. Those time management programs which are secondary to the principal's primary effort must be compatible, and have the ability to synchronize into the total school program. Criti-

cal and careful planning in the area of time management is a must to the principal and his/her building staff.

A principal and his/her building team need to first consider the total amount of time to be consumed within a given time period (academic year, semester or quarter, calendar year, month, week, etc.), and the established goals which the school and its individual units are to attain within a given time period (or periods). This train of thought will most likely enable the principal and the staff to be cognizant of the projected or future time period which must be studied and divided for meaningful consumption (and in the direction of objective accomplishment).

2. Upon the completion of the planning phase, there is need to establish a system of priorities in the areas of the individual objective and the tasks required in attaining the objective. The determination of priorities may require superior-subordinate coordination.

3. High priority tasks should be handled first with secondary tasks consuming those spaces of time that may be in the surplus category or wasted to nonactivity situations. From the principal's administrative unit (which includes the building administrative team) to the departmental or grade level units and down to the various logistical units (clerical, custodial operations, food service, etc.) leaders may well have to delegate some tasks to their subordinates. In order to gain a better grasp of the task performance activity within the given time limits, efforts should be broken down according to the daily routine of the five-day workweek.

4. Within the work cell of individual task performance, time needs to be further divided in order to provide efficiency in operation. Tasks should be classified into the following groups:
- a. Urgent
- b. Very necessary
- c. Necessary
- d. Somewhat necessary
- e. Unnecessary
- f. Totally useless

Elasticity should also be built in to include freedom to handle:
- a. Interruptions
- b. Crisis situations
- c. The return to normalcy

5. In order that the typical leader and his/her subordinates are successful in task performance and the reaching assigned goals, a number of factors should be adhered to. Such as:

a. Immediate engagement of the task.
b. Keeping aware of the total time allotment for task completion.
c. Keeping aware of the rate of time consumption.
d. Requiring teamwork of the entire building staff (administrative, instructional, and logistical).

Time management requires not only the cooperation of the building staff, but also the responsibility and effort of various individuals within the building's personnel structure.

E. STRESS MANAGEMENT

Stress is usually obtained from an environment which to the individual results in causing tension or strain to his/her physical and/or mental well-being. The extreme potency of stress can cause an individual to lose his/her sanity or accelerate one's termination of life.

The upheaval of American society and morality during the 1960s has caused a constant negative societal change which is continuing to carry the present generation into an abyss of degeneration and shame. The school is a microcosm of society, therefore, bringing an assortment of social ills within its walls. There is an ever increasing demand for new tasks, additional paperwork, new training or inservice requirements, new human relations techniques, etc.; however, a panacea has not yet arrived. Innovative procedures for administration, guidance, instruction, logistical services, and computerization have not solved the school's problems or the problems of its personnel. Staff burnout is still present and some personnel tend to use various prescriptions to counter stress through:

1. Leaving the education profession.
2. Taking leave periods (with or without pay).
3. Early retirements.
4. Resignations.
5. Dependency on alcohol, food, tobacco products, and drugs as a release.

Building administration needs to counter the problem of stress which may reside within various members of the staff. Principals may wish to enlist the aid of psychological, psychiatric, or social work experts in assisting in the building stress management program.

In order to move with a stress management program at building level the principal needs to determine if staff production, goal accomplishment, and morale have taken a negative slide. If any or all of these previously mentioned situations exist, the origins of these problems need to be classified. Does the problem stem from school or nonschool situations? School problems are a concern of the principal, however, nonschool difficulties can influence operation within the school scene. These situations can be referred for treatment to assisting agencies within the school organization or to those agencies external to the educational environment.

Once school related problems are identified, measures should be taken to further study and breakdown these issues into cellular blocks to determine possible factors such as:

1. Those problems that are caused through interactions of individuals.
2. Those problems within one's own personality.
3. Those actions that are brought forth by one's environment and culture.

Careful identification and breakdown of the problem will initiate a movement toward reducing the stress situation through program action. Designed activity through:

1. Proper health care.
2. Exercise programs.
3. Recreational activities which suit the personality of the individual.
4. A variety of social activities that are of interest to the individual.
5. Religious activities which are of the individual's choice.
6. Relaxation programmed to individual needs and affordability.
7. Proper planning for work and nonwork situations.
8. Environmental transfer.

Recommendation is made toward the fact of the principal obtaining the assistance of experts to launch, carryout, and maintain (if needed) a program of stress management for the building staff.

Stress management of the staff may require the critical input of psychiatrist, psychologists, and/or social workers to meet individual needs. In many cases principals do not have expertise in these areas to assist building staff members back to normal task performance within the school setting. The engaging of countermeasures to mental and physical problems needs to have the skill of a true professional specialist (psychologist, social worker, or psychiatrist).

F. SUMMARY

The typical school office should so be organized as to handle the flow of administrative task operations throughout all facets of the building's daily operation. Proper office functioning along with proper clerical management by the chief school secretary will promote the office as the center of command within the school setting.

A building's communication scheme will provide for incoming and outgoing communication thrusts through the school office. It is the duty of the clerical staff to route communications materials to those designated units within the building. Communications thrusts, created within the building environment should always allow for a return response by the intended receiver.

Time management is critical to the principal, subordinate leaders, and staff members of the school. The entire leadership unit and building office needs to have input in the construction of the building's time management program (regarding both its instructional and logistical goals and tasks).

The rigors of daily living along with the five-day professional work week can lead building staff members to a point of stress overload. This overload can have an effect upon the individual's mental and physical being. Causes of stress need to be pinpointed and dealt with by specialized professional personnel through countermeasures designed to relieve stress situations.

BIBLIOGRAPHY

Abramowitz, Susan et al. *High School '77: A Survey of Public Secondary School Principals.* Washington: U.S. Department of Health, Education and Welfare, National Institute of Education, 1978.

Anderson, Lester W., and Van Dyke, Lauren. *Secondary School Administration, 2nd edition.* Boston: Houghton Mifflin, 1972.

Archambault, Reginald D., Editor. *John Dewey on Education: Selected Writings.* New York: The Modern Library (Random House), 1964.

Arrowood, Charles F. *Thomas Jefferson and Education in a Republic.* New York: McGraw-Hill, 1930.

Attwell, Arthur A. *The School Psychologist's Handbook.* Los Angeles: Western Psychological Services, 1972.

Bakalis, Michael J. *A Strategy for Excellence; Reaching for New Standards in Education.* Hamden, Connecticut, 1974.

Baker, Joseph J., and Peters, Jon S. *School Maintenance and Operation.* Danille, Illinois: The Interstate Press, 1963.

Barr, Rebecca and Wiratchai, Nonglak. *How Schools Work.* Chicago: University of Chicago Press, 1983.

Barra, Ralph. *Putting Quality Circles To Work: Practical Strategy for Boosting Productivity and Profit.* New York: R. R. Donnelly & Sons Co by McGraw-Hill, Inc., 1983.

Behling, Orlando and Schriesheim, Chester. *Organizational Behavior Theory, Research and Application.* Boston: Allyn & Bacon, 1976.

Black, Jeffrey L. "AIDS: Preschool and School Issues." *Journal of School Health,* Volume 56, Number 3, March, 1986, pp. 93–95.

Burock, E. H., and Smith, R. D. *Personnel Management: A Human Resource Systems Approach.* New York: John Wiley and Sons, Inc., 1982.

Bradfield, L. E., and Kraft, L. E., Editors. *The Elementary School Principal in Action.* Scranton, Pennsylvania: International Textbook Co., 1970.

Bridge, R. G., et al. *The Detrimants of Educational Outcomes: The Impact of Families, Peers, Teachers, and Schools.* Cambridge, Mass.: Ballinger Publishing Co., 1979.

Burke, W. Warmer, Editor. *The Cutting Edge, Current Theory and Practice in Organization Development.* LaJolla, Calif.: University Associates, 1978.

Byrne, David R., et al. *The Senior High School Principalships.* Reston, Virginia: National Association of Secondary School Principals, 1978.

Campbell, Roald F., et al. *Introduction To Educational Administration, Fifth Edition.* Boston: Allyn & Bacon, 1977.

Candoli, I. Carl, et al. *School Business Administration, 3rd edition.* Boston: Allyn & Bacon, 1984.

Carver, F. D., and Sergiovanni, T. J., Editors. *Organizations and Human Behavior: Focus on Schools.* New York: McGraw-Hill, 1969.

Casey, Leo M. *School Business Administration.* New York: Center for Applied Research in Education, 1964.

Cascio, Wayne F., and Awad, Elias M. *Human Resources Management: An Information Systems Approach.* Reston, Virginia: Reston Publishing Co., Inc., A Prentice Hall Co., 1981.

Castelter, William J. *The Personnel Function in Educational Administration.* New York: Macmillan, 1971.

Chisholm, Michael. *Modern World Development: A Geographical Perspective.* Totawa, New Jersey: Barnes & Noble, 1982.

Commager, Henry S. *Jefferson, Nationalism and The Enlightenment.* New York: G. Braziller, 1975.

Compayre, Gabriel. *Horace Mann and the Public School in the United States.* New York: T. Y. Crowell & Co., 1907.

Conant, James B. *Thomas Jefferson and the Development of American Public Education.* Berkeley: University of California Press, 1962.

Constable, Robert T., et al. *School Social Work: Practice and Research Perspectives.* Homewood, Illinois: Dorsey Press, 1982.

Coons, John E., and Sugarmon, Stephen D. *Education By Choice: The Case for Family Control.* Berkeley: University of California Press, 1978.

Corwin, Ronald G., et al. *Perspectives on Organization: The School As a Social Organization.* Washington: American Association of Colleges for Teacher Education: Association of Teacher Educators, 1977.

Crane, Donald P. *Personnel, The Management of Human Resources, Fourth Edition.* Boston: Kent Publishing Co., A Division of Wadsworth, Inc., 1986.

Cremin, Laurence A., Editor. *The Republic and the School; The Education of Free Men.* New York: Teachers College, Columbia University, 1957.

Davis, Keith. *Human Behavior At Work: Organizational Behavior.* New York: McGraw-Hill, Inc., 1981.

Desatnik, Robert L. *Innovative Human Resource Management.* American Management Association, 1972.

Dewar, Donald L. *The Quality Circle Guide to Participation Management* (Quality Circle Institute) Englewood Cliffs, New Jersey: Prentice-Hall, 1980.

Dewey, John. *A Common Faith.* New Haven: Yale University Press, 1934.

Dewey, John. *Democracy and Education; An Introduction to the Philosophy of Education.* New York: Free Press, 1966.

Dewey, John, and Tufts, James H. *Ethics, Revised Edition.* New York: H. Holt & Co., 1942.

Dewey, John. *Experience and Education.* New York: The Macmillan Co., 1950.

Dewey, John. *Freedom and Culture.* New York: Capricorn Books, 1963.

Dewey, John. *Individualism Old and New.* New York: Capricorn Books, 1962.

Dewey, John. *Liberalism and Social Action.* New York: Capricorn Books, 1963.

Dewey, John. *Moral Principles in Education.* Boston: Houghton Mifflin Co., 1909.

Dewey, John. *Philosophy of Education (Problems of Men).* Paterson, New Jersey: Littlefield-Adams, 1958.

Dewey, John. *The Child and the Curriculum.* Chicago: University of Chicago Press, 1959.

Downs, Robert B. *Horace Mann, Champion of Public Schools.* New York: Twayne Publishers, 1974.

Dreyfack, Raymond. *Sure Fail: The Act of Mismanagement.* New York: William Morrow and Co., 1976.

Dworkin, Martin S. *Dewey on Education.* New York: Bureau of Publications, Teachers College, Columbia University, 1959.

Edwards, Newton. *The Courts and the Public Schools; The Legal Basis of School Organization and Administration, Third Edition.* Chicago: University of Chicago Press, 1971.

Eurich, Alvin C., Editor. *High School 1980: The Shape of the Future in American Secondary Education.* New York: Pitman Publishing Corp., 1980.

Filler, Louis, Editor. *Horace Mann on the Crisis in Education.* Yellow Springs, Ohio: Antioch Press, 1965.

Flowers, Anne, and Bolmeier, Edward C. *Law and Pupil Control.* Cincinnati: W. H. Anderson Co., 1964.

Gazda, George M., et al. *Human Relations Development: A Manual for Educators.* Boston: Allyn & Bacon, 1973.

Gazda, George M., et al. *Human Relations Development: A Manual for Educators, Second Edition.* Boston: Allyn & Bacon, 1977.

Goodwin, David. *Delivering Educational Service: Urban Schools and Schooling Policy.* New York: Teachers College Press, Columbia University, 1977.

Greenwood, William T. *Management and Organizational Behavior Theories: An Interdisciplinary Approach.* Cincinnati: South-Western Publishing Co., 1965.

Gustafson, Thomas J. *Microcomputers and Educational Administratin.* Englewood Cliffs, New Jersey: Prentice-Hall, 1985.

Halloran, Jack. *Applied Human Relations: An Organizational Approach.* Englewood Cliffs, New Jersey: Prentice Hall, Inc., 1978.

Harris, Ben M., et al. *Personnel Administration in Education: Leadership for Instructional Improvement, Second Edition.* Boston: Allyn & Bacon, 1985.

Harris, George W., Jr. *Management of the Public School Logistical System.* Springfield, Illinois: Charles C Thomas, Publisher, 1985.

Healey, Robert M. *Jefferson on Religion in Public Education.* New Haven: Yale University Press, 1962.

Henderson, John C. *Thomas Jefferson's Views on Public Education.* New York: AMS Press, 1970.

Heslep, Robert D. *Thomas Jefferson and Education.* New York: Random House, 1969.

Hill, Fredrick W. *School Business Administration in the Smaller Community.* Minneapolis: T. S. Denison, 1964.

Holding, Dennis H., Editor. *Stress and Fatigue in Human Performance* (Wiley Series on Studies in Human Performance, Department of Psychology, University of Durham, England) Chichester, England: John Wiley and Sons, Ltd., 1983.

Honeywell, Roy J. *The Educational Work of Thomas Jefferson.* New York: Russell and Russell, 1964.

Hooker, Clifford P., and Rehage, Kenneth J. *The Courts and Education.* Chicago: National Society for the Study of Education, 1978.

Horne, Herman H. *The Democratic Philosophy of Education.* New York: The Macmillan Co., 1932.

Hoy, W. K., and Miskel, C. G. *Educational Administration: Theory, Research and Practice.* New York: Random House, 1978.

Hubbell, George A. *Horace Mann, Educator and Reformer; A Study in Leadership.* Philadelphia: W. F. Fell Co., 1910.

Hussey, David E., and Langham, M. J. *Corporate Planning: The Human Factor.* Elmsford, New York: Pergamon Press, Inc., 1979.

Hynd, George W., Editor. *The School Psychologist: An Introduction.* Syracuse, New York: Syracuse University Press, 1983.

Jenson, T. J., and Stollar, D. H. *Legal Terms and Phrases Encountered in School Administratin.* Columbus, Ohio: The Ohio State University Center for Educational Administration, 1961.

Johnson, Howard M. *Planning and Financial Management for the School Principal.* New York: Teachers College Press, Columbia University, 1982.

Johnston, A. M., and Harris, G. "Field Trips and Liability." *Tennessee Teacher.* Volume XLII, December 1974, pp. 5–7.

Joiner, Lee M., et al. *Microcomputers in Education: A Nontechnical Guide to Instructional and School Management Applications.* Holmes Beach, Fla.: Learning Publications, 1982.

Jordan, Kenneth F. *School Business Administration.* New York: Ronald Press, 1969.

Judson, Clara. *Thomas Jefferson, Champion of the People.* Chicago: Wilcox and Follett Co., 1952.

Kakabadse, Andrew. *The Politics of Management.* Aldershot, Hants, England: Gower Publishing Co., Ltd., U.S. Printing, 1984.

Kelley, Edgar. *Improving School Climate: Leadership Techniques for Principals.* Reston, Virginia: National Association of Secondary School Principals, 1980.

Kemerer, F. R., and Deutsch, K. L. *Constitutional Rights and Student Life: Value Conflict in Law and Education.* St. Paul, Minnesota: West Publishing Co., 1979.

Klein, Stuart M., and Ritti, Richard R. *Understanding Organizational Behavior,* Second Edition. Boston: Kent Publishing Co., A Division of Wadsworth, Inc., 1984.

Knox County (Tennessee) Schools. *Knox County Food Service Employment Objectives.* Knoxville, Tennessee: Office of School Food Service, 1986.

Knox County (Tennessee) Health Department. *Regulations Governing Food Service Establishments.* Knoxville, Tennessee: Knox County (Tennessee), 1986.

Illbach, Robert J., and Zins, Joseph E. *Organizational Psychology in the School: A Handbook for Professionals.* Springfield, Illinois: Charles C Thomas Publisher, 1984.

Landers, Thomas J., and Myers, Judith G. *Essentials of School Management.* Philadelphia: W. B. Saunders Co., 1977.

Larwood, Laurie. *Organizational Behavior in Management.* Boston: Kent Publishing Co., A Division of Wadsworth, Inc., 1984.

Le Boeuf, Michael. *The Greatest Management Principle in the World.* New York: G. P. Putnam & Sons, 1985.

Lee, Mary D., and Kanungo, Rabindra, Editors. *Management of Work and Personal Life: Problems and Opportunities.* New York: Praeger, 1984.

Lieberman, Myron. *Beyond Public Education.* New York: Praeger, 1986.

Linn, Henry H. *School Business Administration.* New York: Ronald Press, 1956.

Mann, Horace. *Life and Works of Horace Mann.* New York: C. T. Dillingham, 1891.

Maude, Barry. *Practical Communication for Managers.* London, England: Longman Group, Ltd., 1984.

Mead, Margaret. *The School in American Culture.* Cambridge: Harvard University Press, 1955.

Messerli, Jonathan. *Horace Mann; A Biography, First Edition.* New York: Knopf, 1972.

McCarty, M. M., and Cambron, N. H. *Public School Law: Teachers' and Students' Rights.* Boston: Allyn & Bacon, 1981.

McGrath, J. H. *Planning Systems for School Executives: The Unity of Theory and Practice.* Scranton: Intext Educational Publishers, 1972.

McKeon, Richard, Editor. *The Basic Works of Aristotle.* New York: Random House, 1941.

Miller, Van, et al. *The Public Administration of American School Systems, Second Edition.* New York: Macmillan, 1972.

Morgan, Joy E. *Horace Mann: His Ideas and Ideals.* Washington, D.C.: National Home Library Foundation, 1936.

Morphet, Edgar L., et al. *Educational Organization and Administration: Concepts, Practices, and Issues, Fourth Edition.* Englewood Cliffs, New Jersey: Prentice Hall, 1982.

Neale, Daniel C., et al. *Strategies for School Improvement: Cooperative Planning and Organization Development.* Boston: Allyn & Bacon, 1981.

Norton, Marcia N., and St. Paul, Gene. *The Elementary Principal's Resource Book.* Englewood Cliffs, New Jersey: Prentice-Hall, 1985.

Oberteuffer, Delbert, et al. *School Health Education: A Textbook for Teachers, Nurses, and Other Professional Personnel, Fifth Edition.* New York: Harper and Row, 1972.

Oregon, University of—Center for Educational Policy and Management. *Second Handbook of Organization Development in Schools.* Palo Alto, California: Mayfield Publishing Co., 1977.

Owens, Robert G. *Organizational Behavior in Education,* Second Edition. Englewood Cliffs, New Jersey: Prentice Hall, Inc., 1981.

Parody, O. F. *The High School Principal and Staff Deal With Discipline.* New York: Teachers College Press, Teachers College, Columbia University, 1965.

Peterson, LeRoy J., et al. *The Law and Public School Operation.* New York: Harper & Row, 1969.

Pounds, Ralph L., and Brymer, James R. *The School in American Society, Second Edition.* New York: Macmillan, 1967.

Ratner, Joseph, Editor. *Characters and Events; Popular Essays in Social and Political Philosophy.* New York: H. Holt & Co., 1929.

Rebell, Michael A., and Block, Arthur R. *Educational Policy Making and the Courts: An Empirical Study of Judicial Activism.* Chicago: University of Chicago Press, 1982.

Recutter, E. E. *Schools and the Law, Fifth Edition.* Reston, Virginia: National Association of Secondary School Principals, 1981.

Reutter, E. E. *The Supreme Court's Impact on Public Education.* Bloomington, Indiana: Phi Delta Kappa Organization on Legal Problems of Education, 1982.

Rhodes, E. F., and Long, R. P. *The Principal's Role in Collective Negotiations.* Washington: Educational Service Bureau, 1967.

Rickover, Hyman G. *Education and Freedom, First Edition.* New York: Dutton, 1959.

Roe, William H., and Drake, Thelbert L. *The Principalship, Second Edition.* New York: Macmillan Publishing Co., Inc., 1980.

Runkel, Phillip J., et al. *Transforming the School's Capacity for Problem Solving.* Eugene, Oregon: Center for Educational Policy and Management, College of Education, University of Oregon, 1978.

Russell, P. *Jefferson, Champion of the Free Mind.* New York: Dodd-Mead, 1956.

Schultz, Theodore W. *Investment in Human Capital: The Role of Education and of Research.* New York: Free Press, 1971.

Sergiovanni, Thomas J., and Starralt, Robert J. *Supervision: Human Perspectives.* New York: McGraw-Hill, 1983.

Sharp, Clifford H. *The Economics of Time.* New York: Wiley, 1981.

Sidman, Bernard. *Educational Computer Technology: A Manual Guide for Effective and Efficient Utilization by School Administrators.* Palo Alto, California: R & E Research Associates, 1979.

Sieber, Sam, and Wiklder, David E., Editors. *The School in Society: Studies in the Sociology of Education.* New York: Free Press, 1973.

Smith, Payson, et al. *Horace Mann and Our Schools.* New York: American Book Co., 1937.

Schimmel, David, and Fischer, Louis. *The Rights of Parents in the Education of Their Children.* Columbia, Maryland: National Committee for Citizens in Education, 1977.

Shuster, Albert H., and Stewart, Dan H. *The Principal and the Autonomous Elementary School.* Columbus, Ohio: Merrill, 1973.

Stoops, Emery, et al. *Handbook of Educational Administration: A Guide for the Practitioner, Second Edition.* Boston: Allyn & Bacon, 1981.

Sumption, Merle R., and Engstrom, Yvonne. *School-Community Relations: A New Approach.* New York: McGraw-Hill, 1966.

Tennessee State Board of Education. *Rules, Regulations and Minimum Standards for the Governance of Public Schools in the State of Tennessee.* Nashville, Tennessee: State of Tennessee, 1985.

Tennessee State Department of Education. *Tennessee Internal Financial Management Manual.* Nashville, Tennessee: State of Tennessee, 1977.

Tootle, Harry K. *Employees Are People,* First Edition. New York: McGraw-Hill, 1947.

Tredgold, R. F. *Human Relations in Modern Industry.* New York: National Universities Press, Inc., 1950.

United States Constitution, 1791. Amendment V.

United States Constitution, Amendment X, 1791.

United States Constitution, Amendment XIV, 1868.

United States Constitution, Preamble, 1788.

Van Fleet, James K. *The 22 Biggest Mistakes Managers Make and How to Correct Them.* West Nyack, New York: Parker Publishing Co., Inc., 1973.

Wey, Herbert W. *Handbook for Principals; Practical Suggestions for Action.* New York: Schaum Publishing Co., 1966.

Wiles, D. K., et al. *Practical Politics for School Administrators.* Boston: Allyn & Bacon, 1981.

Winters, Wendy G., and Easton, Freda. *The Practice of Social Work in Schools: An Ecological Perspective.* New York: Free Press, 1983.

Wood, C. L., et al. *The Secondary Principal: Manager and Supervisor.* Boston: Allyn & Bacon, 1979.

World Book, Inc. *The World Book Encyclopedia, Volume 7.* Chicago, Illinois: Scott Fetzer Co., 1987.

World Book, Inc. *The World Book Encyclopedia, Volume 15.* Chicago, Illinois: Scott Fetzer Co., 1987.

INDEX

297